# EMPOWERING ONLINE LEARNING

## 100+ Activities for Reading, Reflecting, Displaying, and Doing

Curtis J. Bonk
Ke Zhang

JOSSEY-BASS
A Wiley Imprint
www.josseybass.com

Published by Jossey-Bass
A Wiley Imprint
989 Market Street, San Francisco, CA 94103-1741—www.josseybass.com

Jossey-Bass books and products are available through most bookstores. To contact Jossey-Bass directly call our Customer Care Department within the U.S. at 800-956-7739, outside the U.S. at 317-572-3986, or fax 317-572-4002.

Jossey-Bass also publishes its books in a variety of electronic formats. Some content that appears in print may not be available in electronic books.

**Library of Congress Cataloging-in-Publication Data**

Bonk, Curtis Jay.
    Empowering online learning : 100+ activities for reading, reflecting, displaying, and doing / Curtis J. Bonk, Ke Zhang.
        p.    cm.—(Jossey-Bass higher and adult education series)
    Includes bibliographical references and index.
    ISBN 978-0-7879-8804-3 (pbk.)
        1. Computer-assisted instruction.    2. Internet in higher education.    I. Zhang, Ke, 1973–
II. Title.
    LB1028.5.B598    2008
    378.1'734—dc22

                                                                                                2008009377

Printed in the United States of America
FIRST EDITION

*PB Printing*   10  9  8  7  6  5  4  3  2  1

# CONTENTS

# PREFACE

The increasing popularity of online learning in education and training (Allen & Seaman, 2004, 2005), combined with insufficient instructor development, poor strategic planning, and high dropout rates (Frankola, 2001), generates many challenges and dilemmas for instructors, trainers, and instructional designers. One key challenge relates to the generational differences in learning experiences and preferences among online learners. Learners, especially adults returning to college for additional degrees or certifications, want their e-learning experiences to be personally empowering and highly relevant to their occupations and interests. But so do younger learners who may be highly savvy with the educational technologies that are integrated into such online instruction. However, they may have quite different educational experiences and learning expectations.

With the advent of the Web of Learning (the phrase we use for learning-related uses of online resources and technologies) to supplement a course, deliver most of a course, or handle an entire course or program online, instructors, trainers, and students have increasing needs and expectations (as well as the means) to individualize and customize instruction. As online opportunities proliferate, instructors, instructional designers, and administrators need models or frameworks and rich examples of how to address the many types of learners signing up for their online certificates, modules, courses, and programs.

Corporate training and e-learning guru Elliott Masie (2006) has repeatedly noted that we live in an age of fingertip knowledge, where memorizing lists is much less important than knowing how to access them. There are serious implications for the lowered expectations regarding memorization in our instructional designs. Do we recognize and perhaps even promote the fact that our learners no longer need to memorize most information? And while technology-savvy young learners may be able to navigate efficiently to the needed information, what skills do they need once they locate it? What are the digital learning skills of the twenty-first century, and how might online learning experiences facilitate the acquisition and use of such skills?

We are only at the initial stages of Web use in education and training; the emphasis on fingertip knowledge skills is just one of many trends. Diversity, variety, flexibility, choice, and options—these are key components of the age of online teaching and learning. Instructors who either lack experience in or are more hesitant or reluctant to try online teaching and learning may simply need additional guidance and frameworks to support their efforts (Bonk & Dennen, 2003). Of course, even online experts from time to time need to try out new models and lenses for navigating this enormous Web of Learning. Likewise, a plethora of new centers and institutes for e-learning, blended learning, technology integration, and teaching excellence springing up around the globe have a mission to find, document, and showcase the best online learning practices they can find. Naturally, such centers make use of frameworks, guidelines, and labels for the online learning activities and teaching models that they employ and advocate to others.

Of course, there are myriad reasons why such teaching and learning centers are gaining attention and, for some, increased funding. For instance, as a direct result of the explosion of Web-based learning during the past decade, there are hundreds of thousands of new online instructors around the planet each year who have never been trained or certified to teach in online environments, nor have they taken an online course as a student. Given this dilemma, it is not surprising that in our journeys within North America as well as around the world we have discovered excitement about models, frameworks, stories, and examples of effective online teaching and learning.

The vast majority of those new to this form of instructional delivery simply want to know what works and what does not. Many teachers, trainers, and college professors or lecturers we encounter are worried that they cannot keep pace with the technology skills of their students. They read reports about each new generation of learners having unique learning preferences and experiences that are vastly different from previous ones. Currently, there is extensive discussion about Generation X and Y students and how they each are distinct from the Baby Boomer generation (Oblinger, 2003). In fact, educators such as Chris Dede (2005) from Harvard's Graduate School of Education now discuss and debate the emerging neo-Millennial learners and their technology preferences when they work and learn online.

But the Web of Learning opens avenues for both younger and older adults. As the age range of students widens, instructors need additional assistance and support to address these varied student needs and preferences. In response to this difficult situation, it is important to recognize the rich body of literature that has emerged in the area of learning styles within face-to-face (FTF) instruction (for example, Kolb, 1984; Lawrence, 1993). At the same time, there is a pressing need to extend theoretical frameworks and practical guidance related to FTF settings to promising ideas about integrating online technologies and resources to address varied learning styles, cultural backgrounds, and preferences.

## The Read, Reflect, Display, and Do Model

In response to these fascinating education and technology related trends and mounting challenges, this book introduces an easy-to-apply, practical model—the Read, Reflect, Display, and Do (R2D2) model—that should help online instructors integrate various learning activities with appropriate technologies for effective online learning for a diverse array of e-learners (Bonk & Zhang, 2006). R2D2 is a new model for designing and delivering distance education, and, in particular, online learning. As the title of this book, *Empowering Online Learning*, indicates, it is meant to empower e-learners and e-instructors. (Our R2D2 model is distinct from the instructional design model from Jost, Mumma, and Willis, 1999, with the same name. Our model is not an instructional design model in the traditional sense, and, unlike Jost et al., it is intended for online environments.)

R2D2 is a framework that can help one plan, design, and deliver online courses. The R2D2 model has four distinct phases—reading, reflecting, displaying, and doing—which help address diverse learner needs, backgrounds, expectations, preferences, and styles. The first phase of R2D2 relates to methods to help learners acquire knowledge through online readings, Web explorations, and listening to online content such as the popular use of podcasted lectures which students can download to their iPods or MP3 players or sit and listen to at their desktops. As such, Phase 1 addresses verbal and auditory learners. Phase 2 of the model focuses on thinking and reflective activities such as online blogs, reflective writing, and self-check activities and examinations. In Phase 3, visual representations of the content are highlighted with activities such as virtual tours, timelines, animations, and concept maps. Last, Phase 4 emphasizes what learners can do with the content in hands-on activities including simulations, scenarios, and real-time cases. When thoughtfully designed and effectively delivered, content and activities created from a perspective such as R2D2 are more engaging and enriching for learners.

We have demonstrated the R2D2 model in many presentations delivered across the globe. Audience feedback indicates that the model is highly intuitive and that it works. Equally important, our research in both corporate training and higher education environments indicates that there will be a shifting from text-based environments to more hands-on, collaborative, and active learning opportunities as well as a movement toward increasing online learning activities and tools and features that enhance visual learning (Kim & Bonk, 2006). R2D2 can help with this upcoming shift.

## Goals and Uses of This Book

We have mapped out continua of instructional options from low-risk to high-risk strategies; from low-time to time-intensive activities; from low-cost to highly expensive endeavors; and from heavily teacher-centered events to those that are more learner centered. Based on interactions with myriad online trainers and instructors during our global journeys, it is clear that, given pervasive and rapidly escalating budgetary and accountability concerns related to education and training across all sectors, many online educators as well as their supervisors want to know more about the low-risk, low-time, and low-cost strategies that can be effectively deployed. Of course, some may want to be pushed to the upper edges of these continua and take more risks or spend more time planning and developing online activities. We hope to accomplish both goals with this book: to gently nudge or push ahead the experts and high risk takers as well as those who are hesitant or too intimidated to embed online technologies in their teaching and training practices.

There are many ways to employ this book. For instance, it might be used in technology integration courses at the undergraduate level as well as educational technology master's and perhaps even doctoral-level courses. In higher education settings, this book could be adopted as primary or supplemental reading for courses on instructional design and technology, online course design, technology integration, distance education, e-learning, and the like. At the same time, it could be used in instructor and administrator professional development institutes and workshops related to online teaching and learning.

While all of the 100+ activities discussed in the book can find application in higher education settings, many can also be applied in corporate, government, K–12, and other training and education settings. The book is intended to provide a compass (albeit just one) for instructors and course designers to use when creating or conducting an online class. While the R2D2 model is not an instructional design (ID) model, at least in the traditional sense of ID, it can provide vital assistance in designing online courses. In addition, R2D2 (and the activities detailed here) provides first-timers, whether they are instructors, tutors, trainers, or instructional designers, with a crutch to support their efforts, while more experienced e-instructors might use it as a tool for reflecting on as well as integrating their existing online teaching practices.

# Book Content and Organization

In this book, you will find the following:

- Practical guidance for online instructors, instructional designers, courseware designers, and course management developers and vendors
- A plethora of ways to create engaging learning activities for a variety of learners
- Stories and examples that online instructors can personally relate to
- Useful references with examples on how to integrate free and emerging technologies into active learning experiences for diverse learners

We felt that it was time for a book that both acknowledged the growing importance of the Web of Learning as well as a model for making sense of it in at least a small way. While we realize that the learning styles literature is replete with problems and misconceptions (see Santo, 2006), we designed the R2D2 model as a means for reflecting on and adjusting one's teaching and learning practices as well as a way to address individual students' needs.

Instead of focusing on distinct learning styles or approaches, the aim of this book is essentially to address diverse learner *needs*. The increasing diversity of learners in any learning setting or educational situation places escalating demands and pressures on instructors, instructional designers, institutions, and organizations. In the end, this book is intended to serve as a resource to help such individuals address these diverse learner preferences and needs.

In Chapter One, we introduce the R2D2 model and explain how to use it in different types of e-learning and blended learning settings. In particular, we outline the R2D2 model—Read, Reflect, Display, and Do—and address different learning styles and various generations or types of learners in online courses.

The following eight chapters provide an overview of emerging technologies for online reading, reflecting, displaying, and doing as well as more than 100 practical activities and ideas for implementation of the model. In Chapters Two through Nine, we discuss each type of learning approach and the available technologies that have emerged to nurture or support it. Even-numbered chapters describe the learning styles addressed by each phase of R2D2; odd-numbered chapters provide sets of twenty-five instructional strategies or activities addressing each type of learning. For example, Chapter Two describes how to use this model to address auditory and verbal learners, while Chapter Three presents twenty-five distinct ways to carry this out with variations and extensions from the original example, instructional procedures, and additional advice and instructional considerations, including our sense of the degree of risk, time, cost, and learner-centeredness of each activity.

This sequence is followed in the remaining chapters of the book. For instance, Chapters Four and Five address reflective and observational learning as seen through many online reflective writing and self-assessment activities. Once again, the former chapter describes technology trends and innovative pedagogical ideas related to this type of learning preference, whereas the latter one contains twenty-five activities that can be attempted in a variety of settings. Next, Chapters Six and Seven focus on visual learning tools, resources, and activities. In completing the R2D2 model, Chapters Eight and Nine present a series of hands-on activities such as simulations, games, and scenario learning. Finally, in Chapter Ten, we summarize the ideas from the previous eight chapters while specifically addressing how to integrate all four types of learning activities in effective online courses.

## Caveats Regarding the Web Resources, Tools, and Activities Listed

Key Web resources that are mentioned in each chapter are also listed at the end of the book by chapter. The Web resources listed for each chapter are also subgrouped by category or type of resource or activity. We realize that over time many of these Web sites and associated URLs may change or disappear. And, as fads and trends change, they might also lose their educational appeal and luster. We hope that the reader will understand the dilemma related to attempting to capture interesting educational aspects of a dynamic learning resource (that is, the Internet) with a static document. As the Web of Learning expands, we hope that you will share with us the resources, tools, and materials that you have found educationally impressive and valuable and perhaps used in your own online learning and instruction. We will attempt to maintain an up-to-date list of such Web resources on our own respective homepages.

It is important to also point out that we are not directly endorsing any of the tools, resources, systems, consultants, or researchers mentioned in the book, nor do we offer guidelines or recommendations on how to select from them. Along these same lines, the 100+ activities outlined in this book are simply examples, not prescriptions; please modify, add to, or delete any idea or step mentioned here or combine pieces or kernels of them as needed. When you do that, the 100+ strategies of this book multiply exponentially. It is the intersection among such technologies and pedagogies that is the most valuable. If there is a particular technology or activity that you believe is noticeably absent from this book, please write to us and let us know.

Curtis J. Bonk
*Indiana University*
*Bloomington, Indiana*
Ke Zhang
*Wayne State University*
*Detroit, Michigan*

# ACKNOWLEDGMENTS

Many individuals contributed to the production of this book. We thank a host of people around the globe who have learned about the R2D2 model and have given us their reactions and testimonials regarding its use. We appreciate all those who have attended our workshops and other presentations and provided feedback, friendship, and far-reaching ideas leading to improvements in the original design. The optimistic and energetic among you have supplied us with the fuel to generate this book. A warm thanks to each of you!

There are indeed many kindred souls walking this planet who have decided, at least for now, to explore the area of online teaching and learning. It is you who have made this field grow and who have helped increase the quality and authenticity of online courses and programs. Please, never stop pushing ahead and making a personal dent or mark in the reform and progress of education and human learning! Each of you must continually attempt to make your dents!

More specifically, we thank our editor, David Brightman, and his assistant, Erin Null, who provided guidance for the structure of this book. In addition to the support from folks at Jossey-Bass, we are each blessed with some of the best students and colleagues in the world, who provided candid feedback on our ideas as well as ample encouragement, humor, and resources where and when needed. Countless former students served as colleagues who provided comments and suggestions related to various chapters as we completed them.

We think of each of you daily. In addition, many other colleagues around the planet offered us inspiration, encouragement, ideas, suggestions, advice, resources, and other feedback. Such individuals include John Savery of the University of Akron, Thomas Reynolds of National University, Veronica Acosta-Deprez of California State University at Long Beach, Christina Mainka and Panos Vlachopoulos of Napier University, Mimi Lee and Grace Lin of the University of Houston, Xun Ge of the University of Oklahoma, Jon Dron of Athabasca University, Jay Cross of the InternetTime.com group, Chris Dede of Harvard University, Vanessa Dennen and Hye-Yoon Jung of Florida State University, Julie Young of the Florida Virtual School, Abtar Kaur of the Open University of Malaysia, Ron Owston of York University, R. Lena Lee of Ohio University, Hyo-Jeong So of the National Institute of Education in Singapore, Kyong-Jee Kim of Sungkyunkwan University, Randy Garrison of the University of Calgary, Gilly Salmon of the University of Leicester, Jim Hensman and Andy Syson of the University of Coventry, Siew-Mee Barton of Deacon University, Norah Jones of the University of Glamorgan, Inae Kang of Kyung Hee University, Okhwa Lee of Chungbuk National University, our wonderful colleagues at Indiana University and Wayne State University, and many others who are far too numerous to thank individually here. We thank you all! May each of you find success as well as support the successes of others in the Web of Learning. Finally, we thank our families for putting up with us while we were writing this book.

# ABOUT THE AUTHORS

Curt Bonk and Ke Zhang designed this book based on their more than two decades of combined distance education teaching experience as well as the insights they have acquired from conversations with thousands of individuals during their travels around the globe. Countless questions, issues, and suggestions arose in those conversations that they address in this book. They each have experience teaching fully online as well as in blended environments, courses using videoconferencing, and, of course, face-to-face (FTF) or on-ground courses. In addition, Bonk was involved with correspondence and television-based courses during the 1980s at the University of Wisconsin.

This book would certainly not exist without distance learning. The seeds for this particular book, in fact, began to germinate during a videoconferencing presentation from Bonk to one of Zhang's classes in the spring of 2005. Bonk and Zhang have each conducted extensive research in the area of online learning, in particular, on collaborative teaming, problem-based learning, online mentoring, and national and international trends in online and blended learning in both higher education and corporate training. Their work has also addressed K–12 environments and military settings. Bonk and Zhang are highly interested in the support structures for effective online teaching and learning.

**Curtis J. Bonk** is a former corporate controller and CPA, who, after becoming sufficiently bored with that, received his master's and Ph.D. degrees in educational psychology from the University of Wisconsin. After serving on the faculty of West Virginia University from 1989 to 1992, he arrived at Indiana University (IU) in 1992 where he was a professor of educational psychology for thirteen years and is now in the Instructional Systems Technology Department and an adjunct professor in the School of Informatics. Dr. Bonk was a senior research fellow with the Advanced Distributed Learning Lab within the Department of Defense. He has received numerous teaching and mentoring awards from IU, as well as the CyberStar Award from the Indiana Information Technology Association in 2002, the Most Outstanding Achievement Award from the U.S. Distance Learning Association in 2003, and the Most Innovative Teaching in a Distance Education Program Award from the state of Indiana in 2003. In 2004, Bonk received an alumni achievement award from the University of Wisconsin. Dr. Bonk has presented more than eight hundred talks around the globe related to online teaching and learning and has more than two hundred publications on topics such as online learning pedagogy, massive multiplayer online gaming, collaborative technologies, synchronous and asynchronous computer conferencing, and frameworks for Web-based instruction and evaluation. Two of his previous books are *Electronic Collaborators* (1998) and the *Handbook of Blended Learning Environments: Global Perspectives, Local Designs* (2006). Finally, he is president of CourseShare and SurveyShare and can be contacted at cjbonk@ indiana.edu or via his homepage at http://mypage.iu.edu/~cjbonk/.

**Ke Zhang** moved to the highly recognized Instructional Technology Program at Wayne State University in July 2006 as an assistant professor. Prior to that, she was on the faculty at Texas Tech University for three years. She received her master's of science and Ph.D. in instructional systems from the Pennsylvania State University with a minor in business administration. Dr. Zhang has professionally consulted in areas such as instructional design, organizational change, training, and workforce development with clients like Siemens, Procter & Gamble, Pepsi, and Otis. Her extensive research activities have resulted in dozens of refereed journal articles, book chapters, and conference presentations on topics related to online learning, collaborative technology, problem solving, problem-based learning, e-learning, and computers as mindtools. Ke can be reached via email at ke.zhang@wayne.edu or via her homepage at http://itlab.coe.wayne.edu/kzhang/index.htm.

THE JOSSEY-BASS

HIGHER AND ADULT EDUCATION SERIES

# CHAPTER ONE

# THE R2D2 MODEL

## Read, Reflect, Display, and Do

## The Web of Learning

Given that you have decided to read at least part of this book, chances are you have explored online learning and become enthralled by its tools, resources, and overall educational potential. Other times you probably have experienced extensive frustration and hesitation. As we mentioned in the Preface to this book, we have named the place you have entered many times "the Web of Learning." We use this phrase in an attempt to help online educators, learners, and policymakers focus on what is available or potentially available online for *learning* instead of on the technologies. Within the Web of Learning metaphor, educational professionals can begin to design models and frameworks that can clarify and simplify online educational possibilities. Our hope is that more innovative, engaging, and exciting pedagogy will ensue.

The Web of Learning contains a plethora of educationally relevant and continually evolving resources, tools, and learning materials, many of which are increasingly open and free to the world. What will you find there? Without too much digging, you will discover online games, virtual worlds, simulations, online conferences or professional meetings, podcasts (typically, online audio files that can be downloaded or listened to) on nearly any topic imaginable, community-developed resources such as wikis, cultural and historical information, links to museums, libraries, and learning resource centers spanning the planet, and countless visual records of human history. Any of these resources and materials can be embedded in online courses and programs.

But many educators are stymied when they enter the Web of Learning, and rightfully so. There seems to be an endless number of learning portals and resources relevant to one's courses, a growing number of tools that one can utilize within a course, and thousands of resources that might find their way into online course activities. With so many instructional opportunities, technology tools, and e-learning resources and materials inundating instructors today, it is not surprising that many simply choose to ignore the Web of Learning or use it in the most minimal way possible. To help those who are hesitant or resistant, we offer more than 100 ideas for employing the Web of Learning in fully online and blended courses. And we provide a model or framework for reflecting on and organizing or compartmentalizing such activities.

## The Need for a Comprehensive Online Teaching Model

As noted in the Preface, there is a mounting need to address diverse learning preferences and various generations of learners. It is clear that e-learning tools and learning approaches within the Web of Learning hold exciting possibilities for personalizing the learning experience of young and old, visual as well as verbal learners, and digitally inexperienced as well as digitally savvy online learners. Unfortunately, currently popular online learning courseware of most any stripe or name (that is, course management systems [CMSs], learning management systems [LMSs], virtual learning environments [VLEs], and so on) is severely limited in the means to address the diverse needs of online learners. As most online instructors and students realize, typical online courses rely heavily on text-based assignments and intensive online readings. Course materials, including syllabi, handouts, PowerPoint presentations, assignments, and online discussion activities, are primarily available in written text (though, as Chapters Six and Seven make evident, there has been a recent shifting toward augmenting or perhaps even transforming such activities with visual learning enhancements).

In any online environment today, communications either among students or between students and instructors—the heart and soul of online learning (especially in higher education)—are mostly achieved through written formats such as e-mails, discussion boards, and text chats. The lack of visual tools such as graphics, charts, diagrams, and the like challenges learners who would prefer visuals of some type to help with their conceptualizations, manipulations, and memorizations. Reflective learners may also find text-based readings less engaging, since they tend to prefer to learn through various forms of observation and deep pondering. Likewise, those who resonate with hands-on activities and real-world applications would most likely anxiously look for the same experiences in their online learning tasks and activities. Suffice to say, most online courses, no matter what the discipline, topic, audience, or work sector, are limited in scope and fail to take advantage of the abundant educational opportunities in the Web of Learning.

## The Read, Reflect, Display, and Do Model

For educational progress, it is vital to make sense of this mammoth Web of Learning. The Read, Reflect, Display, and Do (R2D2) model was designed specifically for addressing varied student learning preferences, diverse backgrounds and experiences, and generational differences. Some students may excel with tasks that are visual, while others might prefer hearing the words or reading from electronic or paper-based texts. Still others might want to jump in and try things out for themselves. And some individuals might be happy reflecting on expert models or their own learning journeys. Of course, most often the learning materials and activities are not as discrete as this but instead involve a combination of such approaches (for example, an activity might be both visually intense and hands-on). R2D2 can help there too!

Throughout this book there are dozens of detailed activities and examples related to the four phases of R2D2 along with suggestions on how they might be used with different types of learners and situations. Our primary goal is to divvy up the Web of Learning so that educators, trainers, teachers, tutors, mentors, freelance lecturers, and instructional designers across educational sectors will actively employ it in their own instruction, and not avoid it at all costs. Baby steps, as Bill Murray repeated to himself over and over in the movie *What About Bob?*, are perhaps what many hesitant or resistant educators need. Using pieces of the R2D2 framework is akin to taking baby steps into this extremely daunting yet enticing Web of Learning. At the same time, it can foster giant leaps for those wishing to take more extensive risks in their online teaching activities.

R2D2 arrives in an age that is overflowing with educational transitions. These transitions include the movement from lecture-dominated classes and lockstep or predefined content to the use of learner-controlled hypermedia and exploratory events. In effect, it is a revolution across educational settings, from teacher-centered content and delivery of such content to learner-enabled and learner-centered learning. There is a simultaneous shift from the primary use of face-to-face (FTF) instruction across educational settings and events to one that blends two or more delivery formats while providing a plethora of learning options. There is also an associated transformation, then, from teaching or training only learners whom you can see and physically interact with to teaching anyone located anywhere on this planet (and beyond, of course); with R2D2 your students might go where no online learner has gone before.

As you explore this book, consider it part of a personal pilgrimage into what you can do online in the Web of Learning. This book is purposefully not laced with prescriptions, though we do offer ample suggestions, caveats, and guidelines. As such, it is perhaps most suited to those in the online teaching and learning trenches who are looking for ways to make sense of this somewhat forbidding online world. Nevertheless, this journey into the Web of Learning is meant for everyone. Use what you can and modify, ignore, or discard the rest. Safe journeys!

## On the Road to R2D2

As indicated, there are four phases—Read, Reflect, Display, and Do—within the R2D2 model. Based on the work of many educators who have explored individual differences in learning and associated learning preferences and styles (for example, Kolb, 1984; Fleming & Mills, 1992; McCarthy, 1987), Table 1.1 provides details on the four phases of R2D2, including instructional activities that link to each area and various types of learners: auditory, verbal, reflective, observational, visual, kinesthetic, and tactile. However, nearly every activity discussed in this book addresses, at least in a small way, more than one phase and learning preference or style. Our classifications, therefore, are meant to indicate which aspect is primarily, though not solely, being addressed. If instructors, trainers, and instructional designers involved in distance learning initiatives take these four types of learning preferences into account when designing and delivering online and other forms of distance learning courses, they should experience higher levels of success.

Despite its applicability to instructional designers and the online course design process, R2D2 is not an instructional design model; instead, it is a framework for the design of online learning environments and activities. It is a lens that might be positioned over the top of one's instructional design approaches. The focus is on what instructors can enable learners to do, not necessarily what sequence of steps or procedures to embed within a training event or course.

As evident in Figure 1.1, the R2D2 model aligns well with various learning style and multiple intelligence measures. In particular, it draws on ideas from Kolb's (1984) learning cycle, McCarthy's 4MAT system (1987), and the VARK (that is, visual, aural, read/write, and kinesthetic) learning style model of Fleming and Mills (1992). Like 4MAT, VARK, and many other learning style or preferences schemes, the R2D2 model proposes an integration of

## TABLE 1.1.   LEARNING PREFERENCES, ACTIVITIES, AND TECHNOLOGIES IN R2D2.

| Phase and Type of Learner | Learning Preferences and Activities | Sample Technology Resources and Tools |
|---|---|---|
| 1. Read: Auditory and verbal learners | Auditory and verbal learners prefer words, sounds, and spoken or written explanations. | Podcasts, online PDF documents, sound or audio files, PowerPoint presentations, online portals, course announcements, help systems, FAQs, Webquests, online newsletters, e-books, and online journals |
| 2. Reflect: Reflective and observational learners | Reflective and observational learners prefer to reflect, observe, view, and watch learning; they make careful judgments and view things from different perspectives, including reflection, self-testing, review, and reflective summary writing. | Blogs, synchronous chats, online exams, writing aids, electronic portfolios, asynchronous discussion, reflective writing tools, online review and self-testing aids, expert videos or performances |
| 3. Display: Visual learners | Visual learners prefer diagrams, concept maps, flowcharts, timelines, pictures, films, and demonstrations. | Concept mapping and timeline tools, interactive news, videostreamed content, online videos, virtual field trips and tours, animations, whiteboards, videoconferencing, online videos, interactive news media, online charts and graphs and visualizations tools, video blogs (that is, vblogs), vodcasts |
| 4. Do: Tactile and kinesthetic learners | Tactile and kinesthetic learners prefer role play, dramatization, cooperative games, simulations, scenarios, creative movement and dance, multisensory activities, manipulatives, and hands-on projects. | Simulations, online games, wikis, digital storytelling and movie making, real-time cases, video scenarios, survey research, continuous stories, groupware and collaborative tools, role play and debate tools |

four types of learning activities: (1) reading, (2) reflecting (including reflective writing), (3) displaying, and (4) doing. Clearly, by targeting auditory or verbal, reflective, visual, and kinesthetic learners, R2D2 is highly similar to the VARK method. However, the R2D2 method places more emphasis on reflective activities by emphasizing writing processes and activities in the second phase of the

**FIGURE 1.1. PHASES OF R2D2.**

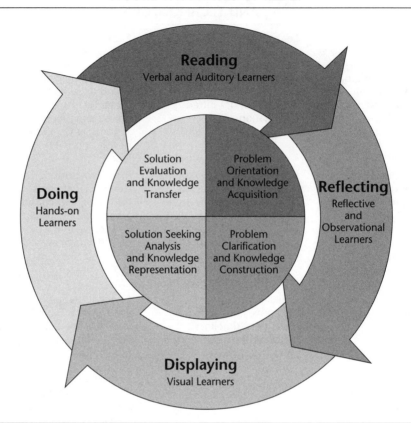

model rather than grouping them with reading, as the VARK model does. In addition, the R2D2 model has a special focus on the application of emerging learning technologies in fully online learning and blended learning.

As shown in Figure 1.1, the first phase of R2D2 (reading) relates primarily to methods to help learners acquire knowledge through such tasks as online readings, e-learning explorations, and listening to podcasted lectures. As such, it addresses verbal and auditory learners. The second phase of the model (reflecting) focuses on reflective activities such as online blogs, reflective writing, and self-check or review activities and self-testing examinations. In the third phase (displaying), visual representations of the content are highlighted with activities such as virtual tours, timelines, animations, and concept maps. The fourth phase of the model (doing) emphasizes what learners can do with the content in hands-on activities, including simulations, scenarios, and real-time cases. When thoughtfully designed and effectively delivered, content and activities created from the R2D2 perspective are more engaging and enriching for learners.

At its core, the R2D2 model is a starting point to help online instructors understand the assorted backgrounds of online learners and become better equipped to address their diversity. Such a model can be used to appeal to the wide-ranging preferences of online learners of varied generations and different levels of Internet familiarity. It also affords users a means to apply the widely available and often free technology tools and resources in many types of online learning activities.

R2D2 may also work well for problem-based learning or in a problem-solving process in general. As indicated in Figure 1.1, the four phases of the R2D2 model introduce a variety of learning activities for the different problem-solving stages, from initial accumulation of knowledge (that is, reading) to reflecting on such knowledge (that is, reflection) to visually showing what one has learned (that is, displaying) to trying out that new knowledge (that is, doing). For example, readings address problem orientation and knowledge acquisition, whereas reflections help with problem clarification and knowledge construction. In addition, activities for displaying learning would be particularly powerful for knowledge representation of the problem or situation as well as solution seeking and analysis. Finally, the doing phase aligns well with solution evaluation and knowledge transfer in the problem-solving process.

Also worth mentioning is the dynamic nature of the model, as events occurring in different phases of the model impact other phases and may cause the learner to revisit steps already deemed completed. As a nonlinear model, R2D2 suggests a dynamic approach to online learning and encourages instructors, designers, and learners to select diverse learning activities strategically from different phases and to incorporate them in various sequences to better address learners' different needs and preferences.

While the journals and research literature devoted to e-learning continue to increase at dizzying rates, there exists a severe lack of practical models such as R2D2 that can help instructors, trainers, instructional designers, and other educational professionals with easy-to-apply learning activities that result in effective and enjoyable online learning.

As will become clear in reading this book, the R2D2 model reaches beyond any given CMS or Web-based learning platform or system. Given the infinite resources available within the Web of Learning, courses designed using this model or framework could offer online learners massive and captivating opportunities for reading, reflecting, displaying, and doing.

## Linking the Phases of R2D2 to Human Problem Solving

While the chapters of this book detail four distinct phases to the R2D2 model—Read, Reflect, Display, and Do—we admit that nearly any instructional activity or approach attempted within the Web of Learning will undoubtedly involve more than one phase. Our four-part classification scheme is simply meant to indicate which aspect of learning is primarily being addressed. If online educators and trainers take these four types of learning and associated learning activities into account when designing and delivering their courses, they would likely experience higher success rates. And, as shown in Table 1.2, they might also use them to foster learner problem solving and the overall human problem-solving process.

The R2D2 model may serve as a framework to guide the design and implementation of a comprehensive problem-solving or problem-based learning environment. In fact, the four phases of R2D2 also represent different phases and steps inherent in human problem solving. For example, a problem-solving process may start with precursory reading activities to help students understand the nature of the problem or make sense of what the problem really

### TABLE 1.2.   SAMPLE USE OF R2D2 FOR LEARNER PROBLEM SOLVING.

| Problem-Solving Stages | Major Tasks | R2D2 Phase and Activities |
|---|---|---|
| Problem statement or definition | Define the task or problem<br>Identify information needed to complete the task<br>Sort and filter through information, find relevant information and data<br>Listen to what experts have to say on a certain topic | Reading |
| Finding paths to solutions | Brainstorm possible sources<br>Evaluate the possible sources to determine priorities | Reading<br>Reflecting<br>Writing<br>Participating |
| Locate, access, organize, and apply information or resources to solve problems | Locate, access (read, listen to, or watch) resources and information<br>Synthesize information to solve problems | Reading<br>Reflecting<br>Displaying<br>Doing |
| Evaluate solutions | Use and evaluate effectiveness of solutions | Doing<br>Reflecting |

is (that is, Phase 1: Reading). Next, the learner might move to Phase 2 with reflective activities to assist in further clarification of the problem and sort out possible problem-solving paths (Phase 2: Reflecting). Third, such a learner might then proceed to tasks involving information organization, analysis, synthesis, and representation (Phase 3: Displaying). Finally, this problem-solving cycle ends with the evaluation and use of the data that the learner has gathered and sifted through (Phase 4: Doing). While these are perhaps the most logical steps, as noted later in the chapter, it is conceivable that the problem-solving process as well as the use of the R2D2 model could unfold in the exact opposite direction.

Phase 1 of the R2D2 model is pithily and purposely labeled as "Reading." In reality, however, it involves much more than simply reading text-based materials. We believe that it is the most comprehensive and complex of the four phases. As noted in Table 1.2, the "reading phase" is the exploration, fact-finding, and knowledge acquisition stage of the learning process. You need new knowledge and ideas in order to have something to reflect upon (that is, R2D2 Phase 2), to visualize and organize (Phase 3), and to apply your learning and make it meaningful (Phase 4). Instead of overloading and boring students with written texts, Phase 1 of the model introduces a wide range of learning activities and experiences to help learners acquire knowledge, including the use of podcasting, synchronous conferencing, instant messaging, and other content-rich events and activities. It is the stage of learning meant to intrigue and engage learners in the learning process, not to bore them or cause them to promptly file out.

Phase 2 of the R2D2 model emphasizes learners' reflective processes, speaking to reflective or observational learners who learn and problem solve from watching or observing others as well as thoughtfully deliberating on expert models and examples. While closely related to Phase 1 reading activities, Phase 2 pays special attention to activities and events that stimulate personal reflection through collaboration and virtual group activities, self-questioning, reflective writing and prompting, and intense and interactive challenges.

Phase 3 of the model, displaying one's learning, is geared to visual learners. This phase of problem solving aims to help online learners not only to understand the content being taught but also to further build their own knowledge base with strategies such as concept mapping, visualization, and advance organizers.

Finally, the "Doing" phase, Phase 4 of the R2D2 model, addresses the crucial need for hands-on experiences in online learning environments, which is probably the weakest link of current e-learning phenomena. The doing phase guides instructors to utilize widely available online resources and technologies for various learning activities. These activities not only meet the expectations of those doers, but, as noted in Table 1.2, also promote knowledge application, problem solving, and other higher-order thinking skills in general.

**TABLE 1.3. LEARNING ACTIVITIES IN EACH PHASE OF R2D2.**

| Reading | Reflecting | Displaying | Doing |
|---|---|---|---|
| 1. Online Scavenger Hunt | 26. Post Model Answers | 51. Anchored Instruction with Online Video | 76. Web-Based Survey Research |
| 2. Web Tours and Safaris | 27. Reuse Chat Transcripts | 52. Explore and Share Online Museums and Libraries | 77. Video Scenario Learning |
| 3. WebQuest | 28. Workplace, Internship, or Job Reflections | 53. Concept Mapping Key Information | 78. Content Review Games |
| 4. Guided Readings | 29. Field and Lab Observations | 54. Videostreamed Lectures and Presentations | 79. Online Review and Practice Exercises |
| 5. Discovery Readings | 30. Self-Check Quizzes and Exams | 55. Videostreamed Conferences and Events | 80. Mock Trial or Fictional Situations |
| 6. Foreign Language Reading Activities and Online News | 31. Online Discussion Forums and Group Discussions | 56. Interactive News and Documentaries | 81. Online Role Play of Personalities |
| 7. FAQ and Course Announcement Feedback | 32. Online Portal Explorations and Reflections | 57. Interactive Online Performances | 82. Action Research |
| 8. Question-and-Answer Sessions with Instructor | 33. Lurker, Browser, or Observer in Online Groups | 58. Design Evaluation | 83. Interactive Fiction and Continuous Stories |
| 9. Online Expert Chats | 34. Podcast Tours | 59. Design Generation | 84. Real-Time Cases |
| 10. Online Synchronous Testing | 35. Personal Blogs | 60. Design Reviews and Expert Commentary | 85. Course Resource Wiki Site |
| 11. Synchronous or Virtual Classroom Instructor Presentations | 36. Collaborative or Team Blogs | 61. Online Timeline Explorations and Safaris | 86. Wikibook Projects |
| 12. Online Webinars | 37. Online Resource Libraries | 62. Virtual Tours | 87. Online Glossary and Resource Links Projects |
| 13. Public Tutorials, Wizards, and Help Systems | 38. Social Networking Linkages | 63. Visual Web Resource Explorations | 88. On-Demand and Workflow Learning |

14. Expert Lectures and Commentary
15. An Online Podcast Lecture or Podcast Show
16. Audio Dramas
17. Posting Video-Based Explanations and Demonstrations
18. Online Sound or Music Training
19. Online Literature Readings
20. Online Poetry Readings
21. Posting Webliographies or Web Resources
22. Text Messaging Course Notes and Content
23. Text Messaging Course Reminders and Activities
24. Online Language Lessons
25. E-Book and Wikibook Reports and Critiques

39. Online Role Play Reflections
40. Synchronous and Asynchronous Discussion Combinations
41. Self-Check Reflection Activities
42. Electronic Portfolios
43. Individual Reflection Papers
44. Team or Group Reflective Writing Tasks
45. Super-Summaries, Portfolio Reflections, and Personal Philosophy Papers
46. Online Cases, Situations, and Vignettes
47. Satellite Discussion or Special Interest Groups
48. Small-Group Case Creations and Analyses
49. Small-Group Exam Question Challenges
50. Reaction or Position Papers

64. Animations
65. Advance Organizers: Models, Flowcharts, Diagrams, Systems, and Illustrations
66. Virtual Field Trips
67. Video Modeling and Professional Development
68. Movie Reviews for Professional Development
69. Whiteboard Demonstrations
70. Online Visualization Tools
71. Video Blogs and Adventure Learning
72. Charts and Graph Tools
73. Mashups of Google Maps
74. Broadcast Events
75. Online Multimedia and Visually Rich Cases

89. Digital Storytelling
90. Online Documentation of Internship, Field Placement, and Practicum Knowledge Applications and Experiences
91. Authentic Data Analysis
92. Online Science Labs and Simulations
93. Simulation Games
94. Simulations and Games for Higher-Level Skills
95. Client Consulting and Experiential Learning
96. Online Tutoring and Mentoring
97. Cross-Class Product Development and Creativity
98. Cross-Class Content Discussions, Analyses, Competitions, and Evaluations
99. Learner Podcast Activities, Events, and Shows
100. Design Course Web Site

## Summary of Activities for R2D2

Chapters Two through Nine of this book elaborate on each phase of the model, with more details on their theoretical foundations as well as dozens of practical applications and examples. Table 1.3 summarizes the twenty-five activities related to each phase of R2D2 that we outline in Chapters Three, Five, Seven, and Nine. We recommend you use this table as a guide for your reading of the remainder of the book. Perhaps check off or circle the strategies that interest you or that you have already attempted. Then come back to this table as you read different sections of this book.

Later in the book, Chapter Ten expands upon this list by including other factors such as time intensity, cost, risk, and duration of the activity. In fact, Chapter Ten reassembles the ideas from the previous eight chapters and therefore, offers opportunities to contemplate the overall framework and power of the R2D2 model. At that time, you might ruminate on whether we met your expectations in designing a model that addresses the learning-related preferences of the highly diverse learners of this planet.

## Further Thoughts on R2D2

Reading, Reflecting, Displaying, and Doing: these are the entry points for the R2D2 model. Each activity addresses a particular learning preference and type of learning. The phases may be applied independently in a lesson if a certain preference is dominant among the targeted learners as well as when a particular type of learning is believed to be the most appropriate. More practically, when attempting to address a diverse student body (or global workforce), instructors may choose activities from more than one of these phases and create a range of e-learning tasks and events for their online courses.

An online activity deemed applicable to a particular discipline, educational group, or age level can often be used substantively within another educational sector or population. With the appropriate modifications, tweaking, and guidelines, most, if not all, of the 100+ strategies described in this book can be applied to any population of learners, educational level, or training setting or situation. At the same time, they must fit with your goals and objectives. Some may require extensive modification before they are useful in your particular setting.

While R2D2 is not an instructional design model, it certainly could be applied as a practical guide for instructors in their efforts to prepare engaging learning materials and activities. For example, an instructor of an online graduate course or a teacher in a virtual high school could put together a lesson plan by selecting and integrating some activities from each of the four phases. Such purposeful decision making would help make sure that varied learner preferences and needs are addressed with appropriate activities and methods. In such cases, these varied learning activities may be carried out in different orders as appropriate. The R2D2 model is not a linear model; thus the learning events do not necessarily sequence from reading to reflecting and then move on to displaying and still later doing.

With continued innovations in educational technologies as well as in technologies not meant for education but that quickly find use there—witness the explosion of educational uses for the iPod—it is conceivable that only a few of the activities in this book will remain viable a decade from now. Tomorrow, next week, and during the many weeks and months that follow, there will be a flurry of ideas from many sources to enhance, extend, and transform the ideas presented here. Without a doubt, the Web of Learning, or its successor, will continue to sprout new learning paths and opportunities. For those concerned with online course quality and effectiveness, it is imperative to be on the lookout for such opportunities. They will appear in a speech that you did not intend to attend, in a footnote of a research paper you stumble upon, in a newsletter from a famous training guru, or in an e-mail or Web log (blog) from a professional organization. Creative pedagogical uses of the Web of Learning can spring up from anywhere. Raise your antennae! It would be fantastic if, in teaching or training online, you discovered one or two, a few dozen, or even hundreds of ideas we have not touched on here; with the R2D2 model, you now have a classification scheme in which to organize these ideas and reflect on their use.

## Some Final Words

The activities in this book are instructional templates or guides, not prescriptions. Think creatively with them. Say "Yes" or "Perhaps" before discounting or thinking "No way" to any of them. Hold off initial judgments or inner voices trying to convince you that this would never work or does not apply to me or my learners. Trust us, they can work nearly anywhere. So give it a go!

If you use any of the online resources or materials related to the 100+ activities that we describe in this book in your courses, training events, or publications, please write to the copyright owner of such materials for permission to use them. Copyright law requires that permission be requested to reproduce copyrighted materials. There are benefits, too, from contacting the original designers of the online resources or materials, since they may have important updates or extensions to share. In addition, they likely will be ecstatic that someone is making use of some of their ideas. When this occurs, expanding networks will form that will focus on sharing educational resources and pushing educational opportunities for the learners of this planet in a positive direction. Keep pushing!

CHAPTER TWO

# PHASE 1 OF THE R2D2 MODEL

## Verbal and Auditory Learners

The educational content offered in the Web of Learning has been repeatedly criticized for relying too heavily on text while providing minimal opportunities to learn from visuals and hands-on activities. It is certainly true that most content initially developed for online learning involved reading or writing activities. Any online learning instructor or trainer will likely have seen her share of asynchronous discussion forums, chats, Web pages to browse, and course announcements. Text, text, text, text, and still more text.

Such text is ideal for those who love to read as well as those with rich vocabularies. And, of course, given that the majority of text originally posted to the Web of Learning was in English, there is a distinct advantage to native speakers of English. But the tide is changing. As Jakob Nielson (2005) pointed out, more than one-third of Internet users now come from Asia. He further noted that sometime in the year 2005—thirty-six years from the first experimental connection in 1969 between a computer in Palo Alto, California, and another in Los Angeles—the Internet grew to more than 1 billion users. Nielson argued that the second billion will take only about a decade to reach, with the vast majority of new users coming from Asia. As that occurs, it is doubtful that the Web of Learning will continue to rely on so much text—at least in English, anyway.

## Continued Shortfalls of "Management" Systems

As alluded to in the previous chapter, the primary delivery systems for online learning (that is, course management systems [CMSs] and learning management systems [LMSs]) are often praised for increased organizational and administrative ("management") efficiencies. However, the truth of the matter is that the focus is on those features that are actually tangential to learning, such as course announcements, online gradebooks and tests, and the posting of online resources and modules. These are the tools that make the administrators being held accountable for such courses salivate and ask for more. However, such features are not tools for learning. We have to demand better. As Van Weigel (2005) argues, "The downside of the CMS is that it inhibits the individual as well as collective creativity of the class participants by forcing e-learning technologies into the familiar classroom categories of lectures, discussions, and exams (with an occasional opportunity to chat with the professor or other students 'after class')" (p. 55).

Weigel further argues that what happens is that there is an overriding focus on accessibility and convenience over pedagogical experimentation and skill development. He believes that the goal of online education should be to foster critical thinking skills, self-confidence, exploration, and the ability to collaborate and learn from peers.

But the overwhelming focus of administrators and vendors is on the online boxes or shells in which to dump content; it really does not matter if you are using course management systems such as Desire2Learn, Moodle, Sakai, Angel, WebCT, Blackboard, or some other system. Despite lawsuits suggesting that one company may have developed some tool or features before others, all these systems lack pedagogically noteworthy capabilities or qualities. This is unfortunate since, as Carmean and Haefner (2002) argue, "Students choose a course for its intellectual content ('mind') and not for its classroom or system container ('matter'). CMSs do not provide a pedagogical platform any more than chalk, chairs, and tables provide the classroom learning experience" (p. 28).

Instead of responding to vendor and administrator hype over some newly designed feature or upgrade, the focus needs to shift to deeper learning principles and tactics (Carmean & Haefner, 2003). For example, in effective online environments, there are important elements like timely feedback on student posts, student engagement in tasks that are closely aligned with the real world, and a sense of challenge in the learning content. Additionally, in such systems, there are built-in opportunities for learner reflection and interaction, learner choice and opportunities to explore personal interests, and respect for individual learning approaches and different backgrounds or degrees of prior knowledge on a topic. And, when appropriate, there might be expert or practitioner interactions and apprenticeships, virtual team projects and performances, and peer, teacher, tutor, or mentor scaffolding and feedback.

Few online courses we have observed actually embed the majority of these principles. In one of our studies conducted on dozens of course syllabi posted to the World Lecture Hall (see Cummings, Bonk, & Jacobs, 2002), only one syllabus incorporated expert or practitioner interactions. Equally problematic, most did not offer sufficient opportunities for learner reflections and explorations. Instead, the vast majority emphasized instructors doing something to the students. But the Web of Learning opens up possible interactions to include learner-practitioner interactions, instructor-instructor interactions, and even practitioner-practitioner interactions within a single course.

## The Curse of Text?

Since the dawn of the first online course, the easiest content to post or catalog to the Web of Learning has been text. There is nearly a decade of research that indicates that instructors will place on the Web of Learning what is easiest to do and what works (Bonk, 2002; Peffers & Bloom, 1999). Traditionally this has meant that text—not rich multimedia—was the primary delivery medium. There is nothing inherently wrong with relying on what works and what one has the time or energy to accomplish. With the advent of Flash animations (that is, online animations, movements, and captivating visual styles created using Adobe Flash animation software) and decreased storage costs, however, the days of text-only Web sites may be numbered. Yet, while text-based Web courses may soon be giving way to rich multimedia and alternative means to represent content, for now, text remains king.

Perhaps there is simultaneously a curse and a blessing of text, resulting from the fact that we are often swimming in it online. Just find the right button and one can upload a Word document, post a course announcement, or link to a Web resource that is loaded with text. Or perhaps you have a PowerPoint slide show loaded with even more text to lock into place and load to the Web. Or maybe there is a text-laden syllabus that simply needs to be converted to HTML (hypertext markup language) format that can then be interpreted and indexed by Internet browsers. And, of course, to start the course, there will undoubtedly be a series of course announcements and associated frequently asked questions (FAQs) posted to the course Web site or sent via e-mail. Most course announcements, of course, will be organizational or managerial in nature, such as reminders or pointers about books, course initiation dates, assignments, passwords, due dates, and course resources. Nothing is wrong with such information, but the Web of Learning now offers much more than that.

As is clear from the preceding discussion, there is an amazing amount of text that students must access, read, and understand in order to find safe passageway into any course. And that is before the course even begins. In some cases, the arrival of text only accelerates from there. What if one has a reading disability or is dyslexic? Will there be support? And, if so, how will such help be provided? Of course, there are government mandates in different countries regarding user accessibility, such as Section 508 of the Rehabilitation Act of 1998 in the United States. Just who will check or guarantee that online courses across educational sectors offer such special help?

## The Blessing of Text?

On the other hand, the heavy reliance on text in online courses may be a blessing in disguise. First, it allows for online experimentation that is not too much different from face-to-face (FTF) courses. Hence, learners are fairly easily acclimated to online courses, since they can find familiar resources, tasks, and activities. Learners in FTF courses have tended to rely on text throughout their educational careers, and so too will their online ones exhibit such tendencies. Second, text is relatively easy for learners to download even when they have bandwidth limitations or constraints. So learners in rural communities as well as third world countries who lack broadband access to the Internet can more readily participate in an online class. Third, electronic text can be read by tools such as the Jaws Screen Reader to help visually impaired learners. In addition, clever (and sometimes entertaining) tools like Babelfish exist to translate such text to other languages with just one mouse click. For example, entering the words "A Web of Learning" into Babelfish and translating it from English to Spanish yields "*Un Web de todo.*" Fourth, new knowledge or learning inroads made can be swiftly communicated through text and shared with others around the planet without too much worry about whether the receivers have the necessary infrastructure to handle a particular task, activity, or resource.

Due to this pervasive reliance on text, there have been a plethora of advances in online teaching and learning (and certainly many drawbacks as well). Because of the throughput possible with text, online educators have experimented with many types of online courses, course experiences, and programs that might not have otherwise been considered, much less attempted. Perhaps this age of online text was a necessary one. Perhaps it is simply a prime example of starting with baby steps and proceeding from there. It is extremely difficult to promote novel uses of the Web of Learning until you are assured that what has been done in the past also can be replicated (at least to some degree) and perhaps improved upon online.

## Phase 1 of R2D2

Phase 1 of the Read, Reflect, Display, and Do (R2D2) model is perhaps more comprehensive and complex than any of the other three phases (see Figure 2.1). This is because it is the exploration and fact-finding stage of the

### FIGURE 2.1. PHASE 1 OF R2D2.

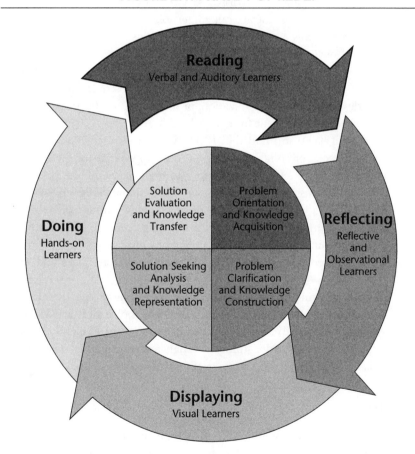

learning process. Given that you must typically acquire knowledge prior to using knowledge, this first phase of the model focuses on knowledge acquisition. Consequently, at least at the present time, it is heavily embedded with text-related activities that tend to favor verbal and auditory learners.

In the Web of Learning, there are myriad ways that knowledge can be acquired—through watching and listening to videostreamed lectures and podcasts, synchronous presentations, online discussions with peers, guest expert chats, and online and paper-based readings and explorations. Clearly, such resources favor auditory and verbal learners. In effect, in Phase 1, you sift through text in electronic reading assignments or on text-laden screens in your online explorations. The format of the readings is constantly evolving as electronic versions become more widely available and accepted. The standards for electronic books remain in a state of flux, though acceptability has been raised as e-book costs have become more affordable and screen display devices more crisp.

If an e-book is not at your fingertips, you may instead decide to listen to audio recordings from experts, including instructor lectures or commentaries. And once complete, you can enter into a series of online discussions and debates with peers who have completed the same or similar sets of resources. No longer must such discussion, however, be restricted to learners from your own designated class, organization, or institution. In the Web of Learning, peers and teachers can appear from anywhere.

Again, keep in mind that R2D2 is not meant to represent every possible learning tactic or combination of learning approaches or methods. Educational professionals, nonetheless, can use it to make sense of the possibilities. And it may not be instructors, trainers, or instructional designers who most significantly benefit from the model; instead, it might more directly influence the learners themselves. If you prefer learning from text or words, or you just happen to find yourself in activities that emphasize text, you might discover that you excel within these types of online learning tasks and resources. For instance, you might prefer learning from online tutorials or some types of audio files. Or you might rely on speaking or presenting online as well as reading the posts of your peers (perhaps using the chat tool within a CMS or LMS or a synchronous conferencing system such as Elluminate, Centra, or Breeze). You might also enjoy talking things through and negotiating meaning, perhaps in online group discussion forums or threaded conversations.

## Podcasting

Technology that promotes and repackages text in different formats and display devices continues to rise. As anyone walking through a college or university setting today would notice, iPods are presently the "in" thing. Because of the convenience of mobile devices such as cell phones and MP3 players (that is, portable devices that allow the user to store, organize, and play audio files), learners of all ages are coming to expect that they can access and participate in different learning modules through these devices. In response, courses at many universities are now offering access to online audio files from FTF lectures (or from specially made podcasts for an online course) that students can download to their MP3 players or iPods. The learners can then listen to, or, if in video format, watch such files when the time is available, including when driving, walking, running, or quietly sitting at a beach or in a park. Learning, then, is extended to every possible waking moment in one's life. But do you, either as a lifelong learner or as an online instructor, take advantage of it?

Podcasting, which typically involves only an audio channel, is rapidly growing in use in online learning in all settings: K–12, higher education, and corporate and military training. In the Web of Learning, there are now designated educational podcast shows that attract daily or weekly audiences, as well as podcast clearinghouses such as Podcast Alley, or, for the K–12 crowd, the Education Podcast Network (EPN). Podcast Alley, for instance, indexes podcast sites; as of August 2006, it had indexed more than 23,000 different podcast sites, nearly 1,000 of which were educational podcasts. Those 23,000 Podcast sites contained more than 830,000 individual podcast episodes. Imagine the educational potential in just this one portal, among the hundreds of thousands, now found on the Internet. How can any educational professional keep track of all the possibilities?

Many refer to an educational podcast as akin to an online talk radio show. But it is perhaps more reminiscent of a public broadcasting show featuring the ideas or work of a well-known scholar or expert. We find that a 5–15 minute podcast of a lecture makes the best use of this technology. And if two or three people can be involved, perhaps in a question-and-answer dialogue, it adds to the interactivity of the session and, hence, to the chance for learner engagement. We typically note three to five controversial or key questions for a chapter or unit and have the person moderating the podcast ask these questions at different moments during the podcast.

With more recent video iPods, there is the capability to juxtapose videoclips against the audio. If you do this, it is called *vodcasting*. Psychologists like Alan Paivio (1991) and Richard Mayer (2003) have long promoted the use of multiple forms of media in learning, such as combining visual and verbal aspects of learning. In psychological terms, this is referred to as *dual-coding theory*. According to this view, there are more pathways or possibilities to retrieve information if you have learned it in more than one format. Of course, there are many caveats here, such as those related to the timing or spacing of such learning and how coherent those materials are. Nevertheless, vodcasting and video-based blogging (to be discussed in Chapters Four and Five) will soon be common educational tools thanks to their power to personally strengthen the learning experience.

A growing use of educational vodcasting is in professional development training. For example, a company named SonoSite offers downloadable training videos to an iPod for dynamic review of various ultrasound techniques. Using such online training, ultrasound practitioners can get a refresher or quick and comprehensive review for any formal training workshops and courses that they might have received. While not intended to replace FTF training, they do enhance and update such training for critical patient procedures and evaluations. The vodcasts provide review materials and technique guides, while exams test such knowledge. It is another example of dual coding and the power of multimedia in action.

Training guru Elliott Masie offers a type of vodcast training as part of his annual "Learning" conference each October and also as part of his frequent interviews with experts during the year. Masie interviews famous people in the training field and posts links to the audio file or podcast from such interviews with a "Listen" icon to click on, a PDF of the text transcript with a "Read" icon to click on, and sometimes a video to "Watch." Clearly, Masie is offering several key options (that is, see it, read it, or watch it) with these multimedia vodcasts so that you can select what is best for you given your available time, learning preferences, familiarity, and interest in the topic. In particular, this should appeal to auditory, reflective, and visual learners. At the same time, Masie is attempting to establish a model for how other educational organizations and institutions around the globe might design their training. Such an approach epitomizes twenty-first-century training; at least at the start of it!

Such techniques and devices allow learners to learn anywhere. And when universities such as Duke and Drexel give away iPods to incoming students, when the University of Michigan is heavily promoting their use in its dentistry program, and when the University of Maryland equips M.B.A. students with BlackBerry devices (that is, a wireless handheld device that supports e-mail, Internet browsing, text messaging, faxing, mobile telephone, and other wireless information services) for promoting communication and organization skills, there is increased media attention, public scrutiny, and instructor experimentation (Blaisdell, 2006). Make no mistake, many students on college campuses are being given free technology when they arrive for their freshman year. And, as an incentive to enroll, potential students are typically shown how different technologies are being incorporated into instruction when they tour college campuses. Yes, the green spaces are wonderful, professors well known, and workout facilities superb, but it is the iPod or laptop that students will write home about or take back with them when their courses are done.

This is the age of technology in learning, and it is now in full view. So when high schools in Miami, Florida, allow flip-flops as part of standard student dress but not iPods (Sampson, 2006), it draws simultaneous public acclaim and criticism. Certainly educators in Miami must have stopped and pondered what flip-flops have to do with a student's education before making such a decision. Perhaps some might even had the gumption to protest such rulings and point out how iPods might be creatively incorporated into the curriculum to foster student attendance and elevate their achievement test scores. Why are school districts afraid to address the use of iPods with progressive curriculum change initiatives? Is this a sign that they are afraid of the Internet? Or do they simply lack frameworks from which to think about better utilizing it?

## Synchronous Conferencing

In addition to iPods, there has been much attention recently given to virtual classrooms or *synchronous conferencing* technologies (that is, technologies that offer real-time presence of the instructor and students and live interactions as opposed to asynchronous or delayed conferencing wherein one can contribute from anyplace and anytime; often synchronous conferencing tools refer to real-time discussion or chat tools). With such systems, one can learn from live online expert presentations, chat discussions on the side, and small-group breakout sessions. As with vodcasting, mentioned earlier, with synchronous presentations from the instructor or a guest expert, the learner has multiple ways to internalize the information, including both visual and verbal representations. Synchronous conferencing tools provide a sense of teacher immediacy that asynchronous discussion forums too often fail to do because of their lack of prompt feedback on student questions and concerns. Online knowledge acquisition may also happen in virtual classrooms or Web conferences, with application sharing, Web touring, surveys and polls, online presentations, and chats.

Synchronous conferencing is definitely on the uptick. A recent study by the American Society for Training and Development (ASTD) indicates that virtual classroom tools such as WebEx and Centra are the most highly employed in training environments (Ellis, 2006). Tools rated lower by training professionals in that particular study, such as Elluminate and Macromedia Breeze (now Adobe Connect Pro), are more often found in higher education settings. K–12 schools tend not to use synchronous tools other than simple online text chat tools such as MSN Messenger or ones provided within their CMS. However, many do rely on free, Internet-based (IP) videoconferencing to exchange ideas with students from other schools and to learn from guest experts. Keep in mind, however, that these types of comparison studies vary widely in their results.

## Instant Messaging and Text Messaging

Instant messaging (IM) and text messaging are also tools that can be used to send content to learners. Already, more than 90 percent of organizations in the business world are utilizing IM in some way (Bronstein & Newman, 2006). According to Farmer (2005), by 2004, employees at International Business Machines (IBM) were sending more than 3 million IMs a day. This high use of IM at IBM apparently sped up company decision making while lowering phone costs and reducing the e-mail load on company servers. It also had a positive impact on employee collaboration and teaming, responsiveness, and overall productivity.

There are numerous reasons to incorporate IM into your training and educational courses and programs. First, there is an increased sense of awareness that others in your course are also online and might be available for consultation or support. For example, the course instructor or tutor is there for questioning. Such availability increases the sense of social presence on the part of the instructor and, therefore, can have a positive impact on student motivation and retention. Second, there is immediate feedback and rapid responsiveness, also known as *instructional immediacy*, that occurs in IM but is much less likely with asynchronous conferencing (that is, technologies that allow one to post from anywhere they have Web access and at any time; typically, there is no real-time interaction expected). Third, such tools are easy and convenient to use. Sure, IM systems continue to expand in tool features and options, but the basic features such as knowing who is currently online, who is away, and so on, are easy to understand. Fourth, Bronstein and Newman (2006) point out that an IM connection is akin to a conversation between two people; however, as these systems keep expanding the number of possible participants, such convenient one-to-one dialogues may evolve into something else. Finally, one can participate in an IM while completing other tasks. In fact, IM is often used to epitomize the multitasking needs and abilities of adolescent youth. Clearly, there are many advantages to incorporating IM into your online education and training plans.

In addition to instant messaging, text messaging using mobile phones and handheld devices is growing rapidly within courses and training experiences. Many schools, universities, and organizations are experimenting with sending content to students on their mobile phones. In Korea, which is known for mobile learning and high bandwidth capabilities, instructors can send video lectures and associated notes to students' personal multimedia players (PMPs) (Kim, 2004).

This is especially handy for students who miss part or all of a class. A PMP allows for many types of content, including voice messages, still images, games, MP3 music, and full motion video. In other parts of the world, instructors, trainers, and course designers are beginning to think of innovative instructional applications through text messaging tools, including polling learners on different topics, sending course reminders, and sharing ideas on books that they have read (Bronstein & Newman, 2006).

In one high school in New Zealand, a teacher is using an inventive system wherein students dial a specific number and receive replies along with notes on the Shakespeare-related content that they are studying (see Dye, 2006). In addition, homework tips, advice, and other relevant content can be forwarded to student mobile devices. Instead of sending or pushing content to students, this program is being advertised as the first "pull" system in K–12 schooling, wherein students actively access information that they want to receive. Like the modern-day equivalent of flashcards, students can replay or study such content in a car, bus, or train as well as at home. While there are small fees involved, approximately 30–40 percent of the students are utilizing the system.

## Recap

Such tools—podcasts, synchronous conferencing, instant messaging, text messaging, and IP-based video conferencing—are all ways to exchange words or text. Certainly, there are many more means for doing so; this is simply a partial list to show why Phase 1 is a critical component of the R2D2 model. As evident, there are multiple means by which to exploit the Web of Learning for highly auditory and verbal learners; in five or ten years, such a list will increase considerably. Since text is a highly familiar delivery mechanism for most learners of this planet, such technologies might be more easily exploited online without student complaints about confusion as to either the technology or the learning activity. While the focus of Phase 1 is on reading, Phase 2 entails greater reflection on such reading as well as writing activities. Before moving to Phase 2 learning, in the next chapter we provide twenty-five activities geared toward Phase 1 of R2D2.

CHAPTER THREE

# ACTIVITIES FOR PHASE 1

## Verbal and Auditory Learners

In this chapter, we present twenty-five learning activities that feature an emphasis on words and text corresponding with Phase 1 of the R2D2 model. The scales below each activity—the Key Instructional Considerations, related to the risk, time, cost, and degree of learner centeredness—are highly subjective and depend on many factors, including the content area, degree of learner familiarity with the Internet, and ages of the learners. Keep in mind that these risk, time, and cost indices are for the instructor, trainer, moderator, tutor, or course developer, not the learner or learning participants.

## Activity 1. Online Scavenger Hunt

*Description and Purpose of Activity.* An online scavenger hunt is a common activity to help students become familiar with the course content and to foster discovery learning by exploring the vast amount of Web resources available on a topic or the technologies (for example, a particular search engine) embedded within it. Scavenger hunts are highly popular in brick-and-mortar classrooms as well as in virtual schools in nearly any discipline. In a scavenger hunt, individuals or groups of learners might be asked to find a set of items in a list or accomplish a set of tasks. The Web is filled with thousands of scavenger hunt examples.

*Skills and Objectives.* Includes exploratory learning, concept review, search skills, and reflection on what is found and what is learned. It can also be used as an early course activity to determine if learners have the proper passwords and access to necessary technology tools and resources.

***Advice and Ideas.*** A scavenger hunt might be most appropriate at the start of an online course or at the beginning of a new unit. Learners can then use the activity to become familiar with the new content. For younger learners or those who are new to online learning, the directions need to be written with more detail. To design an online scavenger hunt, you first need to identify the learning objectives and tasks for the current course topics or chapters as well as the actual content that your learners will explore and find online. Create lists of items to find or tasks to accomplish. Decide whether the scavenger hunt activities will be performed as individuals or in groups. Be sure to define the scope of your topic to fit into your timeline. Select from the Internet learning resources that relate to your topic and organize them into an online scavenger hunt. For example, if you are exploring topics in cost accounting, look for online financial information that explains the key concepts, rules, or principles of the course (for example, earnings per share, capitalized leases, capital gains, prepaid expenses, and intangible assets). Questions and problems for the students might include:

1. Find Microsoft's operating income for the first quarter of 2007. (Answer: $4.47 billion)
2. Was that an increase or decrease over the preceding year? (Answer: An 11 percent increase compared with $4.05 billion in the prior year period)
3. What was Microsoft's overall revenue for the quarter ending September 30, 2006? (Answer: $10.81 billion)
4. Find the assets of Google as of June 30, 2007. (Answer: $14.857 billion)
5. How much cash did it have on hand at that time? (Answer: $4.494 billion)
6. How did that compare to its total liabilities? (Answer: $1.764 billion)
7. Find the definition of *discounted cash flow*. (Answer: The present value of future cash estimated to be generated)
8. What does SSARS stand for? (Answer: Statements on Standards for Accounting and Review Services; statements issued by the American Institute of Certified Public Accountants [AICPA] that specifically relate to review and compilations)

Once the scavenger hunt has been designed, post it, complete with directions and point information, to the Web, or within your course management software, and assign the task. You might give your learners a day, a week, a month, or 30–60 minutes of class time to find their answers. Once the task is completed and you have assessed the outcomes, one way to recognize learners for their efforts is to post high scores or give bonus points for high scores.

***Variations and Extensions.*** Most of the time a scavenger hunt is conducted with resources selected and organized by the instructor. One variation would be to ask learners to find different resources or materials on a given topic or content, and build the scavenger hunt with a collection of learner-generated questions. Alternatively, you might assign an individual or pairs of students to create a different scavenger hunt each week for a set amount of points, using resources found online.

## Key Instructional Considerations

> *Risk index:* Low
>
> *Time index:* Medium
>
> *Cost index:* Low
>
> *Learner-centered index:* Medium
>
> *Duration of the learning activity:* 1–2 weeks

# Activity 2. Web Tours and Safaris

***Description and Purpose of Activity.*** Given that Web resources can overwhelm students, some instructors decide to start a session with a Web tour or *safari* of the course agenda, course modules, and task options. Other instructors might take learners on a safari of online resources that might prove valuable in completing the course. Web tours and safaris seem more common in corporate training when using synchronous conferencing tools, though, once again, they can find use in nearly any online educational setting. Such tours may be facilitated by live instructors, guided by prerecorded narration, or unguided for self-paced activities as needed.

***Skills and Objectives.*** Includes basic or factual knowledge, exploration skills, search strategies, self-directed learning, reflection on new knowledge, and inquiry learning. A key goal of this activity is exposure to learning resources that might be used later in the course.

***Advice and Ideas.*** While a learning safari can show K–12 and higher education students the palette of options that they have in a course, Jay Cross (2007) argues that in the corporate world they add business value to an organization. In effect, a learning safari can be used to excite or motivate learners into a topic or discipline. If the safari is prerecorded, it will be vital to update the resource list every year or two. Be sure to focus on key resources so as not to overwhelm the learners at the beginning of the course.

To create your safari, gather a list of key online resources for a particular course or module. Perhaps ask learners who completed that course in the past if they would add or delete anything from that list. Once the resources have been gathered and evaluated, create a prerecorded learning safari of these resources with a guided narration, or, if possible, conduct a live demonstration of these resources to learners, either face to face (FTF) or using synchronous technology. Alternatively, a list of important resources might be compiled for students to explore on their own with a list of guiding questions or tasks.

***Variations and Extensions.*** Perhaps provide options for the safari in which learners decide which format of the safari that they want to engage in: a live session in a Webinar (that is, a live online instructional presentation, session, or performance), a prerecorded session, or a set of resources for self-paced learning activities. Or create a guided introduction or safari to preliminary or opening materials that students explore on their own.

## Key Instructional Considerations

> *Risk index:* Medium
>
> *Time index:* Medium
>
> *Cost index:* Medium
>
> *Learner-centered index:* Medium
>
> *Duration of the learning activity:* One week as needed

# Activity 3. WebQuest

***Description and Purpose of Activity.*** WebQuest started out as a popular activity in K–12 online learning environments but now finds use in higher education, corporate, government, and military training situations. The idea for the WebQuest originally came from Bernie Dodge and one of his former students, Thomas March, at San Diego State University. In a WebQuest, online resources are arranged for learners to explore and review and then debate ideas, events, and concepts. In effect, the instructor, trainer, or instructional designer finds a set of materials and provides access to them online in a set of activities. The steps are laid out for the learners; the ways in which they can be assessed are posted.

Students might learn a set of concepts and skills and then be tested on them. Or they might explore a topic or area in some depth (for example, modern art or the history of rock and roll) and then afterward complete a predesigned activity exploring different forms of art or rock groups by year or decade. While often used in K–12 education, higher education courses on Web searching, online research, and database management often make use of online WebQuests.

An interesting WebQuest was created by Beatriz Lado for her intermediate-level college Spanish courses at Louisiana State University, in which students need to determine if Valencia, Spain, would be a good place for an exchange program experience (see Web resources). This WebQuest has links to online information, pictures, and other resources related to Valencia as well as an online Spanish conversion dictionary, monetary exchange rate calculators, and weather-related information. The WebQuest introduction informs students that they are about to have an exciting experience. "You will meet the craziest people, eat the most delicious meals and get to walk around one of the most attractive places in the world. . . . And best of all is that you will be able to do it in Spanish." In this WebQuest, students are specialized reporters in areas such as geography, culture, food, and fun related to Spain. They must explore the Web sites listed—here is where the instructor guides the student into online resources and, thereby, constrains the search. Learners have to create a product (for example, a brochure) that convinces the rest of their class that the exchange program should be in Valencia or at least begin there.

In effect, the online resources support student research. As noted in the WebQuest, students work in groups of four, and each person in a group assumes the role of one of four characters in the WebQuest. For instance, Luis Comidillas "loves to eat and cook; he is going to taste everything so he can explain to his friends back home what the ingredients are and how to make the meals he enjoyed in Valencia." Separate online worksheets need to be completed for each role.

The goals of the project include enhancing students' Spanish reading skills, recognizing and producing basic structures of the vocabulary, understanding present and past tense in Spanish, learning about Internet opportunities for learning language, and, of course, feeling comfortable with using technology. An evaluation rubric is provided. In many WebQuests, instructor reflections and advice for other instructors are detailed.

A WebQuest could be considered as guided online discovery learning or it might be viewed as an online lesson plan and a more prescriptive type of instructional approach. The flexible and adaptable nature of a WebQuest as well as its basic structural familiarity (that is, an instructor arranges learning materials for students) and ease of use make it one of the easier methods to teach to instructors new to online environments.

***Skills and Objectives.*** Includes basic or factual knowledge, exploration skills, search strategies, reflection on new knowledge, inquiry learning, and problem solving. Clearly, a wide range of skills can be taught through a WebQuest.

***Advice and Ideas.*** There are many WebQuest examples found in a maze of WebQuest sites and portals (that is, Web sites that provide pathways or points of access to specific content accumulated from diverse sources or locations as well as other personalized capabilities or tools for visitors); often these are highly organized by domain or content area (some are provided in the Web resources section of this book). You might initially start with one of these existing WebQuest templates and after a trial run or two modify it for your own students and content. You might note key revisions in your online notes to other instructors.

Keep in mind that a WebQuest is a great activity to use when wanting to cede some control or ownership over learning to those enrolled in your course. It is also a useful strategy to demonstrate to teachers at the start of a professional development training session or program involving technology, since most will be able to relate to this instructional activity either as an online version of a lesson plan or as a prime example of guided discovery learning. In addition, most instructors will be able to build a WebQuest without too much difficulty. Along these same lines, if you are a trainer of instructors, buy-in for a WebQuest is relatively easy.

***Variations and Extensions.*** We have used WebQuests in the professional development of teachers. In such training, we have had the learners (in this case, professional teachers) design a WebQuest after we have demonstrated various examples to them. The creation of a WebQuest could be used as a required student assignment in any type of class or discipline. Of course, when the student becomes the teacher or designer of the activity, she learns the materials more richly.

## Key Instructional Considerations

*Risk index:* Low

*Time index:* Medium

*Cost index:* Low

*Learner-centered index:* Medium (depends on use)

*Duration of the learning activity:* 1–4 weeks

## Activity 4. Guided Readings

***Description and Purpose of Activity.*** Content explorations are guided when students read from a selection of articles prescreened by the instructor or course developers. Prescreened or preassigned readings might be employed when the learners need more guidance because of their maturity level, content familiarity, or experience with e-learning. A set of questions or issues might be embedded or posted to the Web or to your course management system (CMS) to guide their reading.

***Skills and Objectives.*** Includes basic content information, awareness and comprehension of key concepts and principles, reflection on concepts learned, and time to discuss and debate issues.

***Advice and Ideas.*** Collect readings that relate to your course and organize them by time (for example, week) or content area (topic, module, or unit). If you decide to use them in your course, check to see if your school, institution, or organization has a process for requesting permission to use articles in your class, even if you are simply listing the universal resource locator (URL). You must ascertain the policy of your organization. Once approved, incorporate the articles by providing the relevant Web links for students, with reading activity guidelines and questions related to each article that will motivate their reflection, concept connections, and higher-order thinking skills. You might require students to reflect on these articles in an online discussion forum or in their individual blogs (Web logs) or in a class blog.

Be sure to keep the list up to date and relevant for your students, as online articles are often moved or deleted. Perhaps incorporate activities in which your students nominate articles in addition to those that you have listed. Reevaluate the articles selected before teaching the course again. Once you feel comfortable with this task, you might consider combining articles that you have prescreened with ones that students nominate or individually select. We find that giving students roughly one-fourth to one-third control over content selection works well in motivating them and instilling a sense of learning ownership. However, such control, once again, will depend on the content and the level of students.

*Variations and Extensions.*  Instead of instructor-designed questions or prespecified questions for that week, have the class brainstorm or suggest generic critical reading questions for the article readings (include title of the article) related to the topic for that week. The class might vote on the top three to five questions that will be used to guide the readings. Or perhaps assign a student to come up with the article questions for each week. Such a student would read ahead and post the questions before others started the reading.

## Key Instructional Considerations

*Risk index:* Low

*Time index:* Medium

*Cost index:* Low

*Learner-centered index:* Medium

*Duration of the learning activity:* 4–15 weeks

# Activity 5. Discovery Readings

*Description and Purpose of Activity.*  Such guided reading activities described in Activity 4 also might be more open-ended, where students select articles based on their own course-related interests. In such a situation, a learner might be assigned online reading materials or be asked to find articles that relate to the activities of a particular week or module. The latter approach is perhaps more suited to self-determined or self-motivated learners and online learning veterans; often these are older and more mature adults who expect learning to be relevant to them. Discovery reading activities could be a part of a problem-based learning (PBL) or project-based learning process as well. In an advanced psychology or sociology course, for instance, students might have to produce a final paper at the end of the semester based on research that they design and complete during the semester. In a less advanced course, such as introduction to psychology or sociology, the final paper might simply be a literature review on a personally selected topic, for which they would read articles each week relevant to their final report as well as the weekly course topics.

*Skills and Objectives.*  Includes online searching and browsing skills, article and information filtering, and selection of relevant and personally meaningful materials. Such an activity equips students with twenty-first-century skills related to information search and critical analysis, while simultaneously empowering them with self-directed learning activities. The goal here is motivating and retaining students through choice, goals, and personal relevance.

*Advice and Ideas.* Assign students to search, select, and read a certain number of online articles or other materials for each week or module. To avoid confusion, announce any restrictions or guidelines on topics for discovery reading tasks in advance. Be sure to provide some example articles and reflections as models for learners to follow. To create a community feel, ask your learners to share their findings and reflections in personal blogs, the class blog, or in online discussion forums. In addition, require students to read and respond to a certain number of their peers' reflections. As always, provide guidelines related to how to provide meaningful and constructive responses to learners. Be sure to provide some type of feedback on their reading reflections as well as their course points or grades.

*Variations and Extensions.* Instead of a pure discovery approach, there might be a class portal with links to Web sites that have relevant articles. Such an approach might narrow the search for learners, while also encouraging students to suggest additions and deletions.

## Key Instructional Considerations

*Risk index:* Medium

*Time index:* Low

*Cost index:* Low

*Learner-centered index:* High

*Duration of the learning activity:* 1–2 weeks or 4–12 weeks, depending on the level of student control and type of activity selected

# Activity 6. Foreign Language Reading Activities and Online News

*Description and Purpose of Activity.* Foreign language courses might have students read online newsletters, newspapers, magazines, and other foreign correspondence. Then the instructor might test the learners or have them use their readings in a particular way.

*Skills and Objectives.* Includes learning authenticity, learner motivation and engagement, and skill comprehension and application. A key goal here is to situate student learning in a real context where they can witness the nuances of language use.

*Advice and Ideas.* There are thousands of possible activities here. Start with basic vocabulary exercises and work up to active learning tasks such as student-generated foreign newsletters, personal blogs, or international exchanges. In terms of the latter, if in K–12 education, you might tap into existing online mentoring and peer collaboration programs such as ePALS or iEARN, for instance. If in higher education, you might have to coordinate your own online exchanges by designing pedagogically exciting and relevant activities with colleagues in other countries and universities, as we have done in our own online teaching. For example, Bonk and his colleague, Mei-Ya Liang, are currently studying the use of online news reading, online chats, and personal blogging among engineering students enrolled in an English as a Foreign Language (EFL) class in Taiwan (Liang & Bonk, in review). Each week, students read an assortment of American and other online English-based news and then reflect on the English words and rules that they are learning. They all have a class partner helping with their online activities and reflections. What might enhance this situation would be collaborative partners from an English-speaking country to give feedback to these EFL students. And if you are in a global corporation, you might utilize available global resources and employees (perhaps you have employees at more than one training location) for online language learning activities and feedback. The possibilities for global exchanges are endless. Over time, build a team of international colleagues who might want to collaborate on such activities.

Just as there are myriad possible activities related to this example, there are many possible steps in the process. First, you might conduct a search of related online news media, newsletters, magazines, and Web sites in the target foreign language. At the same time, ask colleagues for their recommendations and nominations. You might also explore award-winning language learning sites such as LangMedia (see http://langmedia.fivecolleges.edu/index.html) for examples of online language learning and use. Second, find appropriate resources and incorporate them into learning activities such as a vocabulary lesson, comprehension test, or language exchange activity. For example, you might use a current online news story from BBC or CNN and have students engage in discussions of them or create glossaries of terms which they share with each other and compare. Third, once learners have been exposed to online language learning lessons, consider having them explore the Internet for similar resources that they might interpret and share.

*Variations and Extensions.* One option would be to have the students translate foreign news or correspondence content to test their language skills as well as their cross-cultural awareness. Another option would be to have them read two or more similar online news stories or commentaries from different resources (for example, Yahoo News, CNN.com, MIT World, and so on) and provide a short summary, integration paper, or presentation on these articles.

## Key Instructional Considerations

> *Risk index:* Medium
>
> *Time index:* Medium
>
> *Cost index:* Low
>
> *Learner-centered index:* Medium
>
> *Duration of the learning activity:* 1–2 weeks, or 4–10 weeks, depending on the activity

# Activity 7. FAQs and Course Announcement Feedback

*Description and Purpose of Activity.* Verbal learners will also appreciate FAQs (frequently asked questions), course announcements, and the archiving or posting of e-mail internally within the CMS or learning management system (LMS) system. Such resources form the basis for shared knowledge within the course. They also provide the seeds for the development of an online community if properly nurtured and managed. Course announcements might be used to introduce upcoming or current courses and activities as well as reflect on what has been accomplished. Frequently asked question sections of a course Web site or CMS/ LMS are intended to clarify potentially confusing aspects of a course and therefore lower learner tension and anxiety. Feedback on them is vital to course success. Students might be assigned to provide feedback on the FAQs, course announcements, and other instructional components of the course at the start or end of the course in a synchronous chat, online survey, or asynchronous discussion thread or online conversation. Such an activity personalizes the course and enhances any other learner-centered activities that are embedded in the course, while also creating a sense of caring and social presence on the part of the instructor.

*Skills and Objectives.* Includes feedback, review of key tasks, and sense of course interactivity and social presence. A key goal is to motivate students regarding assignments and foster their self-monitoring abilities.

*Advice and Ideas.* Review common student questions and concerns from prior semesters or offerings of the course. Ask students from previous semesters what were the key areas of confusion related to the course. At the same time, read through course evaluations for student complaints and issues in need of explanation. Next, organize these questions and concerns into key areas of confusion. Write down answers and responses to these issues. Post these questions and answers or solutions as a series of frequently asked questions. Also consider addressing newly emerged FAQs in a timely fashion by posting them on the course announcements page or by using a course listserv (that is, an electronic mailing list that more than one person can use), class e-mail distribution list, which is typically controlled by the instructor, or class blog.

*Variations and Extensions.* Have learners sign up for a week in which they run the class, including posting course announcements and reminders of upcoming course activities. Or perhaps embed an optional assignment in which a student can design the FAQs for students enrolling in the following semesters or versions of the course.

## Key Instructional Considerations

> *Risk index:* Low
>
> *Time index:* Medium
>
> *Cost index:* Low
>
> *Learner-centered index:* Medium
>
> *Duration of the learning activity:* Weekly or as needed

# Activity 8. Question-and-Answer Sessions with Instructor

*Description and Purpose of Activity.* For effective online learning, students should be able to discuss course concerns, issues, and questions with the instructor using e-mail, text chat, or online discussion forums. Such questions and responses can later be posted to the course Web site for future reference. Alternatively, the instructor, tutor, or moderator might e-mail her responses to students using a course distribution list. Or the instructor might do both—e-mail the questions and responses as well as post them to the CMS.

*Skills and Objectives.* Includes feedback, sense of instructor social presence and instructional immediacy, interactivity, and prompt feedback. A primary objective is to focus student work and answer pressing needs.

*Advice and Ideas.* Set up various times as virtual office hours during which learners can ask questions (especially if coming from different time zones). Consider having learners vote on when these times should be. Come to the session 10–15 minutes before the scheduled time to chat with early arriving participants as well as to test the connection and tool features. Conduct the session using the LMS or CMS chat tool or via a free instant message (IM) service, preferably one with audio conference capacity (for example, Yahoo Messenger, MSN, Skype, and so on). Be frank, but provide a sense of flexibility in your responses to student questions. Try not to be defensive to learner questions and concerns about the course. For questions that appear to be irritating, frustrating, or less pleasant, take a moment or two before responding. Restate key concerns or persistent questions both for those attending the session and for those who could not attend. Be sure to archive the session for possible reuse or analysis. Summarize (or have students summarize) the major questions and answers in a post to a designated online forum, course blog site, message to an e-mail distribution list, or the like. Consider adding some of these questions, where appropriate, to the FAQ section of the course.

*Variations and Extensions.* Create a "Stump the Professor" (or teacher, trainer) activity in which students submit questions related to the class (from practical to theoretical and from common to remote) in an online forum or drop box and the instructor responds to them at designated times each week. Students might be assigned bonus points for asking relevant questions for which the instructor does not have an answer within a set amount of time.

## Key Instructional Considerations

>*Risk index:* Medium
>
>*Time index:* Medium
>
>*Cost index:* Low
>
>*Learner-centered index:* Medium
>
>*Duration of the learning activity:* Weekly or as needed

# Activity 9. Online Expert Chats

*Description and Purpose of Activity.* Your learners may also enjoy online chats with experts, especially when audio (that is, voice chat) is enabled. You might use an LMS or CMS for this or perhaps a chat tool embedded in an online groupware system. Alternatively, you might try out a free instant messaging system (for example, MSN Messenger, Yahoo Messenger, and so on). Expert chats are highly effective and engaging across learning settings, from K–12 to higher education to training environments. We have often utilized expert chats in our respective classes with many fond memories and positive learner feedback and excitement.

***Skills and Objectives.*** Includes course interactivity, feedback, and sense of instructor presence or instructional immediacy. This activity forces students to interpret ideas of an expert and ferret out themes or issues in them. Among the key goals is to connect course material to real-world activities.

***Advice and Ideas.*** Brainstorm a list of possible experts for synchronous chats, or consider asking those who have helped in the past. To enhance learner control and motivation, consider asking students for expert guest nominations. Conduct a class vote if too many people are nominated, and provide students with bonus points for suggesting experts if too few are nominated. Invite the guest expert to interact with your class from a distance (consider having learners invite the experts in for a chat and receive bonus points if successful). Coordinate an open time for most, if not all, learners, as well as the invited expert. Communicate and discuss with the expert(s) in advance regarding the goals, objectives, and expectations for the session (for example, to discuss an article or book that the expert wrote).

Once the speaker(s) and date(s) are set, collect a set of questions from the learners and send these to the expert ahead of time. If it is a FTF class, you might have your students brainstorm a set of questions to ask and then send the list to the expert(s) for review. The expert can later inform you which ones may be the most beneficial or thought-provoking to ask as well as those that she is most comfortable answering. And, if the class is large, the session might be moderated so as not to overwhelm the expert(s) with too many questions at any point in time during the session. Carefully select the communication technologies (for example, LMS, online groupware, or IM) and, if possible, test them with the expert in advance. Introduce the expert to the session at the beginning and facilitate the chat.

When done, archive the session transcript as well as any recorded audio for possible future use (provided you have received permission from the expert) (see Phase 2 of R2D2 for ideas on how to reuse such chat transcripts). Follow up the chat session by inviting learner reflections and sharing these reflections and afterthoughts with the expert(s). Consider posting the session and reflections on the course blog or Web site. Send out thank you notes to the guest expert(s), preferably with input from the students.

*Variations and Extensions.* Ask the expert to return for a second chat experience later in the course, after students have read more of that individual's work. And if the person is well known or an exceptionally captivating speaker, perhaps invite students from other sections of the same class or from similar classes or programs to submit questions to the expert. You might also invite the expert back with one or more close colleagues or research partners, such as someone who helped that person write an important report, journal article, or book. Including two or more expert colleagues might add to the emotional as well as cognitive benefits of the learning experience.

## Key Instructional Considerations

*Risk index:* Medium

*Time index:* Medium

*Cost index:* Low

*Learner-centered index:* Medium

*Duration of the learning activity:* One week as needed

# Activity 10. Online Synchronous Testing

*Description and Purpose of Activity.* Chat tools can also be used for online quizzing of select students to test their understanding of the course content. Some instructors use dynamic assessment, in which each additional testing item is based on previous testing results. In effect, such tests are not related to typical online quizzes that might be stored in a course LMS or CMS, but, instead, they require instructor's real-time interaction with students and grading of synchronous inter-actions and postings. In effect, the teacher posts questions, problems, or issues in a synchronous chat for students to answer, react to, and solve. While these types of activities are in line with social constructivist viewpoints related to teaching and learning, such real-time testing and grading is dynamic, complex, highly flexible, open-ended or semi-structured, and intellectually demanding. It is not a technique for the faint of heart or those with minimal time or who are unfamiliar with online teaching and learning environments.

*Skills and Objectives.* Includes comprehension, quick decision making, dynamic feedback, and application of terms and concepts.

*Advice and Ideas.* Create testing questions or problems appropriate to your topic (these will be open-ended and relatively short answer). For example, in a psychology course, one might ask the learner to "Give me an example of selective memory," whereas in a philosophy course, that same student might be asked to "Describe and define pragmatism." After a relatively quick response, the philosophy instructor might intervene by asking the learner to "provide a few examples of prominent philosophers who promoted pragmatism" and then again by probing further into George Herbert Mead, John Dewey, Charles Peirce, or other popular pragmatists. He might follow that up with questions concerning the definitions and key principles of existentialism and the names of prominent existentialists. Pragmatism and existentialism might be compared to events in the student's own life. Next, ideas from one of Dewey's books that might have been assigned to the class might be discussed in detail.

The psychology instructor, on the other hand, might push on to a topic area outside of selective memory, such as concepts of self-concept and self-perception theory. In effect, the sequence of the online chat test hinges on many variables, including the content area, the goals of the instructor, the responses of the students, and the time available. In effect, this is not typically a multiple choice or fill-in-the-blank type of test.

There are many decisions to be made, including whether or not the test should be timed as well as determining how much time the learners will have to complete the test online (for example, 20 or 30 minutes per participant). Once times are set, you should prepare for the testing activity on your LMS/CMS or some other system. Next, announce testing dates when the testing system will be available for learners, preferably spread over a few days rather than on one single date. Then assign a set of materials or review activities to prepare learners for the synchronous quiz (for example, assign ten issues or questions and perhaps randomly assess each learner on a few of them, thereby limiting plagiarism).

Once the materials have been distributed, assign learners to different testing time slots or let them sign up for the test according to their own schedules. During the test sessions, alternate the test items or randomly select different test items from a fairly large pool of questions or topics so as to reduce possibilities of cheating or collusion. More experienced instructors may use dynamic assessment. To simplify the situation as well as make it more interactive and dynamic, consider having students post their responses every two to three sentences so that the instructor can provide feedback and dynamic assessment on what has been written. In timed tests, provide a reminder for the test taker when it gets close to the end of the session. When the session ends, assign a tentative grade with comments and feedback, if possible, and note any feedback from the learner. Quickly move on to the next learner.

While this is a highly time-intensive task, the amount of time will depend on the number of learners being tested. One might consider having a set number of learners for such designated quizzes and rotating who is being tested. Or, alternatively, if all learners are being tested in this manner on a particular exam, the instructor might conduct only one or two such sessions during a course or term. There are three key benefits from this activity: (1) the students are tested dynamically, since the questions asked depend on previous responses; (2) there is less opportunity for plagiarism, especially if the quiz takers were randomly chosen each week; and (3) feedback to the students is more immediate.

*Variations and Extensions.* Instead of instructor testing, ask students to sign up for certain chat times during which they test partners or team members on their knowledge of a particular chapter. In such an activity, one person is the designated tester who designs the questions and the other is the learner. The next time, these roles are reversed. The types of questions asked (that is, factual, interpretative, application, and so on) might be determined by the instructor or by the learners.

## Key Instructional Considerations

> *Risk index:* Medium
>
> *Time index:* High
>
> *Cost index:* Low
>
> *Learner-centered index:* Low to High (depends on instructor use)
>
> *Duration of the learning activity:* Weekly as needed

# Activity 11. Synchronous or Virtual Classroom Instructor Presentations

*Description and Purpose of Activity.* Live or synchronous online instruction has been successfully used in corporate training for a number of years. However, a huge growth in this field occurred after the tragedy of September 11, 2001. We have personally witnessed the growth of synchronous instruction in our own institutions, in the many types of academic settings that we have visited around the world, and in our respective research projects (for example, Park & Bonk, 2007). Key advantages of synchronous instruction include having social interaction and support from peers as well as the instructor; interactive learning with polls, chats, and surveys; and the ability to archive the session when finished for those who have missed it.

Picture a synchronous class with a live video and audio feed from the instructor in the top left corner of the screen, his PowerPoint lecture notes on the right side of the screen, student names and chat messages in the bottom left of the screen, and a palette of drawing tools at the bottom. If successful, you have imagined how Professor Roberto Garcia uses Adobe Connect Pro in the Kelley Direct online M.B.A. program at Indiana University. To situate student learning, Professor Garcia often will play a short videoclip to anchor his lectures and ideas in a shared experience of his class.

***Skills and Objectives.*** Includes a sense of instructor social presence and instructional immediacy, feedback, interactivity, and focus on critical content. Also helps form a course community.

***Advice and Ideas.*** Schedule topics, dates, and session leaders for synchronous sessions. Be sure to test the system, including password access, familiarity with the tools, and uploading presentation files well in advance. When designing the content, incorporate a few interactive polls and surveys as well as other interactive activities (for example, questions, Web tours, and so on). On the scheduled date, arrive early for system setup and final testing. Do not lecture for more than 15–20 minutes straight. Instead, include many scheduled interactivities in the session. For instance, get learners involved in the synchronous session with activities such as questions and answers, students providing examples or non-examples, live polls, and other events. End with an evaluation of the session. If possible, archive the session.

Keep in mind that there are numerous tools or systems for synchronous online instruction, and they tend to have similar features. For additional ideas related to conducting synchronous sessions in higher education settings, you might consult Jonathan Finkelstein's (2006) book, *Learning in Realtime: Synchronous Teaching and Learning Online*. In addition, if you are in corporate training, you might utilize Jennifer Hofmann's (2003) *The Synchronous Trainer's Survival Guide: Facilitating Successful Live and Online Courses, Meetings, and Events*. In addition, Hofmann has published a series of tips for conducting synchronous training sessions in the online magazine *Learning Circuits* (Hofmann, 2000, 2001).

***Variations and Extensions.*** Part of the time for such synchronous sessions might be allocated for student presentations or lectures. The instructor can then more readily grasp student course connections as well as misunderstandings.

## Key Instructional Considerations

*Risk index:* Medium

*Time index:* Medium

*Cost index:* High

*Learner-centered index:* Medium

*Duration of the learning activity:* Weekly or as needed

## Activity 12. Online Webinars

***Description and Purpose of Activity.*** Many corporations and consulting firms rely on synchronous technology to get the word out about their products or services. Often they will bring in a recognized expert on a topic of interest (for example, how to use blogs or text messaging successfully in the workplace). Such "Webinars," or online seminars, are usually free, though vendors often have a follow-up demonstration of their product(s). Once presentations are complete, there is typically a question-and-answer period. When done, the entire session can be archived for those who missed it.

Webinars are also utilized in K–12 and higher education for professional development as well as many other educational environments and purposes. While writing this book, in fact, we attended many online Webinars to stay current with emerging technologies. For instance, on Thursday, September 7, 2007, Bonk attended a session on Web 2.0 technologies and wikis (that is, software that allows users to collaborate in a relatively quick fashion to create, edit, and link Web pages) that was sponsored by *Campus Technology*, a monthly publication focusing on the use of technology in higher education, and Socialtext, a leading provider of wiki and other Web 2.0 technology (Campus Technology, 2007). In this Webinar, experts such as Howard Rheingold, Stanford professor and author of *Smart Mobs: The Next Social Revolution;* Jerry Kane, assistant professor of information systems at Boston College; and Jeff Brainard, director of marketing at Socialtext, discussed how wikis could be used in instruction. Near the end of the session, they answered participant questions and later posted their PowerPoint slides of their talks to the Web. It was the largest crowd *Campus Technology* had ever drawn for an online Webinar. Three weeks later, Bonk attended a follow-up Webinar from Socialtext on how wikis, blogs, and RSS (that is, Really Simple Syndication (that is, Web postings or sites that one can subscribe to as they are updated rather than having to check on them manually) change how people work.

In each case, the information provided was timely, comprehensive, interesting, and free. With online Webinars, anyone can upgrade their professional skills and competencies without leaving their desk. Webinars can be created by anyone on any topic. The audience for the learning is anyone who signs up and then shows up. Students in a class can be asked to attend one or more Webinars as part of their course requirements and activities. And, as noted later, Webinars can be staged events for a course, program, or institution or organization.

Often Webinars are free sessions with a vendor serving as the sponsor. After the Webinar, the session sponsor normally reserves time to showcase its products. The sponsor typically conducts its own evaluations at the end of the session.

***Skills and Objectives.*** Includes interaction, social presence and instructional immediacy, appreciation of multiple perspectives, feedback, real-world examples and experiences, and presentation of new content and emerging trends. Also, a goal of this task is to involve learners with others in the class instead of strictly relying on instructor-led or self-directed learning.

***Advice and Ideas.*** Decide on topics, dates, and session leaders for the Webinar (for example, "Conducting Business in China: Opportunities for Corporate Training Companies"). A Webinar is similar to a guest presentation; however, it can differ in that it might be created by an organization or institution for anyone in the world to attend and for later review by any class or visitor. Often they are created by vendors who demonstrate their products at the end of the session. An online guest presentation, in contrast, is typically limited to one class or learning situation and normally is not replayed or archived.

Include a few online polls and surveys as well as other interactive activities (questions, Web tours, and so on). Such activities will foster learner engagement and interaction. There are many choices facing the Webinar instructor or presenter in terms of activities—some may involve learner-learner interaction (for example, online chats); some may require learners to interact with instructors (for example, online question and answer sessions); and still others will foster self-reflection and learners interacting with content (for example, document or Web exploration).

Most of the time, a Webinar is created by a professional organization or group. Your class can then sign up to attend it, or, if it has already occurred, you can have your class members watch the archived event during a set week of the course and then discuss it. If, however, you are charged with arranging the Webinar, be sure to announce and market the Webinar using online news forums, e-mail lists of professional groups, and perhaps social networking sites such as Facebook or MySpace. You might also announce it within your organization or institution. Send reminders of the Webinar through e-mail, and post a reminder within your LMS or CMS. Perhaps include a question in the LMS or CMS about whether learners plan to attend the Webinar (assuming it is optional).

Have any invited guests send in their presentation files, Web resource links, or other materials at least two weeks prior to the event. At least one week before the scheduled event, run a practice session or dry run with the presenters. Test the system; load and test resources days or weeks in advance.

On the scheduled date, arrive 15–30 minutes early for the session and conduct final tests of the system and content. Conduct the session with the scheduled interactivities. End the session with a participant evaluation such as an online survey or feedback form. Archive the session for those who could not attend. Perhaps continue to market and showcase the Webinar.

If you need more information and you are in higher education, you might read Jonathan Finkelstein's (2006) book; if you are in a training setting, you might browse the work of Jennifer Hofmann of Insync Training on how to conduct online Webinars (Hofmann, 2000, 2001, 2003, 2004).

*Variations and Extensions.* Start with a question-and-answer session with impromptu presenter comments for 15–30 minutes prior to the designated start of the session. Post the questions raised at this time to a Web site for participants who browse the site later to read through or perhaps make a PowerPoint slide of the list of questions to be shown during the Webinar. Consider having someone as designated moderator or discussant to review the questions or issues raised at the start of the Webinar as a means to prompt continued discussion throughout.

## Key Instructional Considerations

*Risk index:* Medium

*Time index:* Medium

*Cost index:* High

*Learner-centered index:* Medium

*Duration of the learning activity:* Weekly as needed

# Activity 13. Public Tutorials, Wizards, and Help Systems

*Description and Purpose of Activity.* A public tutorial site might be beneficial for e-learning when there are limited opportunities for instructor-learner interaction or when much of the content is self-paced material. Many corporate, government, and military training settings rely heavily on online tutorials. Higher education institutions also depend on them for training students and instructors in new software (including online course tools and systems) as well as for general access to campus information and resources. In any of these situations, the tutorial system or "wizard" may provide the learner with an overview of the resources available for an activity and a visual depiction of how to complete such an activity while also explaining key concepts. Online medical cases often detail critical patient data and decision points while utilizing tutorials to walk the learner through different materials involved in making a proper diagnosis. Tools such as Captivate, Camtasia, and Flash are often used for producing such demonstrations.

***Skills and Objectives.*** Includes feedback, ability to follow directions, concept review, and self-directed learning pursuits.

***Advice and Ideas.*** First determine where learners in your course may need additional support by asking them what resources they think are needed. Have several current or potential learners think aloud as they use your existing online resources.

After determining the kind of help that is needed, conduct a search on the Web for existing tutorials or help systems. If none are available, consider building some type of help system or tutorial. You might need to work with your technology support office or with someone with technology skills who has similar interests. A short and inexpensive PowerPoint show or Flash animation may be all that is necessary. Consider embedding review questions and hints to make the demonstrations more interactive and engaging. When complete, conduct usability testing on the help system or training module(s) and also evaluate their use. You might have potential learners think aloud as they use one or more of the tools or systems that were designed. Sometimes those designing systems take certain steps or procedures for granted; hence, learner feedback is vital for any tool or system developed.

Some organizations have instructional design or consulting departments and sources of funding to help develop training modules. Monies available will often be proportionate to the number of prior or potential learners in the course.

***Variations and Extensions.*** Perhaps embed an optional assignment in which the learners can design a help system for the course or an online component of the course.

## Key Instructional Considerations

> *Risk index:* Low
>
> *Time index:* Low to High (depending on whether using existing tools and resources or developing your own)

*Cost index:* Low to High (depending on whether using existing tools and resources or developing your own)

*Learner-centered index:* Medium

*Duration of the learning activity:* One week as needed

## Activity 14. Expert Lectures and Commentary

***Description and Purpose of Activity.*** While online interactivity is increasingly discussed and highlighted in new product announcements, the Web is often a storage device or container for prepackaged content. Streamed and archived media is one way to standardize key content for the learners. In many cases, there might be spoken expert commentary or narration layered over online resources such as PowerPoint slides, Web site safaris, or other visual representations. Such lectures and commentaries are different from synchronous chat sessions, since they are not question-and-answer sessions. They are also different from most advertised Webinars in that they are not online presentations open to anyone who signs up to watch and participate. Expert lectures can be original content for a specific class as well as repurposed existing content. For instance, the presentation content might come from an existing Webinar that is reused for a particular session or module of a course. In effect, expert lectures might be synchronous or real-time presentations for a class or repurposed content used asynchronously.

***Skills and Objectives.*** Includes reflection, analysis, appreciation of multiple perspectives, and learning content with different delivery mechanisms. Skills fostered include reflection, analysis, and synthesis.

***Advice and Ideas.*** Explore available Webstreamed media on topics related to your class or particular topics. Many universities have decided to videostream and archive course lectures for later use by students, alumni, and guest visitors. Such resources are increasingly indexed online and referred to as "open educational resources" or OERs. Some learners will want access to as many OERs as possible, including "talking head" videos of instructors or experts lecturing on a topic. In fact, our experience indicates that such Webstreamed resources are useful for learners to replay even after attending a FTF session. Of course, any instructor can add to the pool of OER by streaming the more engaging or interactive portions of their lectures. When properly designed, such material can also be used in the recruitment of learners and general marketing or promotion of an online course, program, or organization.

If no asynchronous content is found or developed, explore available Webstreaming technologies within your organization or institution (for example, ePresence TV, MediaSite Live, Polycom, Tegrity, Webcast Group). If a synchronous event with a live expert is required, communicate in advance with the invited expert about the topic, schedule, length, target audience, and so on. Provide relevant information about the expert to learners with a copy of her current vita, personal Web site, or blog link, if available, as well as information about representative professional achievements (for example, publications, grants, awards, patents). Collect a list of questions from learners in advance and make it available to the expert prior to the chat session. Introduce the expert to the class at the beginning of the session and then facilitate the interactions between the expert and students as needed during the session. Conclude the session with key points or issues, and archive it when possible.

***Variations and Extensions.*** Create an asynchronous discussion forum or wiki activity (see Chapters Eight and Nine for wiki-related information) in which the students add commentary about the expert lecture. Or have students gather and post online resources related to the expert lecture and commentary either as individuals or as teams; if as teams, perhaps assign one team to each expert.

## Key Instructional Considerations

*Risk index:* Low

*Time index:* High

*Cost index:* Medium

*Learner-centered index:* Medium

*Duration of the learning activity:* Weekly as needed

# Activity 15. An Online Podcast Lecture or Podcast Show

***Description and Purpose of Activity.*** You may decide to create podcasts of lectures or question-and-answer sessions for one or all units or weeks of an online class. As noted earlier, such podcasts can be downloaded by students to their MP3 players, iPods, or laptop computers or workstations. In addition to personal podcasts, you can provide links to podcast shows or resources produced by others. For example, Chinesepod is a highly popular program for learning Mandarin Chinese online.

***Skills and Objectives.*** Includes motivation and engagement, listening skills, self-directed learning, and exposure to current information and trends. Another key goal of a podcast activity is to identify or reinforce concepts or skills learned in textbooks, lectures, or other resources and extend beyond them. An additional objective is to hear how experts might use a particular idea, concept, or skill or to obtain more current information than provided in text materials.

***Advice and Ideas.*** Decide on a topic that is appropriate for an audio-only (or audio plus video) delivery method. Review related materials and resources on the topic. Decide on key points or issues and create an outline of the talk. Design a set of questions based on the more controversial or interesting aspects of that material. Review issues and questions with the podcast moderator or host, if applicable.

Avoid including too many podcasts of long instructor lectures; we try to limit our podcasts to 15–20 minutes each or less. For instance, Bonk has created short podcasts, each lasting around 15 minutes, for his learning theories class related to the content for the week, such as Robert Gagne's ideas on instructional design and comparisons of human learning and development concepts of Jean Piaget and Lev Vygotsky. He has also developed longer podcasts on emerging technologies in education for distance master's students and alumni of his department at Indiana University.

You can add interactivity to a podcast by using a question-and-answer format. Consider asking your instructional design department to synch up your PowerPoint slides or lecture notes to the podcast(s) to create a more rich and engaging experience. Web sites like Slideshare.net (http://www.slideshare.net/faqs/slidecast) provide an easy-to-use service for syncing audio/podcasts to PowerPoint presentation slides, which they call a "slidecast." Or perhaps provide podcasts for videostreamed lectures as an additional option for learners to listen to after viewing the lecture.

When ready, conduct a podcast session using audio tools such as Audacity, which is a freely available, open source tool, or the popular Garageband from Apple. Such tools allow you to record, mix, play, and edit sounds. You can also insert or add sounds such as music to your podcast, delete part of a sound file, change the playback speed, and combine or mix sounds with such tools. In addition to software, you will need to acquire a microphone for your voice recordings.

After completing the session, you will need to save such files in MP3 format and upload them to a Web site to allow your students and others to download and listen to them. Podcasts can be downloaded and played from your computer workstation or to an iPod or MP3 player for mobile learning.

A podcast newsfeed, or RSS file (that is, a text file that links to your MP3 file), might be created that describes your podcast(s) or provides information about a series of podcasts that interested parties can subscribe to. Link to other relevant and high-quality podcasts and other resources on the topic.

*Variations and Extensions.*  Assign learners to find relevant podcasts on a topic in the field and post them to a class Web site. Next, have students vote on the best ones for each unit or week of the course. The best one or two podcasts for each unit or week can then be posted to a "Best of Podcasts" course portal or Web site that is updated each time the course is taught.

## Key Instructional Considerations

> *Risk index:* Medium
>
> *Time index:* Medium
>
> *Cost index:* Medium
>
> *Learner-centered index:* Medium
>
> *Duration of the learning activity:* 1–2 weeks

# Activity 16. Audio Dramas

*Description and Purpose of Activity.*  Our friends at the University of Glamorgan in Wales introduced us to the notion of the online "audio drama" a few years ago. In contrast to text- or video-based cases, these dramas are case situations that rely primarily on audio. An audio drama is similar to a radio show or a podcast and might incorporate the work of real-world actors and actresses or voice experts to engage students in their listening. We believe that any type of education and training situation can utilize this type of activity.

*Skills and Objectives.*  Includes concept reinforcement, listening skills, problem solving, and analysis.

*Advice and Ideas.*  Unless you are savvy with audio technology, you will likely need support from your instructional technology or training department to produce an audio drama.

Conduct usability testing on one or two sample audio dramas that you might design, or use preexisting ones that you might acquire from a colleague or find at a Web site such as Multimedia Educational Resource for Learning and

Online Teaching (MERLOT) or Connexions. Decide on the content and form of the audio drama you will produce; be sure that the content area selected can be engaging in an audio format. Then prepare the script for the audio drama. Current or former learners can be involved in various roles throughout the production process. Learners can play out the drama, or you may want to hire actors and actresses for the session. Record and edit the session using podcasting software such as Audacity or Garageband, or some other software tool. When completed, pilot test the audio drama with one or more students or with an entire class and later incorporate it into your teaching.

*Variations and Extensions.* Supplement the audio drama with a transcript or textual resource and post them to the course Web site or to iTunes. Or perhaps have students create alternative dramas or scenarios with associated questions or issues to discuss. Another option might be student-generated video dramas that are posted to YouTube or TeacherTube.

## Key Instructional Considerations

*Risk index:* Medium

*Time index:* Medium

*Cost index:* Low to High (costs depend on whether real actors are utilized, the sophistication of the technologies employed, and other personnel required)

*Learner-centered index:* Medium

*Duration of the learning activity:* 1–2 weeks as needed

# Activity 17. Posting Video-Based Explanations and Demonstrations

*Description and Purpose of Activity.* While many types of instructional activities are possible online, one of the more difficult instructional methods to perform online is modeling. It is not particularly easy to model how to solve mathematical, statistical, or science-related problems in online environments. Math or statistics instructors might view this as a serious flaw. However, some instructors use tools like Tegrity to model problem-solving sequences or steps of a process for learners. Using videostreaming tools such as Tegrity or ePresence TV, MediaSite Live, Polycom, or Webcast Group, the instructor can walk a student through the steps of a scientific experiment, medical procedure, or business process. Students can return to the video demonstration for cues or principles that they may not have correctly interpreted or learned in previous viewings. (Note that this technique is also highly linked to Phases 2 and 3 of the R2D2 model.)

***Skills and Objectives.*** Includes modeling key skills and concepts; reviewing or teaching key course concepts; expert guidance; understanding sequential flow or procedures; and skill discrimination.

***Advice and Ideas.*** Decide on content that might be best conveyed through demonstrations, including topics or areas in which students consistently misunderstand content. Create an initial script or storyboard for presentation or demonstration of such content. Ask colleagues to read and react to this script.

When planning the production, contact your instructional design center, training department, or media support personnel to create the video demonstration. The ultimate quality of the video will depend on available resources, time, and video editing experience and expertise.

Dress professionally for the video. Conduct two or three dry runs of the session before filming or recording. Retape if problems occur. Archive the video on the course Web site and consider making it available as an open educational resource for anyone to use. If well done, you might post it to YouTube or TeacherTube and announce or market such materials to colleagues and leaders in the field. Embed student reflection activities around such content while also inserting advice to other instructors on how they might use them.

***Variations and Extensions.*** Perhaps have your learners create text transcripts for different video-based demonstrations and create hyperlinks between common terms or concepts in one or more of them. Consider posting their resulting work to a Web site or a wiki (see Chapters Eight and Nine for wiki-related information).

## Key Instructional Considerations

*Risk index:* Medium

*Time index:* Medium

*Cost index:* Low to High (depends on resources available and required)

*Learner-centered index:* Medium

*Duration of the learning activity:* Weekly as needed

# Activity 18. Online Sound or Music Training

*Description and Purpose of Activity.* The Web stores vast amounts of musical data and information. Musical Acoustics is an award-winning Web site that was recognized with a MERLOT Editors' Choice Award in 2005 as well as a *Scientific American* Science and Technology Award that same year (see http://www.phys. unsw.edu.au/music/). This wonderful resource was designed at the University of New South Wales in Australia. Using materials at this site, students can listen to different types of instruments (for example, violins) and discover how they sound as they age. In addition, they can listen to voice recordings, learn about the acoustics of harmonic singing, and find answers to myriad questions and issues within the field of music (for example, What is a decibel?).

*Skills and Objectives.* Includes discrimination between different sounds, interactivity, learner motivation and engagement, interpretation and classification of themes and patterns, and connecting sounds to specific course concepts or principles.

*Advice and Ideas.* Search for sound files or music-related resources in places such as MERLOT, Connexions, and Jorum. Given the fascination young people have with listening to and sharing music online, you might consider having students browse the Web for audio resources and musical content and nominate sites that have rich educational value or that they simply find appealing or personally meaningful. Incorporate these into a lesson or unit. In addition, consult colleagues who might offer feedback and suggestions for enhancements and extensions on their use.

*Variations and Extensions.* Have learners create a portal of sounds for a particular subject or area (for example, courses on various musical topics such as rock and roll, film critiques, animal science, outdoor education, tourism, or even auto repair). They might record sounds using microphones attached to their iPods, desktop or laptop computers, or digital audio recorders. Really tech-savvy learners might be asked to electronically remix and rearrange the sounds after recording. The portal could be updated each semester.

## Key Instructional Considerations

*Risk index:* Low

*Time index:* Medium

*Cost index:* Low

*Learner-centered index:* Medium

*Duration of the learning activity:* Weekly as needed

## Activity 19. Online Literature Readings

***Description and Purpose of Activity.*** The Web catalogues a plethora of classical literature and houses the work of new and emerging artists, writers, and poets. For example, the complete works of William Shakespeare are now available online at Web sites from the Massachusetts Institute of Technology and Google Book Search. Google Book Search also has the writings of Charles Darwin, John Dewey, and many others. Learners can use these resources to find, read, quote, compare and contrast, and review Shakespeare, Darwin, Dewey, or other writers without having to purchase and lug around a heavy book. They can even read and react to a book written by Dewey in 1910 related to how Darwin influenced educational philosophers such as himself.

***Skills and Objectives.*** Includes information search, exploration, knowledge interpretation, evaluation of literature themes and problem situations, and comprehension skills. The initial goal is simply to learn the content with comprehension and knowledge review questions.

***Advice and Ideas.*** Determine the critical literature content needed. Search the Web for resources and examples. Post them to the course Web site. Assign reading tasks using those resources. For example, students might create hyperlinks among these materials, pose comparisons and contrasts of the literature (for example, Shakespearean plays), and offer class-related comments or annotations for different pieces of famous literature.

There are hundreds if not thousands of pedagogical activities that might be designed with just one of these resources. In the United States, the National Council of Teachers of English (NCTE) has many relevant books, journals, and Web resources related to online literature activities (see Web resources). Be sure that any relevant Web sites have the appropriate copyrights to those materials and review their terms of use.

***Variations and Extensions.*** Consider having students create study guides, supplemental aids, or review notes for online literature that is freely available. Such resources might be created in a wiki (see Chapters Eight and Nine) for others to add to and edit.

### Key Instructional Considerations

*Risk index:* Medium

*Time index:* Medium

*Cost index:* Low

*Learner-centered index:* Medium

*Duration of the learning activity:* Weekly as needed

---

## Activity 20. Online Poetry Readings

*Description and Purpose of Activity.* In addition to English literature such as Shakespeare, many popular sites now exist in the area of poetry (see, for example, Poets.org). Using such sites, instructors and learners can locate a wealth of resources, extensive links to other Web sites, an assortment of curriculum units and lesson plans, biographies of poets, and thousands of stored poems. Instructors might use such a site to begin each class with a different poem or poetic format, have their students create an anthology of their favorite poems, or perhaps have students memorize and recite the poems that they have found online. When such inventive activities are designed with available online resources, the content comes alive and is more meaningful to the learners.

*Skills and Objectives.* Includes information search, exploration, grasping themes, understanding how words sound from the perspective of another, motivation and engagement, and comparing and contrasting different forms of poetry.

*Advice and Ideas.* Search the Web for famous as well as less well-known poetry examples. At the same time, talk to other instructors for examples and ideas. Post resources and materials found to the course Web site and design appropriate learning tasks around them, such as one of those mentioned in the Description. Finally, gather student feedback on the tasks and modify them accordingly.

Once instructors and students are comfortable exploring online poetry sites, the instructor might design an activity that engages them in online poetry competitions. Be sure to share your students' work (with permission, of course)—it might lead to recognitions, stipends, and interesting collaborations.

*Variations and Extensions.* Students might discuss favorite poems in an asynchronous discussion tool or create a podcast in which they read their favorite poems. Alternatively, students might create hyperlinks indicating themes or connections between poems that instructors have posted.

## Key Instructional Considerations

*Risk index:* Medium

*Time index:* Medium

*Cost index:* Low

*Learner-centered index:* Medium

*Duration of the learning activity:* Weekly as needed

# Activity 21. Posting Webliographies or Web Resources

***Description and Purpose of Activity.*** One way to take advantage of possible online learning journeys in Phase 1 of the R2D2 model is to have students post or exchange important Web resources or Webliographies that they have found. A Webliography is a compendium or list of Web links which allow the user to access information in an expedient fashion (Alimohammadi, 2004). These Webliography postings might take place in a designated course Web site or location, a personal blog, or an online discussion forum. Students should not only be assigned to create a Webliography but also be asked to respond to those that their peers have built. In addition, one might have learners evaluate their resources on some scale or continuum, thereby adding an evaluative component to this highly generative activity.

***Skills and Objectives.*** Includes online exploration, self-directed learning, decision making, and digital literacy skills in browsing, filtering, and compiling information. Another focus or goal is to share and reflect on information.

***Advice and Ideas.*** A Webliography is akin to a portal or a window into a topic, person, or place. The body of a Webliography consists of lists of Internet sites with advice, annotations, and qualitative guidelines created by the designer. To create a Webliography, you must browse, find, evaluate, and select relevant Web resources. Next, you create a Web page and choose an appropriate title. An introduction must be written describing the purpose of the Webliography to those who might use or stumble upon it. Annotations might include brief but meaningful descriptions of the links and their relationship to the overall Webliography or reasons for their inclusion. In addition, consider creating an index of the resources in the Webliography, including several keywords.

Dariush Alimohammadi (2004) from Tehran, Iran, outlined the steps in creating a Webliography. She argues that Webliographies with annotations are easier to use. Alimohammadi gives the example of the Edgar Allen Poe

Webliography, which, while originally designed by Heyward Ehrlich in 1997, has continued to be updated and is now a fantastic electronic resource for research on and study of Poe (see Web resources). In this one growing Web site, there are a plethora of relevant hyperlinks to Poe texts, papers, secondary works, commentaries, and indexes. There are also links to class projects, digital media, and historical sites and associations related to Poe.

In your own classes, you might showcase some high-quality Webliographies from previous semesters. You might also embed some type of competition or goal in the activity. List a set of key course topics and concepts. Ask your students to conduct searches of the Web for different concepts listed or to suggest items not in the list. In addition, pair learners as Web search partners who give feedback to each other on their searches. When complete, have students present and discuss their search results. Archive some of the outstanding ones for future course offerings.

*Variations and Extensions.*  Ask students to work in pairs or teams to create their Webliographies. Each team or pair might work on resources for a different team or unit. Teams might critique or give feedback on each other's Webliographies. Alternatively, a second stage may involve team-based usability testing and feedback on the Webliographies created.

## Key Instructional Considerations

> *Risk index:* Medium
>
> *Time index:* Medium
>
> *Cost index:* Low
>
> *Learner-centered index:* High
>
> *Duration of the learning activity:* 2–4 weeks

---

# Activity 22. Text Messaging Course Notes and Content

*Description and Purpose of Activity.*  Educational content is available in multiple formats and delivery mechanisms. And such information delivery is performed by increasingly smaller devices. As a sign of these trends, some instructors are currently experimenting with sending course notes and other content to learner mobile devices such as mobile phones. Students can then practice what they have learned no matter where they are.

*Skills and Objectives.* Includes practice, feedback, concept review, interactivity, and a focus on digital literacy skills such as access and retrieval of information. A key goal here is for students to understand or memorize factual knowledge and terminology.

*Advice and Ideas.* Teaching entails the exchange and communication of thoughts and ideas. Text messaging is an expedient way for this to happen. Text messaging is no longer a novelty; it is now fifteen years old. Because of the recent massive increase in text messaging—in the United States alone it has increased from 81 billion messages in 2005 to nearly 160 billion in 2006—numerous educational applications and interventions are currently being tested or considered (Briggs, 2007).

Some of these messages certainly carry educational value. In the United Kingdom, for instance, a mobile service aimed at students called Dot Mobile condenses the works of famous literature and sends these to students as an aid when they study for exams (MSNBC, 2005). So, Shakespeare's infamous "To be or not to be, that is the question," becomes "2b? Nt2b? ???," and "Romeo, Romeo! wherefore art thou Romeo?" becomes "Romeo, Romeo_wher4 Rt thou Romeo?" In addition to all of Shakespeare works, Dot Mobile offers other famous works of English literature such as Charles Dickens's *Bleak House*. While there are fears that students who read condensed works will never read the original text, or, worse still, use them as cheat notes, those pushing for mobile learning point out that such messaging services might just as easily entice learners into reading the entire book and perhaps even search for other resources from that author or time period. And reading some of a book is often better than reading none of it. Pedagogical activities wrapped around short text messages might include inferring the plot, summarizing key ideas, and using mnemonics to remember themes, scenes, and characters.

Other organizations such as Athabasca University in Canada are using mobile technologies to teach English grammar through text messaging (CBC News, 2007). After downloading their grammar lessons to their mobile phones, newcomers to Canada can study the content and then answer a series of multiple choice or true-false questions. Through these lessons, anyone wishing to learn English as a second language can work at their own pace from a bus, a train, a soccer field, the workplace, or home.

When first considering text messaging in instruction, you might consult with instructional technologists or technology support personnel within your organization or institution as well as local phone service companies. Second, search technology magazines and journals for examples of innovative ideas related to text messaging. Third, conduct a Google search for related articles to find out if anyone has attempted interesting educational applications in mobile computing or text messaging before, and, if so, contact them for advice. A fourth idea would be to propose a text messaging activity to your supervisors or administrators, and if there are any costs involved, write a grant proposal for experimental text messaging activities. The funds might be used to make the text messaging free for all the students in your class, institution, or organization for a specified period of time.

*Variations and Extensions.* Alternatively, make homework tips, advice, and other content available for students to access from their mobile devices. The students, in turn, might rate the resources that they receive.

Text messaging activities might include students writing short summaries of passages that they have read. Such summaries require careful analysis and evaluation of important ideas while reviewing the content. Restating content in one's own words, however few, is a powerful learning tool. And those summaries might be reused in other ways, such as in comparison blog posts of student text entries, course discussion activities, or end-of-course super-summaries of their weekly text summaries.

## Key Instructional Considerations

*Risk index:* High

*Time index:* Medium

*Cost index:* Medium-High (depends on use and service provider)

*Learner-centered index:* Medium

*Duration of the learning activity:* As needed

## Activity 23. Text Messaging Course Reminders and Activities

*Description and Purpose of Activity.* Any training organization or educational institution might use text messaging for supplemental class training, coaching and mentoring, group discussion chats, ask-the-expert sessions, or online office hours (Farmer, 2005). One simple application is the use of text messaging to remind busy students or employees of the courses or programs that they have enrolled in. Such text messaging functions might encourage learners to better plan their time, provide formative feedback or evaluation on different learning experiences to date, or simply promote a specific resource or set of Web resources that students might want to use. Our experience indicates that working adults deeply appreciate course reminders and advice, especially if it occurs in a timely and structured fashion.

***Skills and Objectives.*** Includes organizational skills, prompt feedback, a sense of instructor social presence and immediacy, and instructor-student interaction.

***Advice and Ideas.*** Effective teaching entails the communication and exchange of ideas—this is exactly where text messaging has direct relevance! To speed up the communication, find out if your mobile phone allows for the creation of a distribution list for text messaging (ask your phone service operator how to create one or consult their online help system). The first step, of course, is to gather learners' mobile phone numbers. Once this information has been acquired and distribution lists for messages have been created and saved to your mobile phone, send out course assignment notices and task due date reminders, as appropriate, to learners' mobile phones. Get in the habit of sending these reminders of assignments and due dates once per week at approximately the same time. Learners who are working full time will appreciate your efforts to send task-structuring notices and reminders related to coursework, as well as any useful course summaries or notices you might provide. In fact, text messaging might be the tool of choice for today's mobile learners who tend to respond more enthusiastically to text messages than to e-mail. To evaluate the benefits of text messaging in your classes, give your learners a short survey at the end of the course or term asking them about the effectiveness of receiving weekly course updates and reminders by text messaging.

Be sure to check for any hidden or explicit costs of text messaging to instructors or students, since the costs of text messaging vary significantly by country and service provider. Several of our colleagues have asked their mobile phone providers to sponsor their text messaging ideas and activities. Before commencing on such innovative activities, you might consider obtaining a phone contract with free unlimited text messaging.

***Variations and Extensions.*** Create a weekly polling question or thought of the week for students using text messaging. Responses to these polls or questions could feed back into weekly lectures or course discussions. If, however, your system does not allow you to collect responses, have learners post their responses in an online forum or bring their responses or ideas to an FTF class session.

## Key Instructional Considerations

> *Risk index:* Medium
> *Time index:* Medium
> *Cost index:* Medium

*Learner-centered index:* Medium

*Duration of the learning activity:* Weekly as needed

## Activity 24. Online Language Lessons

***Description and Purpose of Activity.*** In addition to online reading of the news in a foreign language (that is, indirect learning of a language), increasingly the Web is being used to directly teach a language. Sites such as GlobalEnglish, Live-Mocha, and Englishtown have myriad resources for learners (for example, online flashcards, simulations, grammar lessons, voice games, chat sessions, pronunciation labs, progress reports, quizzes, and more). Such online language tools or programs might incorporate online conversation classes, placement tests, self-paced lessons, peer-to-peer practice conversations, and expert mentoring.

The LiveMocha site is the most recent and is based on Web 2.0 principles of sharing, creating friend networks, and joining communities of like-minded people. It is based on both peer support and self-directed learning. Learning at LiveMocha combines interactive games, chat, live video, and reading, writing, and listening exercises to help each other learn. Native speakers not only score your speaking and writing submissions but provide additional learning tips and goals. Points are earned for completing different exercises, and your progress can be compared to friends' in online competitions. It is the combination of the instructional materials, the motivational incentives, and the social networking and interaction with tutors and peers that makes LiveMocha a highly popular and motivational site for language learning. In less than four months of its release at the end of September 2007, it had more than 300,000 registered members. Such explosive growth indicates it has found a niche.

In addition to learning English, LiveMocha can be used to learn French, German, Spanish, Mandarin Chinese, and Hindi. This is just a start. Other languages will be offered soon. And, most important, at the time of this writing, it is free!

While language learning sites already are being extensively used in business settings to teach employees key skills to compete in a global world, there has been an increasing awareness of the importance of multiple language skills for younger learners. The state of Michigan, for example, recently announced the availability of Mandarin Chinese lessons in every high school in the state (Putnam, 2007). And while higher education institutions have been taking advantage of online language resources and lessons for more than a decade, the swell of recent announcements, Webinars, conferences, journals, and organizations related to online language learning is a sign of increased activity there as well.

As online audio becomes pervasive and increasingly inexpensive to store, language learning is also occurring less directly online through online conversations and chats among individuals in different countries or regions of the world. For instance, in Chinswing, users can discuss an array of topics, including finance, religion, relationships, biology and evolution, alternative medicine, and snails and slugs in gardens. These conversational threads take place for free among the people of this planet in any language that they choose. Nevertheless, the vast majority of these threads are in English because many learners are using Chinswing as a tool for improving or practicing their English. While Chinswing was developed as a global message board to encourage conversations about personal interests, hobbies, and hot topics—especially, social, political, and religious topics—such a tool could be used by language instructors and students at all levels in all target languages.

***Skills and Objectives.*** Includes feedback, interactivity, motivation and engagement, skill discrimination, practice, goal setting, and comparison and contrast. Such tools can foster basic language learning skills and competencies to more advanced language use.

***Advice and Ideas.*** The use of online language learning programs is accelerating, especially for popular languages such as Chinese, Arabic, and English. Explore, select, and incorporate online resources, such as podcasts, chats, blogs, and other learning activities, for language learning. For example, if you are teaching Mandarin online to adults, you might browse the resources and links found at Chinesepod.com; or if you have younger learners, check out the online Mandarin program from Michigan State University (see Web resources) (MacDonald, 2006). If you are teaching English in the corporate world, you might explore sites such as GlobalEnglish and Englishtown for examples of what is currently available and possible.

If online resources available for your language-related area or field are limited, you might develop your own or partner with others in such development. To enhance their applicability, be sure to conduct usability tests on resources as you build them. If funding is needed, consider writing grant proposals or requesting resources from superiors. If you lack time or funding to build such resources, you might write to international scholars in the field for their ideas and opinions.

***Variations and Extensions.*** Ask learners to compare language learning resources available at two or more language learning sites. Have them vote on the best free resources to use in class.

### Key Instructional Considerations

*Risk index:* Medium

*Time index:* High

*Cost index:* Low to High (depends if you can use preexisting resources)

*Learner-centered index:* Medium

*Duration of the learning activity:* As needed, perhaps for entire course

---

## Activity 25. E-Book and Wikibook Reports and Critiques

*Description and Purpose of Activity.* The use of electronic or virtual textbooks is proliferating due to reductions in screen size and storage costs as well as enhancements in image display for electronic reading devices. At the same time, free digital text resources and books are finding their way into online courses.

For instance, there are thousands of free books being developed by the Wikimedia Foundation at the Wikibook Web site. Basically, a Wikibook is an online, collaboratively written and edited book by the world community (see Chapter Eight for more details). Naturally, there are many questions about the quality of such online resources and materials. In this activity, an instructor might have learners create reports and critiques related to one or two Wikibooks or electronic books that coincide with different units or modules of a course. The learners might also send questions to a developer or coordinator of a Wikibook (such a person is called a "Wikibookian") and share findings with the class.

*Skills and Objectives.* Includes content knowledge, factual skills, critical analysis, self-directed learning, and exploration. In addition, a key goal is making learners aware of online resources beyond the standard textbook resources and supplemental materials.

*Advice and Ideas.* While Wikibook creation is becoming more widely accepted in higher education as well as other educational sectors, you should explore the Wikibooks Web site for at least a couple of hours to become familiar with it. Such exploration will help you mine it for pedagogical ideas and activities that you can reflect on, design, and share with colleagues. As of August 2006, there were more than 1,000 Wikibooks and 21,000 modules or chapters in development at the Wikbook Web site; however, fewer than 100 books were completed at that time. This Web site contains books on many topics for K–12 students (for example, High School Chemistry, Big Cats, the Solar System, Dinosaurs) as well as adult learners (for example, Technologies for Rural Development,

Reverse Engineering, Immunology, Basic Electricity, Blended Learning for K–12 Schools, Scottish Country Dancing). Recently, the Junior Wikibooks Web site was created by the WikiMedia Foundation to develop and house free books for children ages 8 to 11.

To prepare a Wikibook report or critiques of existing Wikibooks, you should locate relevant Wikibook resources (for example, the books at the Wikibooks Web site). Once the Wikibook resources are selected, assign learners to evaluate one or two books, or chapters within those books, at those sites. Have learners share their reports or critiques in an online discussion forum, a wiki, the course Web site, or a class blog. Consider conducting peer evaluations or critiques of each others' reports. An online instructor might include a discussion of the credibility of such sources and reliability of Web resources after having students explore various resources at this site. (See Phase 4 of the R2D2 model—that is, Chapters Eight and Nine—for additional ideas related to the use of Wikibooks.)

***Variations and Extensions.*** Wikibook reports or critiques might be saved in a database for learners to refer to in later semesters of the course. Comments from the original development team or key coordinator of each Wikibook might also be archived and contrasted.

## Key Instructional Considerations

>*Risk index:* High
>
>*Time index:* High
>
>*Cost index:* Low
>
>*Learner-centered index:* High
>
>*Duration of the learning activity:* 4–8 weeks

# Use and Outlook for Phase 1 Strategies

The twenty-five ideas presented here are just a few brief snapshots of what is possible today within Phase 1 of the R2D2 model. The activities are meant to provide a mental framework that you can use to begin to perceive what is possible in the Web of Learning; they are, for the most part, doable today in any online instructional practices or educational situation.

Humankind will never stop speaking, listening, reading, or thinking. Words and text will most assuredly continue to find their way into the education and training of both children and adults. As such, Phase 1 strategies on the Internet will continue to proliferate in K–12, higher education, corporate, government, military, and informal learning settings.

Phase 1 of R2D2 will never die, though it will undoubtedly be transformed in unforeseen ways. It is also highly conceivable that what will qualify as reading or speaking or listening in five or ten years will drastically change. Is a Wikibook really a book? Is a podcast a speech? Is the online juxtaposition of quotes from two audiobooks as read by the original authors reading or listening? Perhaps it does not matter. What does matter is that there will be no shortage of online content in the form of words or text. The text- and audio-based resources at one's fingertips on the Internet will continue to invite online learners.

## Final Reflections

This chapter presented activities that can help auditory or verbal learners in online environments. As is apparent, there are a variety of ways to help online learners read, listen, explore, and otherwise acquire knowledge online. In fact, there are so many opportunities (that is, hundreds of billions of electronic pages to visit) that trying to implement this phase of the R2D2 model could overwhelm instructors as well as learners.

There are many directions that the Web of Learning, as well as Phase 1 of R2D2, can take. With the emergence of online and blended learning, what is drastically needed are some directions, markers, and signposts for reflecting on the value-added opportunities of the Internet. We hope that this chapter has provided such guidance.

The guidelines in this chapter can help instructors, instructional designers, schools, and training organizations determine how to use emerging technologies for course activities and help support and focus their online and blended learning efforts. A focus or vision is central to smooth running of online courses and programs and student retention within them. The first phase of the R2D2 model lays out a range of learning activities to help with active knowledge acquisition as well as collaborative knowledge construction with widely available learning technologies.

Phase 1 of the R2D2 model is loaded with opportunities. With the learning developed in this phase, learners are now ready to reflect on that learning. As detailed in the next two chapters, such learning opportunities and learning preferences are the focus of Phase 2 of R2D2.

CHAPTER FOUR

# PHASE 2 OF THE R2D2 MODEL

## Reflective and Observational Learners

Once learners have acquired content or ideas from discussions, e-books, online articles, podcasts, videostreamed lectures, and other sources, it is vital that they reflect on such activities. Online reflection is often promoted as one of the key advantages of online learning; especially when using asynchronous or delayed (that is, anywhere, anytime) conferencing for discussion. When learners can contribute to an online discussion or activity at their convenience, they have an opportunity to think more deeply about an idea and for a longer time period. The online discussion forum in the Web of Learning will still be there for them later in the day or at sunrise tomorrow.

Unlike traditional instruction, in which a learner may be allowed a mere 5 or 10 seconds to come up with a response, in online environments, time is stretched in many ways. There are, of course, significant advantages as well as disadvantages for such time extensions. On the positive side, students can gather more data and information before contributing to a discussion forum or analyzing a case or vignette. Also, without having to face competition or pressure from more talkative or expressive peers who tend to dominate the discussions in face-to-face (FTF) settings, learners may feel more comfortable sharing their thoughts and ideas. In addition, they have opportunities to better understand the perspectives of peers, tutors, and instructors before participating. And, given the semi-permanency of the text, they can revisit their postings and change their views if needed.

At the same time, there are likely dozens of negative repercussions to allowing extra time for reflection. A key problem is that learners may get lost in their own reflections awaiting a state of perfection in their thoughts; hence they may not post until they see a glimpse of nirvana or an ultimate due date arrives. Similarly, since the sun never sets on an online course, they may feel a need to keep reflecting well beyond the time their initial ideas or answers would have sufficed. Third, learners who have a tendency to procrastinate will not fare well in asynchronous learning environments. In response, some organizations and institutions design online learning readiness checklists to screen such types of individuals out of online courses and programs.

# Phase 2 of Read, Reflect, Display, and Do

In Chapter Two, we criticized the overriding text emphasis within the Web of Learning. However, having semi-permanent electronic text that is perhaps linked to still other text provides many pedagogically significant opportunities for Phase Two of the R2D2 Model (see Figure 4.1). In fact, it will be difficult at times to distinguish between Phase One (the information gathering stage) and Phase Two (the reflection stage).

## Opportunities for Reflective and Observational Learners

As indicated, the second part of the R2D2 model emphasizes learners reflecting on the content that they have been learning in Phase 1. Thus, it is geared toward reflective or observational learners. You have likely come across such learners in your classes or learning experiences. They may be the quiet ones in FTF classes who often score the highest grades at the end of the course.

Such reflective and observational learners, of course, tend to prefer to observe, view, watch, and reflect on specific learning activities as well as on their overall learning. Instead of shouting out answers or participating in a haphazard fashion to get noticed, they will sit back and reflect on their learning experiences and postpone reaching final conclusions until their ideas have matured or are requested. They are known for making careful judgments and hesitating on offering solutions until sufficient data has been obtained and analyzed. Reflective and observational learners also try to observe and compare information from different viewpoints before making decisions or suggestions. Students exhibiting this style of learning tend to listen to others and learn from models or examples of what is expected.

Such behavior is explained by the social learning theory long promoted by Stanford University psychologist Albert Bandura (1986, 1997). From this perspective, individuals can learn vast amounts of important information from

## FIGURE 4.1. PHASE 2 OF R2D2.

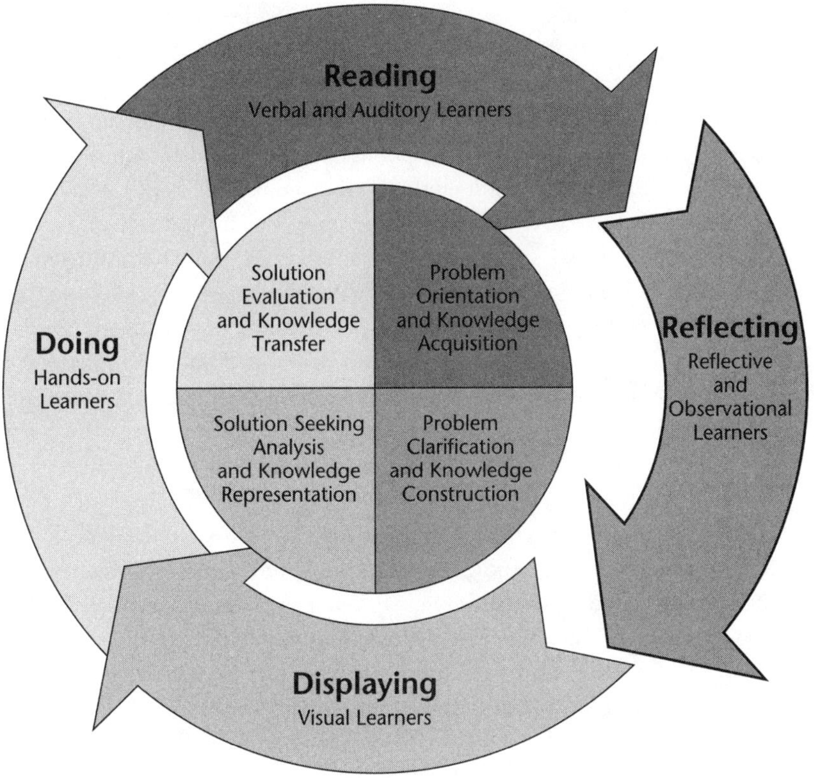

observing others model their own strategies or learned behaviors first. In effect, they can be reinforced for their learning by vicariously watching others in the online course being praised or reprimanded for their opinions and ideas in an asynchronous discussion forum or synchronous presentation. According to Bandura, they can also be directly reinforced by the instructor or moderator. And the learner can provide self-reinforcement. Decades of research from Bandura across countries and communities around the globe indicate the sheer power of learning from observations. Most important, he argues that reflection on those observations is central to learning.

Given the time extensions of asynchronous learning, it may be the ideal instructional approach for reflective and observational learners. Indeed, many different distance learning delivery systems offer reflective learners engaging opportunities that mesh well with their style preferences. Such experiences may be too seldom experienced in FTF classes. Unlike educational delivery mechanisms of the past, the tools and resources found in the Web of Learning can perhaps benefit all learners. With asynchronous discussion forums and threads, for instance, a learner can think carefully and thoughtfully before responding to others or posting a new message.

Of course, these types of experiences are clearly valuable in fully online experiences as well as well as in supplemental activities within an FTF experience. In either case, if the instructional goals are depth of discussion, as opposed to surface-level thinking, there may be distinct advantages to online forums (Henri, 1992). Here, learner rewards or points may accumulate for those who find themes and patterns in the discussion threads, integrate ideas, and create useful metaphors or analogies for others to learn from. Online reflection and discussion remains fairly useless without demonstrations that one has internalized some of those ideas and generated new, high-quality ones.

## Writing Online

Writing is commonly referred to as a tool for thinking (Langer & Applebee, 1987). Many cognitive studies in the 1980s and 1990s showed evidence that writing did indeed impact thinking (Bereiter & Scardamalia, 1987). As a result of such research, many writing-related movements during the past few decades have had an impact on teaching and learning in K–12 as well as higher education settings. The "writing across the curriculum" and "writing process" or "process approach to teaching writing" movements of the 1980s and 1990s are prime examples.

Fortunately, the Web might be thought of as an ideal forum for writing and reflection. A learner can write to her heart's content without concerns about red marks. We find that students often write hundreds of words each week (and read thousands of words of their peers) in online discussion forums. Students typically do not even realize that they are, in fact, writing when they are corresponding online with peers, experts, and instructors through e-mail, interactive chat sessions, blogs (Web logs), and other reflective writing activities. There is no pen. No physical paper to wrestle with.

The Internet, therefore, can be used as a gigantic writing device. Tools already exist to mark up, edit, comment on, and annotate such work. There also are software aids for outlining and organizing one's thoughts and ideas as well as prompting systems that foster reflection on one's ideas as they are written down. For decades, writing tools and systems have helped novice and less experienced writers think about the genre, purpose, and goals of their writing. On top of that, some writing systems foster the sharing of knowledge and ideas in online communities of writers or peer databases. In effect, writing tools exist for self-reflection as well as for collaboration and community. They can focus writers at the word level (for example, spelling aids, grammar checkers, word processors, and so on) as well as the meaning level (for example, Web logs, outlining tools, bibliographic retrieval tools, and so on) (Bonk, Reynolds, & Medury, 1996).

Clearly, online learning has brought a renewed awareness of the availability and importance of such tools and systems while accelerating the focus on writing as a tool for student thinking. It was fortuitous that the Internet emerged as a legitimate and highly valued learning tool in the 1990s after decades of mounting research on writing. While not discounting the importance of text messaging from a mobile phone, the Internet has become the tool of choice for student writing; witness the use of online discussions, e-mail, chats, social networking software, and blogs. Blogging is also being accepted by teachers and schools as an indispensable way to display the evolution of one's thoughts and understandings.

## Blogging

Perhaps more than online course discussions, blogs epitomize how the Web of Learning can address reflective and observational learners. What is a blog, you ask? From one viewpoint, a *blog* (short for "Web log") is an online personal diary or account of experiences or thoughts that can be private or, at the other extreme, broadcast for others to read and comment on. Stephen Downes (2004) argues that a blog is more than that (that is, it is more like personal publishing) because of its personal flavor as well as the chance it provides to extend the reader to other new and relevant resources. In a blog, one not only provides commentary and ideas but also provides hyperlinks to other related resources.

Trey Martindale and David Wiley (2005, p. 60) note that a blog, at its most basic level, is "simply a Website," but blogs are simultaneously an empowering tool for personally publishing one's ideas and communicating them with a worldwide audience. One might blog on any topic, but for online courses, it is typically related to areas such as course readings, course tasks and activities, personal research including one's dissertation progress, field experiences or places wherein one has tried out the content learned in a particular class, and extra course-related work.

While at the start of this century, there were only a few hundred thousand blogs, according to research by Perseus Development Corporation (2005), by 2003 there were more than 4 million blogs (Perseus Development Corporation,

2003) and by the end of 2005 more than 50 million. A year later, blogs were growing at a rate of 75,000 per day, according to *USA Today* (Graham, 2006).

Like podcasting, a significant chunk of these blogs are education related. This tremendous growth offers hundreds, if not thousands, of ways to employ blogs in all areas of education, including K–12 schools, higher education institutions, and nonprofit, military, and corporate training settings. Popular educational blogs include Stephen Downes's Web site "Stephen's Web," which is focused on higher education matters, and Will Richardson's "Weblogg-ed," which primarily addresses K–12 issues and trends. There are also many blogging celebrities in the corporate world; however, it is not unusual for someone in a corporate setting to float in troubled waters after they have posted something in a personal blog that offends someone at work or discloses information that corporate executives find problematic, confidential, or unnecessary.

This stunning growth in the use of blogging results, at least in part, from the plethora of blogging tools and resources available for K–12 education, higher education, corporate training, and personal use. One might use tools such as Pitas, Blogspot, Live Journal, Diaryland, and MovableType. Such tools provide automatic formatting of one's entries or stories, time and date stamp entries, archives of previous posts, search functions, a blog roll that indicates what other blogs a particular blogger reads, a place for reader comments, and simple syndication possibilities (Martindale & Wiley, 2005). Most important, most of these blogging tools are free.

For those wanting to foster student reflection, critical thinking, and knowledge exchange, there is a goldmine of opportunities here. In terms of instructional uses, there might be individual blogs for personal reflections, dyad blogs for paired activities or for creating feedback mechanisms, team blogs for joint assignments, instructor blogs summarizing class activities and events, and class blogs for cross-cultural exchanges. Students might also be asked to expand their blog posts into longer papers or reduce their blog posts into reflective summaries of key points learned. In paired blog activities, we often will assign "critical friends" or "Web buddies" within our classes who give each other weekly feedback on their blog postings. We also require a reflection paper at the end of the semester on their overall blogging experience and associated learning, in which they must comment on the effectiveness of the critical friend task.

Instead of having students use different tools for each blog, instructors might create bloglike tasks by assigning each student in a class an individual discussion thread within an asynchronous conference. We have experimented with both approaches. In the latter approach, we have had students create online resource libraries (ORLs) of additional articles that they have read in a personal discussion thread, using tools such as WebCT, Sitescape Forum, or Sakai.

We typically assign students a critical friend in the class who gives them weekly feedback on their blog postings, and at the end of the semester we require reflection papers on the blogging as well as the blog feedback tasks.

In a nutshell, a blog allows students to generate ideas, reflect on the ideas of others, and conduct personal searches of content related to the class. Given the rapid ability to post new comments and share blogs, they may be the most innovative educational tools for reflection in higher education to date.

## Beyond Blogs

There are numerous other opportunities to foster reflective reading and writing in an online class. Many of these are interactive tasks involving two or more learners, such as a mock trial with the entire class or role-play situations in which all students in a class are assigned a different role or personality (Watkins, 2005). One might also place students in smaller teams of perhaps two to four students in pro-and-con debates or controversial situations that they must resolve. Such conflict-intensive situations will foster cognitive dissonance and, therefore, continued student reading of the positions of others as well as reflection on their own positions. These situations might also promote collaborative knowledge construction, a sense of sharing, and meta-awareness of the critical resources or underlying knowledge base available on this topic.

As noted in Chapter Three, publications from the National Council of Teachers of English (NCTE) contain thousands of examples of writing tasks and techniques that might foster student online reflection. Oftentimes, we simply assign a series of reflection papers as a means to address Phase 2 and allow the learners to pick the type of writing reflection that best matches their interests and competencies. For instance, we might include an individual summary writing task option as well as a collaborative group one. In most collaborative group situations, we require students to give feedback to each other using the "Track Changes" and "Insert Comments" tools within Microsoft Word. We find such feedback and advice to be deeply appreciated by students. Simple advice: peers are a free resource—use them!

The Web of Learning has been used for learner reflection in perhaps every discipline and every type of learning environment, from those involving young children to employees in the workforce. It has been used in internship and field placement reflections in professional schools such as accounting, nursing, optometry, law, education, and engineering as well as in trade-related disciplines and skill areas. In such situations, the learners might be asked to interview their bosses, supervisors, or those they are observing about their job roles and assignments so that students can grasp the demands of a particular occupation.

Learners might also be required to record how certain key concepts, principles, and ideas from a course or training event are encountered and employed in the real world (Bonk, Hara, Dennen, Malikowski, & Supplee, 2000).

When in a real-world placement, internship, or field experience, reflective learners might be asked to record the nuances of how a particular concept or idea is implemented as well as any alternative views and competing ideas and decisions observed that were not discussed in class or found in the course content. When this occurs, students might discern the limits of their book knowledge. If such a real-world experience is not possible, they might be asked to observe video scenarios from real-world situations and reflect on those instead. Such rich online video scenarios can help standardize the content and afford multiple opportunities for reflecting on it. Of course, the use of video-based situations and scenarios is highly linked to Phase 3 of the R2D2 model.

One increasingly popular application is to use the Internet to apprentice students by placing them in professional situations, such as having them watch or listen to videostreams of online conferences, seminars, and institutes. Learners can, in fact, listen to a live or delayed broadcasts while accomplishing additional tasks or engaging in other activities—in effect, multitask. During the past few years, the *Chronicle of Higher Education* has featured online performances of music recitals, theater performances, heart surgeries, and fashion shows (for example, Carlson, 2004; Olsen, 2003; Young, 2003). Before these live events occur, online instructors might provide learners with guide sheets or learning scaffolds to guide their observations and perceptions. Of course, when students begin conducting their own online performances, they would be shifting to the fourth phase of the R2D2 model—"Doing."

As pointed out in the preceding two chapters, the Internet contains a plethora of podcasts and Webinars that students can reflect on. Tools such as Tegrity allow high school or college instructors in areas such as physics or biology to conduct demonstrations of key experiments and problems online. Online storage of such presentations allows them to be reused and replayed, and subtle hints and pointers can be added. Furthermore, instructor notes can be matched with those demonstrations.

Such events and activities will continue to climb in usage in online learning environments, especially in geographic regions with extensive broadband connections (for example, Korea, Netherlands, Denmark, Iceland, Canada, Switzerland, the United States, and the United Kingdom) (Organisation for Economic Co-operation and Development [OECD], 2004, 2005) or in programs where learners typically have such access (for example, working professionals in online M.B.A. programs). Perhaps most important, archived events such as podcasts, videostreamed talks, and Webinars allow those learning at remote locations opportunities to learn that previously did not exist. As indicated, through observations and explorations as legitimate peripheral participants (Lave & Wenger, 1991), such forms of learning delivery can be used to apprentice students into their chosen profession or even to professions that they had not previously considered.

Simple exposure to an expert in any discipline and reflections on their ideas or performances can rouse to life your learning passions and nurture life goals that were not even dreams before. Thus, there is a dire need for profound pedagogical thinking related to reflective learning activities in the Web of Learning. Broadband access will continue to increase, as will the number of humans wishing to learn online as well as those offering their online mentoring services. Not only will this increase access to content, but it will also offer more avenues for online apprenticeship and mentoring as well as self-directed learning.

These trends toward more active and self-directed learning require that reflective tasks be embedded to nudge student internalization and appropriation of new knowledge. Self-reflection, self-check options, review questions, and general learner self-reflections (for example, "Did you know?" activities) are common in large-scale or global online training initiatives such as those from companies like Cisco Systems and Sun Microsystems. Wenger and Ferguson (2006) pointed out that Sun Microsystems teaches more than 250,000 online and FTF students per year at more than 250 training centers in more than 60 countries. Similarly, by 2005, the Cisco Networking Academy had been offered to more than 400,000 students in 10,000 CNA academies in 150 different countries (Dennis, Bichelmeyer, Henry, Cakir, Korkmaz, Watson, & Brunnage, 2006). Our experience researching online courses used by the U.S. military indicates that they also embed such self-checks (for example, firefights, pre- and post-assessments) within their online courses and programs (Bonk, Olson, Wisher, & Orvis, 2002).

There are many reasons for the use of such self-check reflections and performance tests in online courses. When you train hundreds of thousands of learners in countries spanning the globe, there must be some consistency in the content, including a centralized curriculum development approach. In addition, there is a need for quality controls, instructor guides and training programs, continued reviews of program accessibility and cost effectiveness, and some standardization in the assessment procedures. Review and self-check questions are just part of the process. When properly used, however, they provide opportunities for the learner to pause and reflect on the content that he or she is learning.

Examples of such self-checking are also plentiful in higher education. For instance, James Strauss, professor of anatomy at The Pennsylvania State University, created a Web site for student self-testing on the muscular system that received more than 250,000 hits in one month alone (Penn State Live, 2005).

Of course, that was the month of December 2004, which was smack dab in the middle of student final exams. Apparently, college students around the globe wanted practice and support before their finals. The huge response to Dr. Strauss's system indicates that one person can change the world, or, at least, the world of college anatomy temporarily.

Similarly, professors at Indiana University (IU) have developed a system, "Computer-Assisted Learning Method" (CALM), that Socratically interacts with high school and college students in testing them on their chemistry-related knowledge. The goals are to increase students' content knowledge and problem-solving skills. The CALM system is currently being extended to other disciplines such as physics. While originally designed for college students at IU, many high school students in advanced placement and honors courses in the United States now have access to the CALM system. The point is that students crave such checks of their content knowledge—these systems are private, provide instant feedback or suggestions, and are available at any hour. Simply put, students want to know what they know and do not know, and they want to know that now!

In terms of generic testing software, Hot Potatoes from Half-Baked Software is a free online testing software program for educational institutions that are nonprofit and publicly funded. Hot Potatoes includes online capabilities for multiple choice, short-answer, jumbled-sentence, crossword, matching/ordering, and gap-fill exercises. Another commonly used program for test construction is Questionmark Perception, which offers the ability to send test questions to a personal digital assistant (PDA) or online browser as well as offering paper-based tests, instant feedback, a question bank, adaptive branching (that is, questions sent to the learner that depend on previous answers in order to hone in on their ability level), and randomization of questions as well as choices within the questions.

The use of such activities is especially critical in online modules or courses in which there are extensive learner-content interactions yet minimal feedback from instructors, tutors, peers, or outside experts. As mentioned earlier, posting model answers or archiving student work gives reflective learners something to observe as a standard or example of exemplary performance. Online modeling might be especially useful in physical education and outdoor recreation courses, as well as in counseling, teacher training, and any form of emergency preparedness training. Students might also reflect on their online or FTF learning progress and performances in electronic portfolios. Here, they can explore their learning goals, career plans, and course accomplishments.

As with the first phase of R2D2, we see no letup in the sheer number of tools and resources that will be  made available for learner reflection and observations. With larger bandwidth on the Internet, there will be a multitude of animations and visuals for learners to observe and reflect upon. And surely the tools for self-testing, reviewing one's performances, and observing the performances of others will only increase. What seems needed today is research in this area that explores the impact of reflection and observation in online courses on student learning, course satisfaction, and transfer of knowledge to other tasks and topics. Of course, for those in training environments or the workforce, it might be valuable to explore levels of reflection in professional development and how to foster growth within such levels through distance learning.

# Recap

As with Phase 1 of R2D2, there are many tools available in online environments to address student learning preferences—in this chapter, reflective and observational processes and activities. Learners might use online technology tools and aids for (1) blogging about the week's readings, (2) outlining and reevaluating key points for a paper or speech, (3) annotating comments on the paper of a team member or critical friend, (4) pausing and reevaluating content in a videostreamed presentation, (5) summarizing the results of a role play activity, (6) self-testing knowledge of a chapter or a topic, (7) comparing and contrasting different viewpoints in a debate, or (8) providing peer comments on a paper.

Many such Phase 2 tools have been around for decades using various technology delivery formats including desktop computers, laserdiscs, and CDs; their emergence on the Internet, however, has made some of them more apparent and useful. As a way of celebrating this trend toward Phase 2 learning, Chapter Five lays out twenty-five ways to foster learner observation, reflection, and reflective writing online. Those who effectively use such strategies will soon realize that the Internet is an ideal reflective space for ferreting out and sharing thought constructions, critical reflections, idea summarizations, local as well as international collaborations, and a host of other reflective learning options.

CHAPTER FIVE

# ACTIVITIES FOR PHASE 2

## Reflective and Observational Learners

As was done in Chapter Three for verbal and auditory learners, in this chapter we present twenty-five learning activities for reflective and observational learners in Phase 2 of the Reading, Reflecting, Displaying, and Doing (R2D2) model. All of these ideas are intended to offer opportunities for learner reflection and observation, but they may touch on the learning preferences of the other phases as well. In fact, given that reflection is useful at nearly any moment of the learning process, many of these activities have high overlap with the other phases of the model—in particular, with Phase 1. As stated in Chapter Three, the scales provided below each activity are highly subjective but are meant as online teaching and learning guides—not as ultimate truths—for instructors and course designers.

## Activity 26. Post Model Answers

***Description and Purpose of Activity.*** Instructors across academic fields and disciplines use *modeling* as a means to convey information to the learner, typically before the learner has acquired the skills necessary to perform an action or when it would be inappropriate or unsafe for the learner to try it out in the real world. One might model how to solve a difficult mathematics problem, derive a basic statistical equation, conduct an internal audit, dive off a high board platform, use a microscope, search for articles on the Internet, or think through a writing assignment and associated processes. Unfortunately, modeling is one of the more difficult instructional techniques to perform online. Our own research indicates that modeling is a rare occurrence in both K–12 (Sugar & Bonk, 1998) and higher education (Bonk, Malikowski, Angeli, & East, 1998) environments. Some of our more recent survey research indicates that it remains difficult to implement in both higher education and corporate training settings (Bonk, Kim, & Zeng, 2006). As a solution to this problem, some of our colleagues post to the current course Web site model answers that learners provided in previous classes or training situations. Such model answers or examples might also come from the instructor or other experts.

When we ask former students if we can repost their answers or work from previous semesters for new students, they always say "Yes." Interestingly, they typically then say, "But let me make it better first." And that is long after they have received a grade in the course. This would be a rare occurrence in a face-to-face (FTF) course; however, in an online one, learners more readily realize that the audience for their work extends well beyond the instructor to potentially the entire planet.

We have a colleague in a business law department who posts sample answers to court cases from previous semesters. In contrast to the online-learning critics who argue that most online curricula is dumbed-down content, this technique allows instructors or tutors who post model answers to continually raise the standards of excellent performance for a particular class or program.

**Skills and Objectives.** Includes comparison and contrast, observational skills, critical analysis, coaching, and high course standards. Modeling is also part of establishing a community of learners.

**Advice and Ideas.** Take stock of the previous work of your students. Identify tasks for which students typically had many questions or concerns or found it difficult to excel. Select exemplary prior student work that relates to these difficult tasks to share on the Web in the "show room." Obtain permission of the student authors as necessary. Delete all personally identifying information as appropriate. When your students use these examples, you might have them write reflections on how their own work compares to the examples.

Always think ahead to the next offering of the course and save interesting and engaging student work. Ask permission to post ahead of time in case the students move on and you no longer have their contact information. Even for a new course, consider offering model answers or model assignments that you find on the Web or in courses from other colleagues. And during the actual teaching of a course, you might provide model answers right after each unit or module and recognize "unit or module stars" within the current class. In addition, consider making exemplary student work available once the assignments are graded. To motivate more students, try to select answers and examples submitted by different students in each unit or module. Use the course bulletin board, discussion forum, coffee house, or course blog to encourage conversations with students who submitted these examples.

*Variations and Extensions.* Post model answers according to semester or course and have competitions for best answer, essay, product, and so on each time the course is taught. The top-ranked answers or projects might receive bonus points.

## Key Instructional Considerations

> *Risk index:* Low
>
> *Time index:* Low
>
> *Cost index:* Low
>
> *Learner-centered index:* Medium
>
> *Duration of the learning activity:* As needed

# Activity 27. Reuse Chat Transcripts

*Description and Purpose of Activity.* One technique that we have found highly valuable is to reuse and repurpose synchronous chat transcripts. We archive our expert chat sessions both for learners who attended the event as well as for those who could not. The chat transcript might be used for students to reflect on the differences in perspectives from two or more experts, the themes appearing within various chat sessions, or the content that was covered during units or weeks after a particular chat session. It might also be used to reflect on how student views changed after chatting with or speaking to one or more experts. As with the chat activity in Chapter Three, chat reflections can find use in nearly any educational situation or environment.

*Skills and Objectives.* Includes synthesis skills, feedback, sense of social presence and instructional immediacy, comparison and contrast, appreciation of multiple perspectives, and analysis, evaluation, and other critical thinking skills.

*Advice and Ideas.* Invite a selection of experts for synchronous chat events during the course. Coordinate the events, including arranging times and dates and asking about guest preferences for the event. Assign learners to read articles authored by these experts prior to the sessions. When possible, collect questions from course participants ahead of time and pass these on to the expert. Facilitate and moderate the chat session. Archive all chat sessions that take place during the course or unit. (Note that, unless the guest expert has granted permission to make the session public, the archive might be made available solely for students in the course.)

Once archived, you can assign reflective activities around the archived chats. Perhaps have students compare different chats or look for themes across various chat sessions. Students who missed a chat session might be encouraged to write a paper based on one or more archived chats. That paper can then be reviewed by peers who attended the live chat session. At the same time, you can post an asynchronous forum thread for students to discuss what they learned from each live and archived chat.

Experiment with this idea—there are myriad spin-off activities from the use of synchronous chats. This is one task for which the opportunities for apprenticeship and engagement are extremely high, and, ironically, such activities are based on content that many instructors and students might have considered dead or no longer useful. Think about what other given-up-for-dead content might exist on the Web for similar reflections (for example, old podcasts, video-streamed lectures, streamed conferences, expert panel discussions).

***Variations and Extensions.*** Share the chat transcript with the expert who participated and ask if he or she has additional reflections or stories to share. Or perhaps have an expert compare the ideas in his or her transcript to those of other guest experts in the course. You might ask students for their ideas regarding how they might want to use and reuse such content—it might surprise you. They might decide to have class competitions to see which individuals or groups can quote the most from the online chat sessions. You also might decide to have them send their reflection papers to the guest experts or others not even involved in the chat for their feedback and commentary.

## Key Instructional Considerations

> *Risk index:* Low
>
> *Time index:* Medium
>
> *Cost index:* Low
>
> *Learner-centered index*: Medium
>
> *Duration of the learning activity:* 1–2 weeks for each activity

## Activity 28. Workplace, Internship, or Job Reflections

*Description and Purpose of Activity.* Perhaps it is not obvious when first reading the title of this activity, but this idea is highly useful across age ranges. Once he or she is old enough to work, any learner can benefit from posting job reflections online. Young learners might be in an internship experience for which they make use of the course content (or at least observe it being used), whereas older learners might use course content in their current full-time job settings.

Such experiential e-learning is becoming increasingly common. In fact, the myriad opportunities for real-world experiences might be one of the key reasons an instructor, trainer, administrator, or consultant might use the Web in an educational or training setting. When learners are linked to the real world, instructors and trainers can embed reflection activities in which learners interview their supervisors or colleagues about what their jobs entail. The instructor, tutor, or trainer might weave these reflections together in helping learners define an occupation or particular job duty. Learners might also conduct personal reflections on how they are applying key course content.

*Skills and Objectives.* Includes critical analysis skills, reflective writing, and connecting content knowledge from books and lectures to real-world experiences. Another goal would be the comparison of different perspectives or observations and appreciation of the diversity of field experiences as well as the varied application of skills.

*Advice and Ideas.* Assign a set of questions or topics for students to ask their supervisors or others during their internship or workplace experience. Perhaps also ask students to come up with additional questions to think, ask, and reflect upon. Next, ask your learners to post their reflections to an online discussion board or class blog. To encourage learners to read each other's posts, ask them to summarize their reflections and compare them to the posts of their peers, highlighting the commonalities and differences in their observations. Point out key aspects of these experiences that the learners apparently missed or found confusing, and clarify any misperceptions or misunderstandings. Perhaps assign a final integrated reflection paper that spans their workplace experiences near the end of the course.

An instructor can do many things to enhance such a real-world experience. For instance, if learners are having a difficult time in their internship experiences, you can point to the positive posts of other students so that they do not overgeneralize their negative experiences. Too often, learners give up on a field of study when brief or initial internship experiences have soured their taste for it. An additional practice to help learners grasp the broader picture is to share with the class the outcomes or themes from prior semesters or course offerings. You might consider piloting the reflection questions ahead of time or sharing them with other instructors for their candid feedback prior to use.

***Variations and Extensions.*** Assign students partners, and ask them to write joint reflections that summarize commonalities and differences in their observations.

## Key Instructional Considerations

> *Risk index:* Medium
>
> *Time index:* Medium
>
> *Cost index:* Low
>
> *Learner-centered index:* Medium
>
> *Duration of the learning activity:* 4–15 weeks

# Activity 29. Field and Lab Observations

***Description and Purpose of Activity.*** Similar to job or internship reflections, learners might be placed in temporary field assignments, online labs or simulations, or FTF lab activities in which they watch an expert and reflect on his or her performances *prior to* an internship or job experience. These field observations or expert labs act as a safe harbor to test out knowledge and abilities prior to unleashing the learner into the real world. Learners are provided with a set of questions to take with them to the field. Student observations are posted to the Web for comparisons and feedback.

***Skills and Objectives.*** Critical analysis skills, appreciation of multiple perspectives, reflective writing, and connecting content knowledge from books and lectures to real-world experiences. Once again, this activity should help students avoid overgeneralizing an unsatisfactory field or lab experience.

***Advice and Ideas.*** To structure the activity, provide and discuss a set of questions or topics for learners to reflect on each time before they enter into a field or watch an expert video. Ask the learners to summarize their observations and reflections and share them with peers in an online discussion forum or the class blog. Require learners to look for commonalities and differences in their summaries. Instructors or tutors can then point out key aspects of these experiences that the learners missed or found confusing. Consider assigning a final integrated reflection paper across all their experiences near the end of the course.

Perhaps the most effective activities are those that are blended experiences, combining FTF presentations and discussions, field observations, and lab activities in which learners try out some of the content. Such activities are common in teacher education, counseling, school psychology, and other education-related disciplines. They are used in many other professional disciplines, too, including accounting, law, engineering, social work, nursing, and dentistry. Field observations also have obvious applicability in trade industries such as pipe fitting, plumbing, automotive mechanics, and heating and cooling systems maintenance. In effect, this type of activity could be valuable anywhere a learner has a temporary field placement activity or experience.

*Variations and Extensions.* Learners can be asked to post joint reflections with a partner or synthesize their experience across a team or small group. They might also compare their actual field experiences to events encountered in practice lab activities or viewed in a simulation.

## Key Instructional Considerations

*Risk index:* Medium

*Time index:* Medium

*Cost index:* Low

*Learner-centered index:* High

*Duration of the learning activity:* 4–10 weeks

# Activity 30. Self-Check Quizzes and Exams

*Description and Purpose of Activity.* As indicated in Chapter Four, reflective learners like to determine whether they know the content well enough to pass required examinations or course requirements as well as identify areas where they have deficiencies or misconceptions. This is especially true for modules and courses with extensive factual content, such as introductory high school and college courses (for example, introduction to psychology, accounting, or sociology). In effect, students want to know if they know something. An instructor might develop a set of quiz or test questions for students each week. Sometimes textbook publishers provide this for free, or instructors teaching the same course at other institutions or organizations might develop and share such content. With the recent promotion of self-directed learning online, we have seen such activities becoming increasingly common, especially in corporate training and higher education environments. Learners can self-test or self-determine, with computer feedback, whether they are grasping the concepts or not.

***Skills and Objectives.*** Includes key course concepts and facts, feedback, self-directed learning, self-monitoring, and reflection. Of course, the instructor's or course designer's goals help determine the level of exam questions written. Typically online exam questions are written at a factual or declarative knowledge level, though, as Bloom's taxonomy (Bloom, 1956) made evident long ago, they also could focus on comprehension, application, analysis, synthesis, or evaluation levels.

***Advice and Ideas.*** Consider making online self-evaluation a required (or optional) activity in your course. Locate appropriate existing self-evaluation online materials (or develop your own original ones) and make these available for your learners. Provide online quiz, test, or other self-review activities corresponding to each week or module in the course. Decide on the maximum number of times students will be allowed to take these self-evaluation activities, or make them unlimited but with a required minimum passing rate. Consider assigning a paper in which students reflect on their performances and improvements in these self-evaluation activities over time.

Students appreciate these types of self-checking opportunities if tests and quizzes are low in stress and require limited time commitments. Perhaps treat such tests as mastery assignments wherein if students receive a score at or above some criterion (for example, 75 or 80 percent), they receive a set amount of points and are allowed to jump to the next quiz or module. If they complete all the online quizzes with passing scores, they might receive additional points. Also consider allowing quiz retakes as often as possible if this is built into the testing system. You might decide to use the student's last score, average score, or high score.

***Variations and Extensions.*** You could have learners sign up to create all the self-test questions for a particular week, or use a fixed percentage of questions that the learners suggest each week.

## Key Instructional Considerations

*Risk index:* Low

*Time index:* Medium to High (depends on availability of premade content)

*Cost index:* Low (depends on system)

*Learner-centered index:* Medium

*Duration of the learning activity:* As needed

## Activity 31. Online Discussion Forums and Group Discussions

***Description and Purpose of Activity.*** Online discussion forums are now highly familiar events in higher education. Instructors can rely on bulletin boards, online group tools, instant messaging systems, or asynchronous conferencing tools for such discussion. Online discussion forums can be predesigned by the instructor or trainer, be student generated, or entail some combination of instructor and student design. Instructors can make salient certain key concepts or concerns for students to focus on in the content or topic. These online forums might be embedded within an FTF class as a supplemental activity or as a key component of a fully online course or educational experience. Students might be placed into interest groups to avoid such forums becoming too complex.

***Skills and Objectives.*** Includes student reflection and expansion on course concepts and ideas, exploration of topics or ideas of personal interest, critical analysis, interaction, and synthesis. Another key goal is comparison to the interpretations or perspectives of others in the learning experience.

***Advice and Ideas.*** If trying this out for the first time, you must initially decide on the online discussion format (for example, general discussion, debate, small-group discussion, student in hot seat, and so on) as well as the topics for discussion. Once these are determined, provide written guidance in a handout, Website, course blog, email, course announcement, or syllabus posting for learner participation with examples of good and bad posts (for example, what counts as a meaningful post, how to provide critical reviews in a professional manner, and so on). Make available a list of ground rules for the discussion task (for example, how discussion is initiated, how to respond to comments in which one disagrees, the minimum length of posts, and so on). Create a detailed grading rubric and provide it to learners ahead of time. Posting procedures must be clear about when the posts are due, how often students need to post, and how learner participation will be evaluated (for example, the number and frequency of postings, peer feedback offered, quality of posts, and so on). Next, you will need to set up the discussion boards and define peer membership in each group if there is more than one group. For example, you might assign students to groups based on projected occupations or interest areas.

Be sure to provide guidance on how to use the system, or offer a live training session, if applicable. If various student roles are assigned, specify their roles or assignments clearly. Instructors and tutors facilitate and moderate discussions as needed.

You might consider the three-sentence rule: require students to post a minimum of three sentences, since the first sentence that students often post tends to be an agreement with a previous post and the next sentence is often an opinion such as "I believe that . . ." or "In my opinion," instead of a critical analysis or insightful comment. In the third sentence, online learners often provide something meaningful and display some depth within their thinking. While we prefer quality over quantity in student posting behaviors, our own research indicates that just telling students to write three sentences minimum or to fill the screen before submitting their post has gone a long way toward enhancing critical thinking, interactivity, and depth within our online discussion forums.

There are a slew of other caveats and guidelines for effective online discussion forums. For instance, assigning due dates is important, since many students will require such task structuring and guidance, especially those known to procrastinate or who are new to online learning. In classes of fewer than forty students, group size for an online forum might range from seven to fifteen students. We find that a typical discussion group is about twelve to fifteen students, since some students will procrastinate until the last minute while a few students will jump in early. While that is a rule of thumb, you might get by with one discussion group for classes of fifteen to twenty students. Continual experimentation is vital.

Keep in mind that there are entire books and special journal issues filled with advice related to this topic (for example, Collison, Elbaum, Haavind, & Tinker, 2000; Palloff & Pratt, 2001; Salmon, 2000, 2002). Authors of such books and articles note that it is crucial for instructors to model the posting behaviors that they expect of their students. In addition to instructor modeling, providing discussion guidelines, examples, and due dates is critical for student success (Dennen, 2005).

***Variations and Extensions.*** As a means to empower students, have them brainstorm a few topics (or all topics) for several weekly class discussions; the instructor might still control the discussion topics of most weeks.

## Key Instructional Considerations

*Risk index:* Medium

*Time index:* High

*Cost index:* Low

*Learner-centered index:* High

*Duration of the learning activity:* 10–15 weeks of course

## Activity 32. Online Portal Explorations and Reflections

***Description and Purpose of Activity.*** As was pointed out in previous chapters, there are likely thousands of reflection activities already posted to the Web. Students might be assigned to review or evaluate a specific online portal of information related to a course topic or learning module. Such content might be indexed at learning object repository or shareable content sites such as Multimedia Educational Resource for Learning and Online Teaching (MERLOT), Connexions, or Jorum. Or learners might be asked to browse through a specific activity or set of activities in a designated course from the Massachusetts Institute of Technology open courseware initiative or from some other university that has made university-level course content and associated activities available for free to the world community. Maybe there is an unique portal of information that the learners might browse before coming to an FTF meeting. Or perhaps the learners might be directed to specific learning resources and portals that an instructor or organization has created or pooled together and placed in a learning management system (LMS) or course management system (CMS).

Such types of activities are powerful catalysts for reflection on what learners know as well as what they do not know and can prompt a series of activities to help them learn this material in meaningful ways. Once again, such exploratory Web activities can find applicability in any educational situation or audience—this is one type of activity wherein the sheer power of online and blended learning comes into view and is easily justified.

***Skills and Objectives.*** Includes exploration, self-directed learning, motivation and engagement, reflection on course concepts, and analysis skills.

***Advice and Ideas.*** Search the Web for exemplary and award-winning materials or portals related to your class or topic of interest. You can search designated sites that professional organizations, book publishers, vendors, or government agencies in your field have indexed. For instance, the Department of Education and the U.S. federal government have made many rich educational resources available for teacher training as well as for student learning of math, science, and technology. When in doubt, try resources such as MERLOT or Connexions or simply conduct a search in Google or Yahoo! on your topic. The subject area communities in MERLOT often provide quick access to high-quality materials in a particular subject area or discipline. Instructors who are adventurous and have simple HTML (hypertext markup language) programming skills or help from an instructional design, media, or training department or staff might create your own well-organized portal of resources on a topic with an annotated list of the exemplary materials and resources you find. Those without programming skills or support might utilize easy-to-use and free online tools such as Squidoo to assemble a set of Web resources on any topic and share your expertise with the world. Many other powerful content management systems exist, such as Drupal, Daisy, Joomla, Mambo, Netvibes, Pageflakes, and WikiMedia (see a list of free and open source content management systems at http://en.wikipedia.org/wiki/Comparison_of_content_management_systems).

Once you have selected resources from places such as MERLOT, implement your explorative and reflection activities with them. For example, have learners, individually or in small groups, browse and observe demonstrations or simulations (with necessary scaffolding questions and guidelines) that have been posted within the portal. You might ask your students questions about the relevance of each resource or portal to the course content. Learners might also be required to reflect in an online discussion forum, blog post, or reflection paper on the principles or concepts embedded, explicitly or implicitly, across two or more resources. To foster student interaction and discussion of the resources, incorporate collaborative tasks such as a virtual debate, hot seat activity (where one student is in the hot seat for the week and must answer other students' questions), or general discussions. In addition, students can provide feedback to the designers of selected online resources or learning object portals.

Keep track of the sites that students found useful and index them. Consider creating a shareable database of student reflections and comments. Perhaps expand such resource listings by working with other instructors who teach the same course in your school or institution or at other locations around the globe.

***Variations and Extensions.*** Ask students to find two similar online learning resources and compare the quality of them using a predesigned rubric or assessment index. Or have them post a joint evaluation with a partner or team.

## Key Instructional Considerations

> *Risk index:* Medium
>
> *Time index:* Medium

*Cost index:* Low

*Learner-centered index:* Medium

*Duration of the learning activity:* As needed

---

## Activity 33. Lurker, Browser, or Observer in Online Groups

***Description and Purpose of Activity.*** One technique for fostering learner reflection and taking advantage of rich, real-world content is to have students join an
online bulletin board, usergroup, or discussion forum related to the profession that
is the focus of the online course or training material. For example, a student in a
public health course might join an established community health or wellness group
in Yahoo! Groups, Google Groups, or MSN Groups. Alternatively, they might create a new group using one of these tools or systems. If joining an established group,
students might be asked to assume the role of a *lurker* (someone sitting in online
without directly participating much, if at all) or observer within such a group and to
take notes on their observations. The required role might change as students progress
within the course.

***Skills and Objectives.*** Includes observation, analysis, and reflection skills. Of
course, a key goal here is simply to learn how to watch, observe, and, in the case
of online audio files, listen.

***Advice and Ideas.*** Identify appropriate professional organizations and their
Web sites, blogs, e-mail lists, discussion forums, and archived discussions. Assign
learners to be lurkers in an online forum (or blog, e-mail list, and so on) of one
of the resources or organizations identified. You might use a different name
other than *lurker,* such as *browser* (Salmon, 2002), *listener, novice, trainee,* or *quiet
participant.* Provide clear instructions on what student should do and behave,
together with a set of key questions to reflect on. Have learners post their daily,
weekly, or monthly reflections and observations of the discussion group. Ask
learners to individually or collaboratively identify the commonalities as well as
differences in their observations, and discuss questions such as why commonalities and differences would exist. Assign and collect learners' final reflection
papers based on insights gained from the task. Where appropriate, add peer or
expert feedback within the task.

Consider having students think about how they are mentored or appren-
ticed into that particular discipline or subject area from this activity and what
they recommend happen next.

*Variations and Extensions.* Ask students to be lurkers in two or more different online groups and compare the tools and resources available in each as well as their experiences and learning gains.

## Key Instructional Considerations

*Risk index:* Medium

*Time index:* Medium

*Cost index:* Low

*Learner-centered index:* High

*Duration of the learning activity:* 4–8 weeks

# Activity 34. Podcast Tours

*Description and Purpose of Activity.* Some museums are making tours of their contents (for example, art exhibits) available for visitors to download to iPods, MP3 players, and mobile phones (Sloan, 2006). In some cases, comments from the artist are embedded in the podcast or are optional components of it. Instructors in areas such as art, history, archeology, and anthropology might search the Web for museum and other related types of tours that students can explore to learn course content or extend their learning beyond the course. While such activities have more obvious applicability in K–12 and higher education settings, as podcasts become increasingly common and accepted, those in training settings will undoubtedly discover creative and timely uses of them as well.

*Skills and Objectives.* Includes listening skills, expert modeling, analysis skills, and learning of basic facts and information. Also, such activities prime knowledge needed for later activities.

*Advice and Ideas.* Search the Web for podcast tours within your discipline. Perhaps concentrate on some of the major podcast sites, such as Podcast Alley, the Education Podcast Network, and Podcasting News, or others specifically pertaining to your profession. Provide students with a list of available podcast sites that are relevant to your course content. Also, consider asking them to locate similar sites and add them to the list. Ask students to explore podcast tours with other content-related learning activities (for example, reflection questions, exploratory learning, discovery learning, and so on). Have learners write and share their reviews or summaries of what they have found. Consider having learners construct evaluation criteria and rate these resources for their overall educational value.

Podcast tours are bound to be a growing area where informal learning meets formal academic learning. Consider embedding course tasks wherein students find and index podcast tours, or have one or two student volunteers find such content in lieu of one of their class assignments. A more elaborate strategy would involve students creating their own podcast tours of course content.

***Variations and Extensions.*** Ask students to locate and recommend podcasts from education-related organizations such as museums, libraries, zoos, parks, foundations, news agencies, and so on, as well as from other sources, that link to course concepts.

## Key Instructional Considerations

> *Risk index:* Medium
>
> *Time index:* Medium
>
> *Cost index:* Low (assumes content is preexisting)
>
> *Learner-centered index:* Medium
>
> *Duration of the learning activity:* 1–2 weeks

## Activity 35. Personal Blogs

***Description and Purpose of Activity.*** Learners can be asked to create and maintain blogs or online diaries of their learning during a course (those new to blogging might read the Educause Learning Initiative (2005) article on "7 Things You Should Know About Blogs"; they might also explore the Web resources at the back of this book for links to free blogging tools such as Blogger, Diaryland, Pitas, TypePad, and Xanga). Instructors might ask students to post personal reflections on one or more of their weekly readings. They also can post Web links, personal profiles, and pictures to their blogs. Each student in the course could be assigned a critical friend or Web buddy who provides feedback on those reflections.

Different types of activities might be embedded in the blogging task. For instance, students might be asked to write summary papers or nutshells of their learning from the blogs. Alternatively, they could be asked to expand on key or recurring ideas or themes in their blogs, add details to previous posts, or write personal reflections on the feelings, confusions, or experiences expressed in one or more of their blog posts. While we see blogs extensively used in higher education, learners of nearly any age or stripe can benefit from reflecting on their learning in a blog.

***Skills and Objectives.*** Includes concept analysis, interpretation and integration skills, reflection skills, summary writing, writing as thinking, motivation and engagement, self-directed learning, and personal exploration on items or areas of interest.

***Advice and Ideas.*** Assign the blogging task. Consider asking for student input on their preferences for the task. For instance, they might vote on whether to make their blogs private or public as well as whether to link to them within the CMS or LMS. They might also decide on what percentage of articles related to the class are to be self-selected for their blogging reflections and what percentage are preselected by the instructor, tutor, trainer, or course moderator.

Before students begin blogging, select one or two easy-to-use blogging tools and demonstrate how to use them. Be sure to provide learners with sufficient information, materials, and resources on each of these blogging tools. You could model how to reflect within an online blog. Perhaps give learners some freedom in choosing the blogging tool that they find most appealing or useful; for instance, experienced bloggers might be allowed to continue using the tool(s) that they are already comfortable with. To foster feedback, interaction, and peer review, assign critical friends or Web buddies for the blogging task. Toward the end of the course, require that students prepare a reflective blog on their overall blogging experience in this course.

Instructors, tutors, or moderators could create a course blog Web site where course resources and materials are shared with students. At the same time, student blogs might provide starter materials for final course papers as well as a shared space for students to summarize and disseminate their learning. In effect, blogs can help students generate ideas as well as evaluate them. And successful blogs from previous semesters might be archived and linked to as examples or models (with appropriate permissions). Of course, the instructor should continually reevaluate the use of blogs within a class.

***Variations and Extensions.*** List many of the possible educational uses of a blog, such as those just mentioned, and have the learners discuss and decide on the options that best work for them.

## Key Instructional Considerations

*Risk index:* Medium

*Time index:* High

*Cost index:* Low

*Learner-centered index:* High

*Duration of the learning activity:* 8–15 weeks

## Activity 36. Collaborative or Team Blogs

***Description and Purpose of Activity.*** Blogs might also involve collaboration or virtual teaming. Students can be assigned partners to jointly summarize their progress on a project, joint reading assignment selections, and other experiences in their team blogs. The blog becomes a place for other teams to offer comments as well as for the instructor to provide feedback.

In addition, there might be international exchanges through the blogs. For instance, a class may work on a project or solve a problem, and their work may be recorded in their class blog. Foreign language courses can create international language exchange experiences between classes in different geographic regions of the world. Foreign language instructors can use blogs for reflections on individual or paired online news activities among students in a class. Such bloglike reflections might be prepared using a specific blog software system or site or embedded in asynchronous discussion threads in a CMS or LMS.

While such activities were abundant in K–12 and higher education settings early on, corporate and government training personnel are increasingly finding useful ways to adopt blogging in their courses. Of course, there is sometimes overlap and a fine line between personal blogs used in business to promote or discuss products and those for reflecting on learning-related gains.

***Skills and Objectives.*** As with the previous activity, some of the skills fostered include concept analysis, interpretation, and integration skills, reflection skills, and personal exploration on items or areas of interest. In addition, there would be emphasis on sharing and appreciating diverse perspectives on content.

***Advice and Ideas.*** Follow the advice and ideas in Activity 35 on "Personal Blogs" as necessary. In addition, discuss the collaborative blogging task thoroughly with the class. Articulate the purposes, procedures, and expectations of the task, and provide a period of time for student questions and answers about the task. Consider providing a list of FAQs (frequently asked questions) as necessary. Demonstrate useful final products of this assignment from previous semesters or similar courses, if applicable. Set up the blogging site(s) and link them to the course Web site or course blog or the LMS/CMS. If it is an international exchange, have the class name the class blog site for collaboration and interaction purposes. If you decide to use small-group blogs, there should be links within the course homepage to each group blog. For semester or longer blogging activities, periodically have learners write reflections on their experiences and share them on the collaborative or team blog. For a shorter-duration blogging activity, require that students complete their final reflections on the course blog site or Web site by the end of the blogging task.

You might also attempt to design international exchanges or small-group blogging activities. To accomplish this, network with others at international conferences for possible cross-cultural exchange programs or write to colleagues who might be interested in such an activity. If research is involved, be sure to clarify the roles and responsibilities of each party. Archive international collaborations for later demonstrations.

***Variations and Extensions.*** Pose competition activities for the team blogs, such as assigning bonus points for the teams that have the most creative, most comprehensive, and most informative blog sites.

## Key Instructional Considerations

>*Risk index:* Medium
>
>*Time index:* High
>
>*Cost index:* Low
>
>*Learner-centered index:* High
>
>*Duration of the learning activity:* 8–12 weeks

# Activity 37. Online Resource Libraries

***Description and Purpose of Activity.*** Bonk created the online resource library (ORL) idea in the fall of 2004 when he was teaching a course on learning theories. An ORL is highly analogous to a personal Web log or blog, but it combines features of asynchronous discussion forums and blogging. In an ORL, the instructor or learner develops a location where students can post their learning reflections with their names or other identifying information on them, typically in an asynchronous discussion thread of a CMS. The learner then uses that thread to record her course readings and exploratory activities. Posting may occur for a particular unit or section of the course or throughout the entire term. Feedback is provided later from the instructor, experts, or peers. In effect, each student in the class has a specially designated discussion thread dedicated to his or her article readings and reflections, and it is here that others can read their ideas, viewpoints, and learning journeys while providing feedback and suggestions. Keep in mind, too, that much of this activity relates to Phase 1 of the R2D2 model.

***Skills and Objectives.*** Again, there would be an emphasis on concept analysis, interpretation, and integration skills as well as reflection skills. ORL activities also foster student exploration in areas of personal interest, self-directed learning, and motivation and engagement.

***Advice and Ideas.*** Inform students of the ORL activity and pair or group them with feedback partners based on certain criteria (for example, interests or backgrounds), or perhaps pair them randomly. Create individual discussion threads for each student. Monitor weekly progress and provide intermittent feedback. Near the end of the course or ORL activity, have students write summaries of what they learned from the ORL activity. Grading might include points for the overall quality of student ORLs, quantity of articles reviewed online, quality of blog summary papers, and the amount and level of peer feedback provided.

To help reduce student tension about a novel task like an ORL, consider including student testimonials from previous semesters or courses that can attest to the benefits of this task. Perhaps invite former students in for a chat to discuss their views on this task and to provide advice and recommendations for new students. In addition, you might list ORL threads from previous semesters for new students to browse.

***Variations and Extensions.*** Consider having learners from more than one class or location in this activity as a way to generate additional perspectives and commentary.

## Key Instructional Considerations

*Risk index:* Medium

*Time index:* High

*Cost index:* Low

*Learner-centered index:* High

*Duration of the learning activity:* This could be a 1–2 week activity or a 6–12 week activity.

# Activity 38. Social Networking Linkages

***Description and Purpose of Activity.*** There has been skyrocketing growth related to social networking and other Web 2.0 tools during recent years (Nielsen/NetRatings, 2006). In response, many colleges and universities are making strategic decisions to attempt to tap into their popularity among students (Savarese, 2006).

At the course level, instructors might experiment with the mass appeal of this technology by embedding a general activity through which students get to know each other better using social networking software such as Friendster, YouTube, Blogger, Xanga, MySpace, or Facebook. Students might be asked to sign up for one or more of these services. Ask them to post at least one reference or comment related to their present class or course content in any social networking or blog tool that they use. In addition, you might require learners to find people, postings, blogs, and so on that relate to the course content and then create a Webliography (see Chapter Three) of such resources. Finally, you might require your learners to generate reflection papers based on what they have found.

***Skills and Objectives.*** Includes exploration, personalized learning, socializing, sharing, and collaboration. This is a good social ice breaker that can foster a sense of community in the course.

***Advice and Ideas.*** Ask students to establish a free social networking membership if they have not yet established one. Then, with the learners' consent, gather a list of the users of different social network systems and make it available to the class. Generate a list of conduct ground rules for the class. At the same time, discuss possible issues related to unprofessional conduct in their social networking communications. Ask learners to use the networking software to find classmates as well as other people with similar professional or personal interests. In addition, ask them to make special notes regarding individuals who have interests, however slight, related to course content. Perhaps have them write to such individuals with inquiries related to the course content or the profession. Finally, you might require students to write reflection papers or collaborative papers based on what they found.

Once again, this is a growing area—experiment with it and see what works. Caution students against posting content that might not be professionally appropriate given that classmates and other people will view it.

***Variations and Extensions.*** Assign students to link to one person in the course as a "friend" in their social networking site. Ask them to correspond with that individual weekly, preferably within the social networking system. Alternatively, you might ask students to link to everyone in the course as a friend.

## Key Instructional Considerations

*Risk index:* High

*Time index:* Medium

*Cost index:* Low

*Learner-centered index:* High

*Duration of the learning activity:* 1–3 weeks

# Activity 39. Online Role Play Reflections

*Description and Purpose of Activity.* In Chapter Nine, we will discuss how to assign students to an online role play activity in which they must assume different roles or duties. These roles might involve course participation (for example, questioner, commentator, devil's advocate, summarizer, example giver, naysayer, and so on) (Watkins, 2005). Alternatively, the roles might require that students take on the attributes of specific people or personas (for example, Paul McCartney, Mozart, Jane Goodall, Sigmund Freud, Anna Freud, and so on). An online role play could also entail specific personality roles (for example, extravert, optimist, pessimist, introvert, and so on). And students might role-play as if they were experts or known people in the field of study related to the course. While such activities relate to Phase 4 of R2D2, we are now at Phase 2, which entails reflection and writing on one's learning pursuits. Keep in mind that while the R2D2 model appears linear in nature, it is interactive and recursive, with each phase impacting or leading to other phases; a reflective activity can come after a hands-on one and vice versa.

It is important, therefore, both during as well as at the end of the role play situation that the learners reflect on how the event went overall. How effective were they in their roles? What might they do differently next time? Students might complete self-assessment forms in which they assign themselves points for their respective contributions to the online role play. In professional development situations, learners might also reflect on the roles assumed by characters in a video scenario or computer-generated online simulation.

*Skills and Objectives.* Includes perspective taking, creative expression, insight, concept analysis, and concept review.

*Advice and Ideas.* Carefully select the content or topic for which a reflective online role play would be beneficial. Design your own creative role play activity or find a prepackaged one from an online publisher or a conference you attend, with modifications as appropriate. Define the roles with sufficient detail and provide guidelines for the students as necessary (for example, how or when to start, how to interact, how to respond to each other, and so on). Set up the role play platform in the LMS/CMS.

Before commencing with the role play activity, inform the learners that there will be a final reflection paper on it. Make learners aware of the reflection assignment guidelines and final grading scheme. Assign learners to specific roles or have students sign up for them. Once all these steps have been completed, facilitate the online role play activity; for example, nudge discussions that seem slow to start, intervene in heated exchanges, and summarize or weave postings roughly once or twice per week (see Salmon, 2000, 2002).

After the role play is completed, provide an opportunity for learners to address the conflicts or disagreements between the role they played and their own thoughts or views. They might do this in an online feedback form, e-mail posts to the instructor, or reflection papers. End the activity with student reflections (for example, papers or online discussion) on what they learned from participating in the role play. Perhaps provide examples of reflection papers from previous courses or semesters. To nurture student reflection and feedback, consider the use of self-assessment and peer assessment activities. The points allocated for self- and peer assessment will vary based on the length and complexity of the activity as well as the instructor's discretion.

***Variations and Extensions.*** Experiment with different types of online role play activities. You might offer students a choice among several different online role play options. Instead of assigning roles or designing different roles to select from, allow students to create their own roles or personas. Such choices and options will enhance student participation and ownership. Another option is to create a system whereby students sign up for online roles that are changed every few weeks. To foster participation among normally shy students, you might choose to make the roles anonymous. You might also have students play different roles in an online debate on a hot topic or major issue within the field.

Final reflection papers on these activities can be shared online in the CMS or LMS. Options for reflection papers include students sharing and grading each other's reflection papers, team reflection papers, or paired reflections. Students might also post reflections for students in future semesters to read. Finally, learner reflections might also offer advice for improving the activity.

## Key Instructional Considerations

*Risk index:* High

*Time index:* High

*Cost index:* Low (unless purchasing a role play system)

*Learner-centered index:* High

*Duration of the learning activity:* 1–2 weeks

## Activity 40. Synchronous and Asynchronous Discussion Combinations

***Description and Purpose of Activity.*** One of the most interesting and engaging online instructional activities we have ever attempted involves combining synchronous and asynchronous activities related to the work of one or more experts. Students will often strongly disagree with a viewpoint of an expert after reading one or more of their publications or interviews. However, when offering an opportunity to meet them personally in a synchronous chat or online videoconference, these same students will often find themselves agreeing with all or most of the views of that individual. In effect, they find that one article or publication does not represent all the ideas of an individual and that interests, findings, and perspectives of experts change over time. This technique is a real eye opener! And it is one that would make our top-ten list of online learning success stories.

***Skills and Objectives.*** This task entails a heavy dosage of perspective taking while offering the potential for cognitive dissonance and debate. It also fosters critical analysis, reflection, communication, insight, student interaction, and comparison and contrast.

***Advice and Ideas.*** Make a list of prospective expert chat guests for the course. Perhaps allow students to nominate and vote on them. Provide relevant information about the experts to learners, such as the expert's current vita, personal Web site or blog links, if available, and representative professional achievements (for example, profile, publications, grants, patents, and so on). Assign readings or other activities related to the work of upcoming speakers. Collect questions from learners and make them available to the experts in advance.

Hold an asynchronous discussion or reflection forum on the guest expert's work. After the asynchronous discussion has been open for a set amount of time, conduct a chat session activity (see Chapter Three for procedures for a synchronous expert lecture or chat). When done, thank the guest and, once he or she has departed, debrief with your students. Have them reflect on how their ideas and thoughts about the guest expert or their points of view may have changed as a result of the combined asynchronous and synchronous activities.

This technique can be used to discuss ideas with several book authors. (However, be careful not to invite too many guests to a particular synchronous chat session.) When done, you might share the results of this blended approach with colleagues and ask for suggestions for expanding or modifying it.

*Variations and Extensions.* Perhaps try this activity twice—once utilizing a synchronous session with the guest expert first, followed by an asynchronous discussion or reflection activity; and once using an asynchronous discussion to focus on an expert's articles or ideas, followed by a synchronous expert chat or presentation. Have students reflect on which format they found more engaging and powerful for learning.

## Key Instructional Considerations

*Risk index:* Medium

*Time index:* Medium

*Cost index:* Low (depending on need to purchase software)

*Learner-centered index:* High

*Duration of the learning activity:* 1–2 weeks for each instance

# Activity 41. Self-Check Reflection Activities

*Description and Purpose of Activity.* Michael G. Moore (1989), Ellen Wagner (1994), and other scholars have discussed the types of interactions possible on the Web. Moore highlighted the importance of learner-learner, learner-instructor, and learner-content interactions. Others have added additional forms of interaction to the equation, such as learner-interface interaction (Hillman, Willis, & Gunawerdena, 1994) and learner-self interaction (Soo & Bonk, 1998). In terms of learner-self interactions., it is vital for online learners to be metacognitively aware of their learning progress and strengths.

As indicated in Chapter Four, large online learning programs from Sun Microsystems, Cisco Networking Academy, and the U.S. military often embed self-check, review, and other types of learner-self reflections. While it is relatively easy to add such questions into an online course, they should be purposefully and thoughtfully embedded.

*Skills and Objectives.* Includes concept review, reflection, concept attainment, comprehension, feedback, and problem solving.

*Advice and Ideas.* Identify the topics or specific content where learners tend to be confused or struggle in the course, based on past experiences or observations in the current course. Brainstorm, perhaps with colleagues, a series of self-check questions or other self-assessment instruments. Decide with team members and available instructional designers how to incorporate these self-directed learning materials into the learning experience (for example, when and where to embed them). Conduct a simple pilot test of these questions or instruments with a couple of potential students or with colleagues and refine them accordingly.

Embed self-check reflection activities in the course and gather feedback from learners on their effects. Be careful, however, not to simply insert learner self-questions—make sure that they are needed first. Perhaps you can design thinking scaffolds or reflection sheets for learners in FTF classes based on their online activities.

*Variations and Extensions.* Have learners generate self-check questions for each other. Perhaps have teams create competitions of self-check and review questions, with bonus points for groups who are the first ones to answer all of another group's questions or problems successfully or for the groups who answer the most correctly.

## Key Instructional Considerations

>  *Risk index:* Low
>
>  *Time index:* Low
>
>  *Cost index:* Low
>
>  *Learner-centered index:* Medium
>
>  *Duration of the learning activity:* As needed

# Activity 42. Electronic Portfolios

*Description and Purpose of Activity.* You can find software on the Web to collect and catalogue your work in electronic portfolios. Using such software, students can reflect on their academic progress or growth as well as their other educational experiences during their college careers.

An e-portfolio might contain career objectives, a résumé, sample work, lists of notable achievements and accomplishments, links to an electronic repository of student papers, and pictures and reports from job placements, internships, or study abroad experiences. It might also include personal reflections on the contents found in the e-portfolio, external evaluations, and other artifacts or indicators of what the person has done or might be able to do in the future (Young, 2002a). As noted in a report from Educational Pathways (2005), there are numerous tools and systems for creating an electronic portfolio.

While marking one's growth in an e-portfolio is more commonly associated with K–12 and higher education learners, corporations and government agencies are increasingly interested in such tools and practices thanks to the growing attention being paid to knowledge management as a vehicle for maintaining and enhancing the performance of an organization or institution. The fast pace of change, combined with predictions of great numbers of employee retirements during the coming decade, makes the tracking of learning and associated learning growth a lifelong learning matter.

*Skills and Objectives.* Includes reflection, integration of ideas, analysis of strengths and weaknesses, and creative expression. E-portfolios help learners envision and plan for their long-term growth and learning opportunities. They also focus the learner on their accomplishments and the products that they can produce during a learning experience that can help them obtain jobs or other opportunities in the future.

*Advice and Ideas.* First you should find out if your organization, institution, or school uses a particular portfolio tool. The next task is to receive appropriate training on the use of this tool, if needed. Develop relevant portfolio tasks for the learners in your course, with sufficient guidelines and grading criteria. Guide learners in the portfolio building process as necessary.

Consider providing example e-portfolios. Sometimes an organization or institution might have an online portal of high- and low-quality e-portfolio examples. If these are not available, you might browse the e-portfolio Web resources provided at the end of this book, including resource-rich ones such as the Electronic Portfolio Consortium Web site, Helen Barrett's Electronic Portfolios Web site, and some of the e-portfolio vendor sites listed there. In addition, The Pennsylvania State University provides a variety of sample e-portfolios for disciplines such as music education, engineering, kinesiology, business administration, communications, and agriculture (see Web resources). And this is just one university among hundreds, if not thousands, of educational organizations that are engaged in such activities. A simple Google search will quickly reveal a plethora of such sites.

In addition to the showcase of skills, knowledge, and products placed in the portfolio, require an overall reflection component during the portfolio activity. Perhaps have students write reflection papers detailing their intellectual or scholarly growth over time or comparing and contrasting their growth with one or more peers. Evaluate the effectiveness of the task or activity, and modify guidelines accordingly for future reference.

There are many guidelines that people such as Helen Barrett provide for the use of e-portfolios. For instance, instead of waiting until the end of the course to review student work, be sure to provide times during the course when student portfolios are shared and evaluated. In addition to a midclass formative review, perhaps have a final student portfolio day on which the class explores and evaluates all of the portfolios and provides appropriate feedback. Experts and practitioners might also be asked to review and provide feedback on them.

***Variations and Extensions.***  Assign students to critique each others' portfolios or to make one or two suggestions for improvement. Alternatively, assign them to write reflection papers in which they compare the learning growth in their own e-portfolio to that of one or more other students in the course or to prior student portfolios.

## Key Instructional Considerations

      *Risk index:* Medium

      *Time index:* High

      *Cost index:* Medium (depending on system)

      *Learner-centered index:* High

      *Duration of the learning activity:* 12–15 weeks (typically entire course)

# Activity 43. Individual Reflection Papers

***Description and Purpose of Activity.***  As detailed in Chapter Four, the Web allows for many types of online writing and reflection activities. First, students might be asked to write *abstracts* or *summaries* of different articles read. Such an activity would rise in value if students posted their summaries for others in the class and received feedback from one or more peers or perhaps even external experts or practitioners. Second, they might read resources about a hot or emerging topic or pressing issue and then write a *trend paper* related to it. Third, they might write a *pro-and-con paper* corresponding to a particular theory, model, plan, idea, or principle. Fourth, the instructor might conduct formative course evaluations on the course content or lectures by asking students to write *minute papers* summarizing what they learned or did not learn from a particular lesson. A minute paper could be sent via e-mail or using a CMS or LMS drop-box. A *muddiest point paper* is similar but requires students to focus on comprehension problems and unclear points in the course, not necessarily what they learned or internalized.

With these examples, we have only scratched the surface of the possible for this online activity. There are countless other types of reflective writing activities that an instructor or trainer might design for an online course.

***Skills and Objectives.*** Includes analysis, reflection, interpretation, summary writing, writing as thinking, communication skills, information synthesis, and knowledge integration.

***Advice and Ideas.*** The first step is to select the types of writing tasks that meet your course goals and objectives (Bean, 1996). Given the range of writing assignments possible, your choice may be a key factor in learner success. Once they are selected, prepare detailed directions for the selected writing tasks. Assign the writing tasks, with appropriate guidelines (for example, length requirements, due dates, collaboration or feedback partners, resource or reference requirements, and so on). Provide links to sample writing products from past or similar courses. Perhaps ask students to act as "critical" or "constructive friends" for feedback on each other's work. If assigned, you should post instructions on critical or constructive friend roles and responsibilities (see North Central Regional Educational Laboratory, 1997). In terms of grading, it is best to share the criteria, dimensions, and scoring frameworks or grading rubrics with students ahead of time. Such assessment criteria might be negotiated with students. In addition, your written feedback should be timely and specific. You also might consider regrading rewritten work.

***Variations and Extensions.*** Students can create a set of such reflection papers and the class can anonymously vote on the best ones. The winning papers are automatically entered into a class online Hall of Fame that can be used as examples the following semester (with appropriate winning student permissions, of course). As an alternative to such competitions, students might self-nominate their work to be included in a set of reflection papers that is packaged as an online book or a growing compendium of student work. To strengthen the final products, instructors and peers might serve as editors and reviewers of such work before it is posted online.

## Key Instructional Considerations

*Risk index:* Low

*Time index:* Medium to High (depending on number of tasks assigned as well as the number of students in the course)

*Cost index:* Low

*Learner-centered index:* High

*Duration of the learning activity:* As needed; perhaps 1–4 weeks for each writing activity

---

# Activity 44. Team or Group Reflective Writing Tasks

***Description and Purpose of Activity.*** In addition to individual papers and reports, the Web facilitates virtual teaming and many other collaborative acts in online courses. Such team assignments might be facilitated through the LMS or CMS system with team assignment tools, team workspaces, drop boxes, and URL (universal resource locator, or Web address) sharing. The same set of reflection papers as detailed in Activity 43 might be assigned but instead as a paired or team-related task. Of course, when students work in teams on their reports, papers, and other reflections, the assessment criteria should look not only at the final group product but also individual contributions to the collaborative process and outcome.

***Skills and Objectives.*** Includes collaboration and teaming, writing as thinking, communication, comparison and contrast, appreciation of multiple perspectives, audience awareness, and information synthesis and evaluation.

***Advice and Ideas.*** Assign students to online teams in a course LMS, CMS, or asynchronous discussion forum. If the students are in a designated cohort group taking some of the same courses every semester, you might allow them to form groups based on previous experiences, or you might not allow them a choice, since some students may always end up with nonparticipating partners. If new to online teaching or online group learning activities, you may want to experiment with different teaming options for various types of group tasks.

Consider assigning specific leadership and management roles within each group or have students select from a list of possible roles (for example, group leader, coordinator of team Web site, document editor, Web resource finder, technology guru, and so on). Provide a team contract template or set of guidelines (Zhang & Peck, 2003) and have each team discuss and build their own team contract with all members agreeing to it. Ask groups to post their respective contracts on the group or course bulletin board for an easy-to-use, visible reference and metacognitive aid. In addition to the showcase of skills, knowledge, and products with group information for each team, create a team workplace in the LMS, CMS, or asynchronous discussion forum for ongoing group discussions and debates. When and where feasible, you should moderate online synchronous and asynchronous meetings of the groups (for detailed advice related to online moderation, see Salmon, 2000, 2002). Of course, you should evaluate work turned in by the respective groups, since students typically will not take seriously work that is never graded. Consider changing group memberships at the end of each task or after a certain period of time.

Of course, there are advantages to both students and instructors when selecting this task—students benefit from the combined expertise of their group members, and instructors have reduced grading pressures. The latter point is not an indication that online instruction is easier than FTF, but often just the opposite, since unlike their expectations and experiences in traditional FTF settings, students want and expect feedback on nearly everything that they post or submit online. Instructors who attempt to provide feedback on everything students write or submit online will likely be overwhelmed and perhaps headed to the hospital with a nervous breakdown. To avoid such problems, encourage and promote meaningful peer feedback and support.

*Variations and Extensions.* Have drafts of such team papers due at specific times during the course and assign different teams to provide feedback.

## Key Instructional Considerations

> *Risk index:* Medium
>
> *Time index:* Medium to High
>
> *Cost index:* Low (depending on tools required to foster group interaction)
>
> *Learner-centered index:* Medium
>
> *Duration of the learning activity:* 3–8 weeks

# Activity 45. Super-Summaries, Portfolio Reflections, and Personal Philosophy Papers

*Description and Purpose of Activity.* Another way to foster reflection on course content is to design some type of overarching course mastery reflection assignment. For instance, we have had our students write super-summaries of approximately 2,500 to 3,500 words on what they learned in the online class. However, we required that the students include a minimum number of direct quotes from peer postings in the weekly online discussion forums. We did this to make sure that they read and reflected upon at least some of the online discussion postings.

A second idea here is to assign a personal philosophy or macro-reflection paper related to what learners have internalized from the course and how their life views may have been affected. Once again, we often require our students to pull out specific ideas or examples posted to the online class in their papers. Third, we have assigned students to write reflection papers on the material in their e-portfolios. To focus their efforts, we detail specific aspects of the e-portfolio that they are to address in their reflection papers. In each case, students condense what they have learned in the course into a type of learning or personal growth statement.

***Skills and Objectives.*** Includes knowledge synthesis, reflection, integration of thoughts and ideas, communication, information synthesis, writing as thinking, critical analysis, evaluation, and insight into themes and macro points of view.

***Advice and Ideas.*** Decide on the type of overarching reflective writing activity with which to end the course or unit. Perhaps give students a few choices or options. Assign the writing tasks with sufficient guidelines, grading criteria, and resources. To reduce student tension and concerns, be sure to provide models and examples of the final reflection task. As a means of monitoring task progress, require learners to share their drafts by a preannounced date. In addition, conduct peer reviews on the drafts during a predetermined period of time. Randomly assign feedback partners, or, if critical friend partners have already been created for the course, perhaps use them instead. To foster a sense of community as well as individual accountability, have learners share their final drafts in the LMS/CMS or course blog. Provide written feedback together with grading details. Save high-quality examples as model answers for the future. When done, continue to brainstorm and design other summary tasks and activities.

***Variations and Extensions.*** Ask the students to include a set number of Web links in their super-summaries or philosophy papers that the reader can click on while reading an electronic version of the paper.

## Key Instructional Considerations

*Risk index:* Medium

*Time index:* Medium to High (depending on course enrollment)

*Cost index:* Low

*Learner-centered index:* High

*Duration of the learning activity:* 3–15 weeks (might be ongoing for entire semester)

# Activity 46. Online Cases, Situations, and Vignettes

*Description and Purpose of Activity.* Posting of online case studies or situations to the Web can foster student analysis and evaluation skills. Online cases have wide applicability and acceptability, especially with adult learners who have the experience base to relate to them and perhaps provide personal stories or situations that extend beyond them. In practice, cases tend to be used in professions such as engineering, law, business, education, optometry, dentistry, and nursing.

*Skills and Objectives.* Includes critical thinking and analysis, inferencing skills, comparison and contrast, evaluation, and internalization of concepts and principles. A key goal is to understand how and where course principles can be applied (that is, learning in a context).

*Advice and Ideas.* Conduct an online search for existing case materials related to your topic. If many such cases are found, ask your prior or current students for their opinions of them; perhaps conduct usability testing of these cases with a couple of them. If online resources are scarce, consider producing custom cases for your course. Such custom case creations might require collaboration with other experts in the field. If you are using an existing case that does not have multimedia components (for example, sound, animation, video, pictures, simulations, and so on), you might find related online audio or animations to enhance or augment it. If you are creating your own case, consider incorporating multimedia in the case scenario to enhance the sense of reality and level of engagement.

If time permits, you might read through existing research related to the use of cases in online environments, especially in your field or course topic. Check the footnotes and references of such articles for references to any key resources used in case creation. Perhaps write to the authors of relevant research or practice articles—they might know of existing online case problems or situations that are available for anyone to use.

Once the cases are selected, embed stimulating questions and pointers within each case situation or task. Embed learning activities (for example, information presentation, conceptualization, discussions, reflections, and so on) at specific anchoring points or after adequate explorations of these cases. If you created the materials, conduct pilot tests with one or two former participants of the course or with close colleagues. Gather learner feedback on the use of these case materials and refine as needed.

*Variations and Extensions.* Consider saving the case solutions from previous versions of the course and have students critique or respond to them.

## Key Instructional Considerations

> *Risk index:* Medium
>
> *Time index:* Medium to High (depending if applicable case material exists and is usable)
>
> *Cost index:* Medium to High (again, depending on resources available)
>
> *Learner-centered index:* Medium
>
> *Duration of the learning activity:* 1–4 weeks

# Activity 47. Satellite Discussion or Special Interest Groups

*Description and Purpose of Activity.* In online courses with large enrollment or in large FTF settings, satellite discussion forums using asynchronous conferencing can be established through which students can pursue personal areas of interest. Instead of instructors, tutors, or trainers deciding on topics of interest, in satellite discussion groups, students can nominate the discussion areas of interest and participate in the forums where they have at least some interest. Near the end of the course, students can be asked for feedback on the activity or for a personal reflection on what they learned from the satellite discussion group activities. The satellite interest group (SIG) strategy may promote an online community of learning or community of practice; as such it could apply to K–12, higher education, or corporate training situations. Here, students have more voice in the course activities, and, hence, there is a sense of learner empowerment.

*Skills and Objectives.* Includes multiple perspectives, communication skills, self-directed learning, reflection on content, idea generation, idea evaluation, and feedback on thoughts and ideas.

*Advice and Ideas.* Conduct an FTF brainstorming session, synchronous chat, or online poll to identify key areas of interest to the learners within the scope of the course. Establish SIGs on topics or interest areas that have more than a specified number of votes or interested learners (for example, you might set a lower limit of ten). Set up appropriate communication channels with technologies of your choice for these groups (for example, asynchronous forums, synchronous chats, text messaging, wikis, or course blogs). Monitor and moderate these discussions as necessary. Archive the discussions at the end of the semester or course experience.

There are a plethora of guidelines for online discussion groups in education. Gilly Salmon (2000), for instance, suggests a maximum of about thirty participants per forum, though more if browsers or lurkers are included. She also suggests that a moderator or someone coordinating the subtopic summarize the input every ten to fifteen participant posts. An instructor might offer bonus points to discussion leader volunteers in different forums. Instructors or moderators should occasionally provide learners with feedback within the satellite posts. Instructors might also recruit more advanced learners or practitioners to particular discussion forums for feedback.

*Variations and Extensions.* Perhaps require students to be members of at least two of the online satellite discussion forums. You might also include a few bonus questions on an exam related to the satellite discussion.

## Key Instructional Considerations

> *Risk index:* Medium
>
> *Time index:* Medium
>
> *Cost index:* Low
>
> *Learner-centered index:* High
>
> *Duration of the learning activity:* 4–12 weeks

# Activity 48. Small-Group Case Creations and Analyses

*Description and Purpose of Activity.* Students can design cases for other courses, schools, or universities to solve. These might entail regional or global collaborations. Such case situations may be based on personal experiences or field observations.

Such tasks and activities place greater power in the hands of the learner. Learners are more motivated with the sense of realism embedded in learner-designed cases than with prepackaged cases that have been solved over and over by learners many times in the past. While this does not imply that Harvard Business School types of cases no longer have applicability, it does mean that there are now more options for online learning and learners, many of which place the learner front and center within the learning experience or at least give the learner a more prominent and crucial role in such learning.

*Skills and Objectives.* Includes creativity and idea generation, insight, communication skills, course interactivity, connections between course concepts and experience, reflection on application of concepts, evaluation and analysis skills, feedback, perspective taking and appreciation of multiple viewpoints, and collaboration.

***Advice and Ideas.*** Assign students to small online teams using certain criteria (for example, background, interest areas, learning preferences, learning schedule, and so on). Be sure to provide sufficient guidelines on case-building tasks, including pertinent examples and additional resources as necessary. For instance, many online students need deadlines for posting their cases. In addition, some students require warnings that those who procrastinate will receive limited feedback from their peers. An instructor might also point out that the more controversial they make their case titles or particular discussion thread headings, the more likely they will receive responses.

Ask each team to create and post a certain number of case situations throughout the semester and comment on a given number of peer cases. For this task to succeed without much resistance, you will need to supply guidelines and examples on how to respond to peer cases with meaningful and constructive feedback. To foster a cycle of reflection and interactivity, you should have each team summarize the postings related to their particular cases and evaluate the solutions provided. Perhaps include a final capstone sharing event using videoconferencing across the sites involved in creating the cases.

Case learning is a common way to build expertise. As an enhancement to the process, consider recruiting experts and practitioners for occasional student feedback. For instance, Bonk once had a high school physics teacher from Ann Arbor, Michigan (self-named in his posts as "the Mentor from Michigan"), who had a Ph.D. and apparently longed to help college-level students in an undergraduate educational psychology course that Bonk was teaching. Amazingly, he provided feedback on nearly every student case problem or discussion thread for a span of more than two years (literally thousands of case postings) and he did this for *free*! Such volunteers are out there waiting for you to find them—so take an hour or two and contact people in your network for leads to such people. It will be worth the effort.

Those in corporate, government, nonprofit, and military settings might build a virtual library with relevant cases and examples along with commentary and insights from experts both within the company as well as those who are recently retired. The use of cases in such settings is a powerful strategy for knowledge management and organizational knowledge sharing. People in the military, in particular, retire at a relatively young age and have a wealth of knowledge and experience to lend to the case creation and solution process. As a example, a few years back, Bonk was involved in the evaluation of the Armor Captains Career Course (AC3-DL) with personnel from the U.S. Army

Armor School in Fort Knox, Kentucky, and the U.S. Army Research Institute in Washington, D.C. (Bonk, Olson, et al., 2002). The AC3-DL program uses synchronous and asynchronous online learning as well as FTF delivery mechanisms to train assistant operations officers at different command units such as the battalion level as well as captains to command entire armies. Not too surprisingly, myriad case and scenario learning situations are embedded in the AC3-DL program. In partial response to the high attrition Bonk and his colleagues found within the program, attempts were made to increase learner feedback in a timely and authentic manner, including using synchronous chats with retired officers. Such veterans possess a rich store of case knowledge that can be insightfully used to apprentice younger or less experienced learners.

***Variations and Extensions.*** Provide guide sheets, questions, or templates for students to use to design cases. Also, provide examples and perhaps even an online Web site of the best cases from previous semesters or versions of the course.

## Key Instructional Considerations

*Risk index:* Medium

*Time index:* High

*Cost index:* Low to Medium (depending whether using existing tools within the LMS or CMS)

*Learner-centered index:* High

*Duration of the learning activity:* 1–3 weeks

# Activity 49. Small-Group Exam Question Challenges

***Description and Purpose of Activity.*** Allowing students to design exam questions is one way to motivate them to study the material. In addition, such an activity is a prime example of a learner-centered approach that empowers learners to control some aspect of the course activities or content while working collaboratively and discussing key concepts and principles within the content. At the same time, the exam challenges can foster a healthy dose of competition. When successfully implemented, such an approach builds ownership and pride for learning. And the work generated during one unit, one semester, or one course experience could be used in later iterations of the course. In effect, the course builds with learner-generated content.

*Skills and Objectives.* Includes collaboration, feedback, interaction, critical analysis, insight, concept review and attainment, and critical analysis and reflection.

*Advice and Ideas.* In this task, you would assign students to teams or small groups to solve case situations or problems that might later appear on their exams. Salmon (2000) suggests that the instructor post one or two example questions to each discussion group and ask for their solutions. Ask each team to solve these questions or problems with knowledge and skills acquired in the course. Be sure to require teams to review and provide feedback on others' respective solutions. Groups might also suggest one or more questions or case problems for the exam and provide appropriate solutions. Instructors or tutors can then select one or more of these for course quizzes and examinations. Such a technique will foster student engagement and interaction. Consider assigning bonus credit for suggesting exam questions that are adapted for future use. In addition, groups whose cases or questions are used might be verbally acknowledged and congratulated.

Our research indicates that such online exam resources are heavily used just prior to the exam. Consequently, the instructor might explore ways to reward early and frequent participation.

*Variations and Extensions.* Mark the cases that were ultimately selected on the exam for students who enroll in later semesters or versions of the course. Provide an online explanation of why those cases were, in fact, selected. Such a rationale or purpose might help students grasp the key issues, concepts, or principles that the instructor is attempting to convey.

## Key Instructional Considerations

*Risk index:* Medium

*Time index:* Medium

*Cost index:* Low

*Learner-centered index:* High

*Duration of the learning activity:* 1–2 weeks

# Activity 50. Reaction or Position Papers

*Description and Purpose of Activity.* Have students write reaction papers to different controversies, dilemmas in the news (Watkins, 2005), quotes, or trends. Position papers force learners to reflect on their learning experiences and make sense of them. By having learners take a stance, they reorganize their knowledge and form new connections and insights.

*Skills and Objectives.* Includes knowledge rehearsal, reflection, communication and presentation skills, course interactivity, sense of cognitive dissonance, critical analysis, writing as thinking, feedback, synthesis, and knowledge reorganization and idea linkages.

*Advice and Ideas.* Locate controversial materials, heated debates in the field, and/or key quotes. Organize these materials in a meaningful way and post them to the course Web site or blog. Next, ask students to pick the viewpoint that they wish to further explore and react to in a position paper. Provide sufficient guidelines on the position or reaction paper task. To manage student progress, be sure to assign task due dates and review drafts as appropriate. After evaluating student products, collect exemplary work for future use as model answers.

Save news clippings of controversial issues in your field when not teaching the course, as they may become useful later on. Perhaps have students search for and find key controversial issues for the field. Save those as well.

*Variations and Extensions.* Perhaps require the learners not only to post a position paper but also a counterposition related to papers of one or more of their peers in the course. Students might then be asked to write rebuttals to any counterposition papers of their peers or to debate them in an asynchronous discussion forum or live classroom situation.

## Key Instructional Considerations

> *Risk index:* Medium
>
> *Time index:* Medium
>
> *Cost index:* Low
>
> *Learner-centered index:* Medium
>
> *Duration of the learning activity:* 1–2 weeks

# Use and Outlook for Phase 2 Strategies

As with Phase 1 of R2D2, there are countless ways to embed pedagogical activities for reflective and observational learning into your teaching. Some of the strategies mentioned in this chapter are individual and private, whereas others are highly collaborative and social events. Decisions on which type of strategy—individual or collaborative—will depend on the level of the course, the experience of the students, the tools selected, and the risk-taking nature of the instructor, trainer, teacher, or instructional designer.

Phase 2 of R2D2 is a purposeful opportunity for learner evaluation of the knowledge gained in Phase 1. As pointed out in Chapter Four, innovative tools and systems for writing and reflection have been around for decades. In fact, tools for outlining a paper, summarizing one's learning, annotating or commenting on the ideas of another, organizing thoughts, sharing knowledge, juxtaposing ideas, and fostering reflection on the purpose, audience, and goals of that writing were developed and extensively researched more than two decades ago (Bereiter & Scardamalia, 1987; Daiute, 1986; Salomon, 1988; Scardamalia, Bereiter, McLean, Swallow, & Woodruff, 1989).

Such writing tasks and competencies remain critical today. What is new is that online environments are more subtle in encouraging students to write; chatting (that is, writing) online is second nature for digital natives. And there are no red marks to slow them down! We often find our students writing hundreds of words each week without hesitation or complaint. So while a plethora of writing-related tools, theories, and techniques were abundant in the 1980s, such wide acceptance of writing as a part of one's courses was not as pervasive as it is now in the twenty-first century. Today, learners write in their blogs, in their online discussion forums, on their social networking sites, and in their comments on the posts of others. They are writing all the time!

While such writing activities may be more central to course success today than in the past, it is important to remember that decades of research on writing have provided a general understanding how online writing tools and activities can influence the cognitive processes of both younger and older writers (Flower & Hayes, 1981; Hayes & Flower, 1986; Scardamalia & Bereiter, 1986). What is unique in the twenty-first century, however, is the millions of people who, within the Web of Learning, can use these writing tools and strategies to augment, extend, and link their thoughts and insights to the ideas of others around the planet in novel and thought-provoking ways. As such tools become more prevalent and popular, so, too, will the informed applications of Phase 2 of R2D2.

## Final Reflections

We are admittedly a tad biased when it comes to Phase 2 of the Read, Reflect, Display, and Do model. Bonk's dissertation was on the use of procedural facilitators, or, more specifically, critical and creative thinking prompts in writing, as well as the use of a keystroke mapping program that allowed him to replay students' keyboard entries and watch students' thoughts unfold over time (Bonk & Reynolds, 1992; Reynolds & Bonk, 1996). He also conducted a series of studies in the late 1980s and early 1990s related to summary and essay writing that stemmed from his interests and beliefs in writing as thinking. In many ways, online tools and resources found today with the Web 2.0 are critical extensions of those efforts.

As such, we view Phase 2 as a perhaps the key "cog in the wheel" of student learning. Unfortunately, we also realize that too often it is an area that is either ignored or undervalued by online (as well as FTF) instructors, teachers, or trainers. So it is perhaps fortuitous that as the Web of Learning continues to mature, more focus will undoubtedly be placed on second-phase learning. If instructors simply allow students to explore the ever-increasing amount of online content without reflection, learner tension and hesitation will be a common byproduct. Will this result in increased outpatient visits, psychiatric counseling, and hospital beds for online learning students and instructors? We certainly hope not. Let's keep such risks in mind, however, as we turn to Phase 3 and the focus on the visual representation of one's learning.

CHAPTER SIX

# PHASE 3 OF THE R2D2 MODEL

## Visual Learners

Probably everyone reading this book has been helped in some manner by a visual representation of a learning-related model, framework, principle, or concept or by a task that significantly challenged you to create such a model or framework. Perhaps you find some of the figures and tables in this very book to be where you concentrate your time. It is conceivable, in fact, that when you opened this book, you immediately went to this chapter—Chapter Six—to satisfy a need or curiosity related to visual learning.

When we ask audiences which aspect of the Read, Reflect, Display, and Do (R2D2) model resonates most with them, it is invariably this third phase, emphasizing visual learning, with the fourth phase (hands-on learning) not far behind. While we are fans of reflective writing, extensive reading assignments, opportunities to try out concepts and ideas, and online social interaction and collaboration, we also have visual preferences. It is likely that our visual preferences are a reaction against our overwhelmingly text-based pasts. At the same time, such inclinations may also reflect the types of learning resources and materials likely to permeate future online learning environments. We certainly hope so!

### Phase 3 of R2D2

Phase 3 of the R2D2 model focuses on how learners can represent what they have learned or are in the process of learning (see Figure 6.1). It also makes salient how to foster learning from visual representations, depictions,

## FIGURE 6.1.   PHASE 3 OF R2D2.

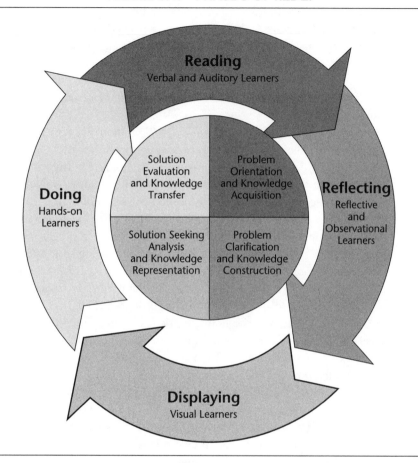

and overviews or summaries of others. While it targets those who might be considered visual learners, it should not be discounted for any learner. Visuals provide another track on which learning can occur. And when combined with other forms of learning, as noted in the discussion of dual-coding theory in Chapter Two, learning is more richly stored and readily available (Mayer, 2003; Paivio, 1991). For instance, when a visual depiction or animation is combined with text or audio, learning can be more deeply processed.

Thus, learning in Phase 3 is concentrated on visual supports and representations. Phase 3 learning, therefore, might include pictures, animations, videos, graphics, flowcharts, diagrams, charts, schematics, simulations, or maps.

Learning in this phase of R2D2 can involve the manipulation of mathematical and scientific data and symbol systems found in algebra, statistics, chemistry, or physics. Of course, there is once again overlap with the other phases of R2D2. For instance, Phase 2 learning also entails showing learners a macro-representation of a concept, principle, or idea and having them reflect on potential uses of it. And, as will be discussed in Chapter Eight, Phase 4 learning includes simulations and other visual displays that learners manipulate, resolve, and explain.

As with the previous two stages of R2D2, there are a plethora of strategies that can be called upon in distance learning environments to address learners who prefer this type of learning or who are ready for this stage of the R2D2 learning process. For instance, an animation of a concept might be embedded in a learning module for spur-of-the-moment selection if the learner desires it. Or an online trainer, tutor, or instructor might use an interactive whiteboard when chatting with students or when presenting in a synchronous conferencing Webinar or other "live" online event. In employing such a tool, the instructor might visually direct students' attention with arrows, boxes, numbering, and different uses of color, notation, and highlighting. For asynchronous courses, learners might also be asked to browse through an online repository or library of videoclips that illustrate how a particular strategy or principle is used in the real world. And as demonstrated in the activities in Chapter Seven, professional schools such as architecture, engineering, dentistry, business, nursing, and education often rely on video cases and scenarios to display key concepts in action.

Remember that R2D2 is a problem-solving approach as well as a means to understand how to more successfully employ the Web of Learning in online teaching and learning. There must be at least some indication that learners have acquired and appropriated the requisite knowledge and perhaps generated knowledge that was not directly intended.

How do you know that learners know? One way is to assign tasks wherein learners are asked to represent their learning in the form of timelines, taxonomies, concept maps, flowcharts, Venn diagrams, and other forms of visual representation. And when such visual displays are electronic, the learner can continually edit, modify, and transform them. Additionally, virtual knowledge representations can be revisited at later moments in the semester, course, or learning experience, perhaps for interesting pedagogical uses by the instructor, tutor, or trainer. At the same time, virtual displays of knowledge create opportunities for students to share and critically evaluate ideas while mentally gauging their learning to date against that of their peers or learning partners. And, of course, such representations can be part of a learning portfolio that learners revisit in later courses or years within a program of study.

Visual representations are not only vital in that they enable learners to display what they have learned; they are also helpful in the knowledge acquisition process. Many software tools and systems have been developed to enhance visual learning opportunities in online environments. While, as argued in Chapter Two, the Web of Learning has been used primarily to present text, the avenues for online visual displays are swiftly increasing.

Many institutions and organizations use animations as a key aspect of their online training (for example, to demonstrate blood flow in the human body in an anatomy class, cash flow analyses in a financial accounting class, or the randomization of subjects to groups in a statistics class). Dr. Valerie O'Loughlin at Indiana University, for instance, has spearheaded the creation of more than a dozen human embryology animations to explain cardiovascular, limb, gastrointestinal, urinary and reproduction, and head and neck development. While time consuming to create, she has received extensive positive feedback and praise while helping simplify the sometimes arduous process of teaching human gross anatomy, especially the complex processes of the development of a human embryo (Fecarotta, 2007). These animations are now featured in the Multimedia Educational Resource for Learning and Online Teaching (MERLOT) and are used in anatomy classes around the globe.

In addition to their many applications in higher education settings, animations are growing in use in other adult learning settings. For example, corporate training departments employ animations and simulations to showcase customer service procedures and sales training. Military training departments now utilize animations to clarify how different weapons or machinery operate as well as for high-level strategic planning and tactical maneuvers.

While the educational uses of animations continue to mount, fully online and blended learning courses might also provide comprehensive organizational aids and overviews or partially completed visual templates for learners to complete or fill in. Additionally, students might utilize the rapidly growing number of online video scenarios and videoclips to anchor student learning in a situation that can be replayed, compared, and extended. Witness the rapid growth of short educational videos in YouTube and Google Video, as well as those in the recently announced TeacherTube site that was developed by fourteen-year teaching veteran Jason Smith and his younger and digitally savvy brother, Adam, with the explicit goal to "Teach the World."

While accessing music, sports, news, and entertainment videos online is well known (see CNN.com video, for instance), it is not too surprising that there are thousands of freely available online educational videos (for example, MIT World), including many excellent presentations by leading figures. Harvard Business School has indexed videoclips of such notables as Peter Senge,

John Seely Brown, and Chris Dede forecasting the future of distance learning and addressing many of the topics included in this book. There are also several highly informative technology-related Google videos featuring Alan Kay (for example, "Education in the Digital Age"). Kay is one of the founding fathers of object-oriented programming and a computer visionary who helped define the basics of laptop and tablet computing. Instead of learners traveling to a conference to hear a keynote from Kay, Senge, Dede, or Seely Brown, they might hop online and watch one that Google, YouTube, Yahoo! Video, or some other service has indexed.

Of course, there are the persistent questions related to how to use such videos. For instance, what is to stop instructors from relying on such expert videos for all lessons and deciding never to lecture in class again? And what is wrong with such an approach if the contents of the experts are of high quality and are relevant to one's course content? Will there be instructor and tutor protests over such approaches since, if conducted on a mass scale, many stand to lose their jobs? Such questions have been raised each time there has been an innovation in instructional media or noteworthy changes in educational delivery formats. However, the possibilities for making use of international experts in a field of study are more pervasive and compelling today.

Clearly, visual representations are a key aspect of the Web of Learning. Visuals are used both to display concepts and ideas to learners as well as to have learners display their learning back to the instructors or those in charge of the learning process. Visual learning opportunities will not subside anytime soon. The trends of the past few years indicate that institutions and organizations offering online training or learning experiences need to take stock of what is possible visually and include such activities as a key component of their online teaching and learning plans.

## Structural Knowledge, Meaningful Learning, and Mindtools

During the past few decades, educators have been devoted to finding ways to make learning more relevant and meaningful for learners. For instance, in a book on knowledge structures, David Jonassen and his colleagues outlined numerous techniques and approaches for conveying, acquiring, and assessing structural knowledge, while simultaneously detailing the prevailing research on such methods (Jonassen, Beissner, & Yacci, 1993). They noted that there are a multitude of mindtools (that is, tools for improving or enhancing cognitive functions or performances of the learner) and techniques that instructors can use to represent knowledge in visual ways and that learners can use to display to instructors what they have learned or are in the process of learning. Such techniques and tools include advance organizers, categorization schemes, concept mapping, and mind mapping.

Jonassen argues that the use of mindtools is on the rise in education. However, their use is not always straightforward, since mindtools scaffold different types of reasoning processes. Equally problematic, there is a wide assortment of such tools to choose from. For instance, tools for graphing knowledge, searching online for needed information, organizing thoughts through concept mapping, modeling complex processes, creating or scanning databases of knowledge, and visualizing learning with rich multimedia and hyperlinked knowledge structures can enhance your learning beyond basic knowledge consumption levels (Averill, 2005).

Such mindtools provide the means for learners to construct knowledge, dynamically assess it and change it, and express their ideas in unique ways. These tools require learners to reflect on what they know or are in the process of learning as well as organize that knowledge in meaningful ways. Using these tools, learners can begin to recognize patterns in learning, categorize and organize their knowledge, identify underlying assumptions and key ideas or principles, and hypothesize findings or predict results. In effect, such tools might take over some of the more tedious or mundane aspects of learning, thereby allowing learners additional mental resources for their critical or creative thinking pursuits.

## Advance Organizers

In the same camp as Jonassen's work on mindtools and knowledge structures, David Ausubel (1978) long ago pointed out that knowledge is hierarchically organized and that we need to find ways for new learning to be subsumed under or anchored within prior learning experiences. He suggested that new information is going to be meaningful to the extent that it is anchored (that is, attached or related) to what learners already know and understand. A key part of this effort is finding ways to link prior learning experiences to new concepts and ideas. No longer is the most efficient path to learning one that has learners repeating concepts and ideas verbatim or in arbitrary ways. When effort is not made to link new knowledge with existing cognitive structures, the result is often inert or unconnected knowledge. Scholars such as Jonassen and Ausubel argue that it is the connections and relationships drawn among events and objects that are vital for higher-order thinking and knowledge retention.

Ausubel promoted the use of advance organizers as a pedagogical aid for instructors, trainers, and instructional designers to help learners organize and relate concepts being learned. They help learners assimilate and accommodate new learning into their internal schema or create new schema when needed. In essence, advance organizers provide the initial scaffolding or priming of knowledge for later learning, in part, by guiding learner attention to key elements or aspects of that learning. This scaffolding enhances the chances that the specifics or details will stick. Advance organizers might also provide key insights or make learners aware of unique relationships. They might best be used when the material being learned is unfamiliar to the learners or when an organizational aid provides crucial contextual information for the learners. In addition, advance organizers are useful when the learners will be tested for higher-level concepts and not simply be asked to recall basic facts. They do not guarantee learning enhancements, however, since advance organizers might be incorrect or they might focus the learners so much that they miss out on opportunities for spontaneity and creative insight.

Advance organizers come in many different types and formats. For instance, they might compare the similarities and differences of two or more religions, such as Christianity and Buddhism, or show the advantages and disadvantages of new types of hybrid cars. They might illustrate the flow of electricity or compare features of a laptop computer to the human brain. An advance organizer might be a quick animation or simulation of a process such as driving a car or a helicopter. It might also be something as pithy as a saying, quote, or joke. A highly effective advance organizer might be something that was recently salient in the news and pertinent to the topic under discussion. Perhaps even more powerful are analogies and metaphors such as "Teaching is like gardening" or "Think of your hard disk as a filing cabinet," since they help students see patterns or relationships among seemingly disparate ideas or principles. In effect, advance organizers involve anything that can prime knowledge and help learners subsume new learning under prior learning.

Among the most common advance organizers are those that involve some type of graphic organization, classification, or categorization. A company organization chart is an advance organizer to someone interviewing for a job. A comparison and contrast table of art periods and key artists or historical events is an advance organizer for a student studying art history. A map can serve as an advance organizer by indicating migration patterns of birds or butterflies, typography of different land regions, or the direction of ice flow near the geographic North Pole prior to encountering learning content on one of these topics.

Across these examples, advance organizers are previews of the learning content. They illustrate key distinctions prior to delving into the specifics of a module or lesson. They are particularly effective when the material is difficult, abstract, complex, or novel for the learner or when they illustrate relationships or linkages among seemingly unorganized data or highly complex information.

As indicated, there are many choices for advance organizers; one can represent information in timelines, taxonomies, Venn diagrams, sequence chains, flowcharts, or some other form of visual representation. Timelines, in particular, are a useful tool for scaffolding students' later learning. A timeline might highlight core sections of an online course or learning module. The Learning Tools project from the University of British Columbia (UBC), for instance, provides an interesting open source timeline tool that instructors can employ for their advance organizers (see Web resources). This tool enables instructors and instructional designers to construct interactive timelines with multiple media such as pictures or image files as well as sound and movie files.

Such tools provide those on the instructional side of the fence with a window into how well learners understand the chronological aspects of key information or concepts. In effect, they offer a way to sort through masses of data and depict a learner's understanding at a key moment in time. Not all timeline tools are created equal, however, since some timeline tools can only handle textual information, whereas others, such as the exciting one from UBC, embed multimedia components. There are countless ways to use such tools as advance organizers and learning aids in Phase 3 learning.

Other online resources and tools that can function as advance organizers include virtual tours and virtual fieldtrips. As Ausubel might have suggested, a virtual tour or field trip of a city, geographic region, or event might set the stage for later learning. Once demonstrated or used, the learner is primed for additional content related to the online tour or field trip. Such tools and resources not only foster student knowledge construction or design and associated generative thinking, but they also force students to evaluate their learning to date and critically reflect on key aspects of their knowledge.

## Concept Mapping

Based on the work of David Ausubel and others on advance organizers, schema theory, and prior knowledge, Joseph Novak at Cornell University promoted concept mapping as a mechanism for displaying one's learning of new concepts and ideas (Novak & Gowin, 1984; Novak & Musconda, 1991). Concept mapping is a means for visually representing ideas as networks of concepts. Through concept mapping, linkages between terms and the direction of such linkages are displayed. These links can be nondirectional, unidirectional, or bidirectional. They can show simple associations between terms as well as more complex causal or temporal relations. To add value or clarity to one's concept maps, such linkages or relations can be labeled or detailed by the learner.

There are many approaches to concept mapping. An instructor might assign learners to create a concept map summarizing key points of a chapter, lecture, module, or lesson. A concept mapping assignment might emphasize learner idea generation and brainstorming of what they have learned. If the focus is on generating ideas from a key word or central concept, it might be considered an *idea* or *mind map* as opposed to the more hierarchical concept map. Or, alternatively, the task or assignment might force learners to explore logical relations among concepts. Instructors or tutors typically assign concept-mapping tasks so that they might better understand learner misunderstandings or misconceptions. These maps might be graded for connections made, organization, hierarchy, causal relations, details, correct macropropositions (that is, key points or concepts) and micropropositions (that is, details), and overall relations.

There are many tools for concept mapping and idea representation, a number of which are presently free. For instance, the open source tool Visual Understanding Environment (VUE) from Tufts University is free to download and use. More important, VUE includes a "Pathways" feature that enables learners (or instructors) to create custom trails through particular nodes in a map that they intend to highlight.

Another tool for such knowledge construction and sharing is the concept-mapping software from the Institute for Human and Machine Cognition (IHMC) at the University of West Florida. The homepage of the IHMC Cmap Tools specifically notes that educators and educational institutions can download and install this software on as many machines as they desire. A key objective here is for learners not only to construct knowledge maps but also to navigate the knowledge maps of peers and to learn to critique visual displays and knowledge models. Of course, another crucial goal is to share and edit knowledge maps. With the IHMC tool, such editing can be conducted in a real-time or synchronous fashion.

A third free concept-mapping tool is called FreeMind, which promotes itself as a tool for supporting project management, essay writing, brainstorming, course management, note organization, Internet research, and the maintenance of small databases of information. FreeMind is an open source tool that has been available for free downloads since at least 2001.

In addition to these free concept mapping tools, there are a maze of commercial products in this area. For instance, there are tools such as MindMapper, Visual Mind, Mind Genius, BrainMine Standard, MindManager, and Inspiration (and Kidspiration for younger learners). Most of these tools were not designed for online or distance learning environments but instead were intended for individual or project team use on stand-alone machines. They typically are not Web based! Ironically, Web-based concept-mapping applications such as

FreeMind, IHMC, and VUE are the free and open source tools. Small wonder that educators find the Web of Learning intriguing while many commercial software vendors find it ominous—the software is often free and easily accessible.

## Visual Portals and Repositories

As documented in previous chapters, there are thousands of online educational portals filled with images, movies, animations, and other visual representations of content. For instance, you can find in MERLOT award-winning sites such as the Valley of the Shadows, which details a gold mine of content related to the Civil War in the United States. This site contains an impressive array of information, including maps and images, census information, diaries, newspapers, soldier records, and church records for different time periods before, during, and after the Civil War. The Valley of the Shadows is applicable to middle and secondary students as well as college students.

Also featured in MERLOT is a fascinating and award-winning Web site titled DNA from the Beginning. This site explains the concept of DNA through text, relevant pictures of famous scientists in the field, video interviews, and animations. Also presented are audio files, online linkages, biographies of famous people in the field, and problems. While DNA from the Beginning is most relevant to middle and secondary students, there are many potential uses for introductory college classes.

DNA from the Beginning and the Valley of the Shadows are just two examples of portals that are rich with visual media. Perhaps more impressive are online portals of digital libraries, museums, zoos, planetariums, and institutes that offer access to millions of pictures, movies, animations, and other types of visually rich information. They might spur both formal as well as informal learning. The Museum of Online Museums (MoOM), for instance, indexes museums from around the planet. Here one can explore exhibits of classical art and architecture, jigsaw puzzle collections, advertisements, and interior designs. Similarly, a site Bonk and his colleagues developed, LibraryShare.com, allows you to peruse the contents of hundreds of public libraries, online libraries, and university libraries. Just one of these sites, the New York Public Library Digital Gallery, contains more than 550,000 images that were digitized from primary resources such as vintage posters, historical maps, rare prints, photographs, and illustrated books (see Figure 6.2). Given these visual treasures, it is not too surprising that the New York Public Library won an award as a Best Research Site for 2006 from a panel of international museum professionals. This expert panel noted the depth of content, high quality of that content, and ease of content accessibility and navigation. There are many such digital libraries today.

### FIGURE 6.2. HOMEPAGE FOR DIGITAL GALLERY OF THE NEW YORK PUBLIC LIBRARY.

Used by permission of The New York Public Library, Astor, Lenox and Tilden Foundations.

For example, in the A's, one might explore digital libraries related to African writing systems, African American female writers, or ancient inventions.

## Virtual Tours

Visuals might also be presented to learners as a series or sequence of concepts that learners might explore, engage with, or navigate through. In fact, in recent years, the Internet has been increasingly used for virtual tours of concepts, battlefields, geographic regions, or places of interest in face-to-face (FTF), blended, and fully online courses.

How might this play out in real life? Well, a geologist at Western Wherever University (WWU) might display land formations in Nova Scotia using video taken from a walking tour of key sites as well as helicopter flyovers of more difficult terrain. At the same time, an archeology professor three classrooms down the hall might take students on a virtual tour of a Mayan ruin and require them to explore a Web site that has 360-degree panoramic views after class. During the next period, a WWU history professor in a building a short walk away might be displaying archways, columns, buildings, and entire cities of ancient Rome using computer-generated three-dimensional (3D) views (Guernsey, 2005). And a few weeks later, he might take his students to explore the wonders of ancient Egypt using a new Web site called Discover Babylon (Foreman, 2006).

The archaeology and history professor are not alone. A colleague of theirs over in the WWU economics building might design a virtual tour of oil wells and underlying supply potential around the world while linking to Google Maps to demonstrate a key point in an introductory economics course. Over lunch that day with a tourism instructor, the economics professor might explain how to use Google Maps or some other online tool to highlight different points of interest in a geographic region, country, or community. And they all might attend a luncheon presentation on how virtual tours, timelines, and field trips are being used on the WWU campus.

## Art, Design, and History Online

Clearly, those involved in nearly any field now have stunning resources to back up their presentations or to support and extend student conceptual learning. In the award winning Omnium Project developed in the College of Fine Arts (COFA) within the University of New South Wales in Australia, art and design instructors showcase and compare visual examples of their students' work as well as that of well-known creative experts worldwide. The Omnium Project, which was founded in 1998, fosters collaboration among individuals around the planet with the chance not only for peer or instructor feedback, but also for internationally recognized art and design experts to question, probe, and provide timely feedback on student designs in progress. Simply put, Omnium is a collaboration tool or system with which learners can post their creative designs and ideas and receive feedback from others. Not surprisingly, it is also being promoted as a platform for fostering human creativity.

In terms of creativity, the Omnium Project attempts to teach students the creative problem-solving process so that they can be creative in their designs as well as in their everyday lives. In fact, each year Omnium hosts a seven-week online design event called Creative Waves in collaboration with the International

Council of Graphic Design Associations (Icograda), the world's governing body for professional graphic designers. In Creative Waves projects, students from around the globe who are interested in graphic design, photomedia, and visual communication can post their work to the Omnium online galleries and receive feedback from internationally known experts and other teachers and mentors.

Creative Waves is a huge multicultural community of novice and expert designers—a place ripe with apprenticeship opportunities. Since 1998, more than 5,000 students, educators, and professionals from more than forty countries have participated in various fully online Omnium projects. Unlike the dreary aspects of most course management systems and virtual learning environments, the visuals embedded in Omnium courses are impressive and highly engaging. For those who are interested, Omnium software became available as an open source option in 2007.

There are many creative tools for art, design, and architecture; Omnium is but one example. Art instructors can now take learners on 3D tours of art in virtual worlds like Active Worlds. Or they might send students on a virtual tour of the Louvre or to some other museum found in MoOM. The Timeline of Art History from the Metropolitan Museum of Art in New York City includes an online tour of art that is chronologically based across different cultures or geographic regions. In addition, this tool allows scholars, students, educators, or anyone else to explore different art themes. Thus, it combines notions of virtual tours with a timeline to guide your particular tour.

Similar to the Timeline of Art History, the Theban Mapping Project (TMP) allows users to explore aspects of ancient Egypt. In TMP there is an interactive database of more than 2,000 images and models for each tomb in the Valley of the Kings. In addition, there are videos, timelines, and article resources illustrated with photographs as well as giant aerial photographs displaying the surrounding topography. Information is continually updated and added to this site. And that is not all. There also are impressive drawings and maps, narrated tours, 3D recreations of tombs, and the ability to zoom in and out on different architectural features. Clearly the visual opportunities within the Web of Learning are endless!

## Other Visual Tools and Resources

Some techniques for visual learning relate to technologies mentioned in previous chapters. For instance, with the emergence of video iPod technology, videos can be part of podcasting. Along these same lines, videos are now often embedded in blogs. One educational example is the use of adventure blogs, including captivating sites such as the Poles and ExplorersWeb. Such highly engaging sites might include special news stories, blogs of explorers in their travels, and many thrilling pictures and videos documenting their journeys and accomplishments. And for the athletically minded, there are Web sites and adventure blogs for the North Pole and Antarctic marathons.

Most of these adventure blogging sites have pictures showing the explorers or adventurers in action. In addition, some of these adventure sites embed PowerPoint presentations and videos of explorer treks or scientific experiments within minutes or hours of occurrence. For example, Andrew Revkin, a well known and extremely prolific science reporter from the *New York Times,* often posts stories that are linked to narrated PowerPoint slides providing an in-depth look at key scientific experiments or procedures being conducted in Greenland, Antarctica, or the geographic North Pole. Even though the authors do not personally teach courses wherein we can directly use this type of content, such scientific forms of adventure learning are simply amazing! Adventure blogs are another unique empowering tool for e-learning.

It is the authenticity and currency of such content that inspires learners. In effect, adventure Web sites and other visual resources and tools bring students directly to the content. Equally important, students can see concepts in action with original commentary instead of simply learning about it from secondhand sources. As noted throughout this chapter, the visual displays are a key part of that engagement process.

While probably less current, online animations are also increasingly used to bring learners more directly into a discipline. An animation can be played to illustrate a concept more clearly, paused to give the learner time to reflect on it, and replayed when the learner has specific questions or concerns. For instance, an animation might display the laws of supply and demand in an economics course, inventory control and supply chain management in business management, and weather patterns and movements in meteorology. Such tools are also common today in medical training (for example, animations of cardiovascular or digestive systems) and hard science areas such as biology, chemistry, and physics. As with video cases and virtual tours, mentioned earlier, both adventure blogs and animations situate student learning in a real-world context that can apprentice novice and less skilled learners into the day-to-day activities and decision making of an expert (Brown, Collins, & Duguid, 1989; Collins, Brown, & Newman, 1990).

Visualization tools might provide a sense of community, personal identity, or social presence among the participants. For example, LearnByDoing is a group-based learning environment that facilitates participant chat discussion. With LearnByDoing, participants in such chats can embed their pictures within the chat as well as post agenda and employ other visual cues to augment their posts.

And when the chat is completed, users can browse through an assortment of visually based summaries of the session. For instance, a visual representation of individual posts in some type of nodal structure can indicate which members different participants tended to interact with. If one student grabs a particular node and tugs at it, others in the same community or social network will also travel with it. In effect, it provides an external representation of a previously hidden online community. Additionally, by displaying each session participant in a different color and highlighting the colors that were active during different moments of the chat session, the LearnByDoing system can indicate when different participants were active in the session. Of course, many such tools will emerge during the coming decade to help visual learners in various distance learning situations and environments.

Before ending this section of the chapter, it should be pointed out that there are numerous online tools to enlarge, shrink, rotate, or superimpose objects and artifacts. Magnifying the head of a pin, rotating an artifact in a museum, zooming in on a chart or map, and overlaying symbols or marks on terrain in a military exercise are techniques that offer learners different ways to investigate data and make sense of it. As noted in Chapter Four, content annotation and marking tools focus the learner on critical content. Such highlighting, annotating, rotating, and magnifying tools also might help visually impaired learners as well as those who suffer from attention-deficit/hyperactivity disorder (ADHD).

During the past decade, the Internet has gradually become a highly visual tool. As stressed innumerable times in this chapter and throughout this book, it provides online learners with the ability to visually tap into current events or replay old ones in ways that previously were not possible or even imagined. The technologies for these visual depictions of concepts or events are continuing to become more available and easy to use. However, there is a pressing need for still more tools and toolkits that facilitate ways to visualize online learning and that might foster opportunities for learners to be more self-directed in their online learning pursuits.

# Recap

The third phase of R2D2 provides learning content in a format that is attractive to many learners. Viewing concepts in action or represented in some type of visual format is powerful. The forms of representation are endless—perhaps it is a sequence of pictures, perhaps it is a model, or perhaps it is a map. Visual representations offer contextual clues for better understanding of new concepts and principles as well as provide valuable problem-solving insights. The visuals may be designed by the learners themselves to indicate their understanding of a concept or degree of progress with a course or module.

Online visual activities such as virtual tours offer quick overviews that anchor student learning in visual representations that can be discussed, revisited, or replayed later to further emphasize key concepts or principles (Cognition and Technology Group at Vanderbilt, 1990). Or perhaps the same visual representation can be reused in different contexts to display multiple concepts. When used in this fashion, the online tutor, instructor, or trainer can assume the role of learning consultant or guide for that learning (Bonk & Cunningham, 1998).

As noted in Chapter Four, increasing the throughput or bandwidth capabilities of the Internet will hasten the use of animations, videos, and other rich visuals in online environments. It is an area that is just beginning to be realized in online learning environments. Consequently, examples and guidelines may be the most vital for this phase. Just like the reflective and observational components of learning in Phase 2, Phase 3 learning is ripe for both pedagogical experimentation and research.

As shown throughout this chapter, visual displays draw students into the learning environment and help them better understand concepts that they might have read about (Phase 1 of R2D2) or reflected upon (Phase 2 of R2D2). In Phase 3, learners continue to grapple with major concepts but begin to internalize their learning through visual conceptualizations provided by others. Even more important than working with premade content is having students form their own visual depictions and representations of the content that they find relevant and noteworthy. Such activities are vital, since active knowledge construction is more likely to be remembered than passive reception of prebuilt knowledge structures (Cognition and Technology Group at Vanderbilt, 1991).

In a nutshell, online opportunities for visual learning continue to proliferate. Tools available for creating virtual tours, field trips, timelines, concept maps, animations, and videoblogs (vlogs) are just some of the ways to realize Phase 3 learning. Chapter Seven details twenty-five online learning strategies for the visual learning possibilities of Phase 3. Some of the activities presented in Chapter Seven will be immediately implementable in most online learning situations, while others may require greater bandwidth, special funding, and increased familiarity and comfort with online learning. Seek out and find what will work best in your present situation!

# ACTIVITIES FOR PHASE 3

## Visual Learners

In this chapter, we present twenty-five online activities for Phase 3 (Display) of the Read, Reflect, Display, and Do (R2D2) model. Some of these suggestions are more suited to younger learners; others are geared toward more mature adults. While visual learning is highlighted, many of these ideas could just as easily apply to one of the other phases of the R2D2 model. As will become apparent, at least a dozen of these can be employed in face-to-face (FTF) or traditional classroom environments as well as in blended or fully online settings. As with the activities presented in Chapters Three and Five, these twenty-five ideas are just a starting point for the reader—there are likely hundreds, if not thousands, of additional ideas that could be used for visual learning in online environments.

Some of the activities presented focus on the visual learning tools and technologies in the Web of Learning, whereas others are more focused on a particular instructional strategy or activity. We also caution that some of the search tools we mention for visual examples or ideas may lead to sectors of the Internet that are not educational; therefore, be sure to leave your browser in a safe search mode when searching for high-quality visual content that might be useful in your online courses.

As in Chapters Three and Five, a rating of key instructional considerations appears at the end of each activity.

# Activity 51. Anchored Instruction with Online Video

*Description and Purpose of Activity.* In anchored instruction, there typically is a short "anchoring" event in the form of a video that instructors and learners watch and then can later revisit and reevaluate (Cognition and Technology Group at Vanderbilt, 1990) (see Figure 7.1 for an example). Short snippets of movies such as *Raiders of the Lost Ark* have been used to teach math and science principles by replaying and analyzing the clips while exploring questions like, "How many Indiana Joneses is the pit wide?" "How long is the airplane?" "How big is the idol?" and "Could Indiana Jones have replaced the gold statue with a bag of sand?" The intent is to create a problem-solving context or environment

## FIGURE 7.1.  A VIDEO ANCHOR IN AN ONLINE CLASS.

using these short video snippets. Such anchoring situations spur student interest in the topic being taught while allowing them to better define problems and more flexibly use their knowledge.

Increasingly, there are online tools and services for finding video-related content, such as Google Videos, Google Images, MIT World, Yahoo! Video, YouTube (recently bought by Google), TeacherTube, MSNBC Video, BBC News: Video and Audio, BBC Video Nation, and CNN Video. With the explosion of online news and educational reports, there are fascinating opportunities for anchored instruction activities in online courses. For instance, if one were asked to teach a workshop or course on leadership, there would be dozens of free videos in these sites that could be used. Perhaps the hard part of this task is not in finding videos for anchoring instruction but in selecting the most powerful ones for learning key content.

Using Google Video, BBC News: Video and Audio, CNN Video, or one of the other resources mentioned, an instructor can have learners watch a series of videoclips related to topics such as petroleum engineering, business ethics, fitness training, or tax accounting. Of course, the instructor should prescreen such videos beforehand and categorize them by the concepts or principles explicitly or implicitly embedded in them as well as the type of thinking skills or competencies that they might address.

In the spring of 2003, for example, Bonk was asked to present online engineering content to teacher educators at Tufts University in Massachusetts, because new state laws were requiring engineering-related content be included in classes from pre-kindergarten through grade 12. Key engineering and technology concepts and principles, including those related to materials, design, and development, were in fact being linked to new Massachusetts Science and Technology/Engineering Curriculum Frameworks. This new mandate was a bold move on the part of Massachusetts politicians and educators. Naturally, Massachusetts teachers as well as teacher educators were getting nervous about how to implement such groundbreaking plans and curriculum initiatives. Despite the fact that Bonk's knowledge of engineering was somewhat laughable (even though his father was an engineer), within a few hours he found a plethora of free engineering-related videos, cases, images, and other Web resources that might be used for pre-K–12 education. The online videos, in particular, could be used to anchor young learner instruction in discussions of the problem-solving processes of different types of engineers. Some were purposefully created to encourage young learners to view engineering as an exciting field of study. As with anchored instruction, the messages in such videos could be reused and replayed to help students of all ages perceive that they, too, could someday lead an exciting life as an engineer.

Now, a few years later, the technologies of choice might be video embedded in a podcast or "vodcast." For instance, a growing number of educational vodcasts that can be watched online or downloaded to a computer or an iPod are available from iTunes U from Apple Computer. Also important, many of these are free! For instance, in hopes of nurturing innovative uses of technology in schools, the University of South Florida has uploaded a series of free short vodcasts of technology integration lesson plans in a variety of subject areas to support teaching and learning in K–12 classrooms (for example, ecosystems, fighting obesity, solar cooking, discovering dinosaurs, poetry creations, and clay animations). If you teach hard sciences, iTunes also stores many vodcasts from the Massachusetts Institute of Technology, such as those in chemistry (for example, topics such as sublimation, filtration, and recrystallization).

Today the Web offers even much more video content to address such needs. In fact, with the recent plethora of online video content, anchored instruction should become a staple of online instruction across educational settings and situations. It is a concept that should be prominent in online learning instruction across educational sectors.

***Skills and Objectives.*** Includes reflection, critical analysis and evaluation, observational skills, and grasping the application of concepts, rules, and procedures in action.

***Advice and Ideas.*** There are millions of online videoclips on the Web that have some relevancy to teaching and learning. In most topic areas or courses, you will quickly find more videos than you can possibly use in one term or semester. To avoid being overwhelmed, consider indexing or rating the ones you find. Perhaps develop your own videos if none exist or customize and reuse existing ones after obtaining necessary permissions. Assign students to watch selected videos with guiding questions from the instructor for reflection and discussion. The type of assignment will depend on the type of course delivery format—face-to-face (FTF) with Web supplements, blended, or fully online. If there are FTF components, for instance, students might be asked to select interesting online videos to show at the start of class and then discuss as a group. An instructor might also display a short videoclip from YouTube, TeacherTube, or iTunes and then wrap the rest of her lecture around it with cycles of questions, comments, and revisits of key portions of the video. In online classes, online videos might take the place of lectures or supplement instructor videostreamed lectures and course notes. In all these cases, the videos anchor the instruction in key concepts, principles, and theories.

Short 5–10 minute videos that anchor learning in noteworthy situations, vignettes, or scenarios are perhaps best for most topics. The instructor can come back to such scenarios or vignettes in the video at timely moments in a lesson and ask the learners to find key features or concepts. However, be sure to prescreen anything you intend to use online. As online video content explodes, your pre-screening episodes will also increase. Consider e-mailing or contacting colleagues for ideas about what might be available. Of course, fair use copyright guidelines should be followed carefully for educational uses of existing video clips (more information is available at the Creative Commons, the Center for Intellectual Property at the University of Maryland University College, or the Copyright Management Center at Indiana University/Purdue University at Indianapolis). Be sure to evaluate the effectiveness of your use of these videos. For instance, based on your resulting course experiences, consider using a blog or online database to record your own rating of each video's educational value for the users and subject areas you teach. Make this available for others around the world to browse and react to.

*Variations and Extensions.* Create a student feedback form for the video anchors as a means to determine which ones are the most effective and why. Perhaps create a ranked listing of the video anchors in accordance with student feedback from previous semesters. Such rankings might address not only student satisfaction or engagement but also any controversial issues or discussion topics created as well as video quality, length, or course appropriateness. Videos rated below a certain level could be replaced.

## Key Instructional Considerations

> *Risk index:* Medium
>
> *Time index:* Medium to High
>
> *Cost index:* Low to High (depending on need for custom videos)
>
> *Learner-centered index:* Medium
>
> *Duration of the learning activity:* As needed

# Activity 52. Explore and Share Online Museums and Libraries

*Description and Purpose of Activity.* As noted in Chapter Six, online museums and digital libraries store millions of historically significant and meaningful pictures, videos, and other visuals that simply await imaginative use. Online museums and libraries are available for thousands of different topics and subject areas. To take advantage of such online resources, instructors might ask learners to explore online museums and digital libraries for visual content related to their online class or module. Such pictures or videos can enhance or help bring to life text-related content used in a course as well as lectures and other course materials.

***Skills and Objectives.*** Includes visual understanding, discrimination skills, exploration, and comparison and contrast. Another key goal is to realize the wealth of free visual content available on the Web.

***Advice and Ideas.*** There are thousands of online museum and digital library sites. Consequently, your learners will undoubtedly require some guidance in sorting through them. Provide students with guide sheets, job aids, or task templates to help them focus their efforts where needed. Furthermore, you might explore one or more sites and share what you have found with the class. Modeling enthusiasm, curiosity, and a thirst for new knowledge will swiftly rub off on your students.

One possible learning activity would be to provide links to digital libraries and museum portals or to specific links related to your course or discipline. If there are dozens of such sites, assign a different one (or set) to each student or group, or have them indicate the sites they prefer to explore by completing an online form that lists all the relevant sites you have found. Perhaps leave a space for additional sites that the learners might come across or know of.

Once sites are reviewed, ask students to create presentations, reflection papers, or critiques of these sites. In these papers, they might reflect on relevancy of the resources to course concepts, how the online resources extend their knowledge, and what similar types of resources could be used or developed in this class. Or assign a learning task that would require higher-order thinking skills, such as problem solving, decision making, evaluation, and so forth, and ask the learners to complete the tasks after exploring the digital library or virtual museum. Require students to generate conceptual linkages between the videos and any text-related readings in their papers or presentations. Also ask them for justification of major conceptual linkages in their papers or presentations. Invite peer sharing and critiques on these conceptual presentations.

***Variations and Extensions.*** Ask students to find similar images or media content from two or more sources and compare and contrast such resources or explore themes. If this is a blended course with some FTF meetings, the instructor might ask students to present what they have found. Or if it is fully online, the instructor might have the learners post reflective summaries with links to online resources that they have browsed and found personally relevant or an annotated bibliography of such resources. Finally, the instructor might create a gallery or database of resources that online learners continue to update and evaluate each semester.

## Key Instructional Considerations

*Risk index:* Medium

*Time index:* Medium

*Cost index:* Low

*Learner-centered index:* Medium

*Duration of the learning activity:* 1–2 weeks

# Activity 53. Concept Mapping Key Information

***Description and Purpose of Activity.*** Students might be required to create concept maps or visual representations of key information or knowledge gained from the course or learning experience. To guide their efforts, they might use one of the tools mentioned in Chapter Six, such as Inspiration, MindMapper, Visual Understanding Environment (VUE), FreeMind, or Cmap.

In our own courses, we often have students create a set of three to five concept maps representing different weeks, chapters, lectures, or modules of the course. Students place key information or macropropositions near the top of their maps and micropropositions or secondary information below them. Linkages between terms as well as descriptions of such linkages are essential for understanding what the student has internalized. In addition, depicting causal relationships is crucial in certain disciplines or topics. We also typically ask our students for reflective papers on their concept maps in which they verbally document their personal growth or understanding during the course. If it is a blended class with FTF events, they might be asked to discuss their concept maps or knowledge structures in a formal presentation, conference-like poster session, or student panel debate. We have also held course auctions of student artwork (that is, concept maps) after FTF poster sessions. Students whose work has mustered the highest bids from their peers typically receive course bonus points.

***Skills and Objectives.*** Includes knowledge integration and synthesis, concept review, visualization of learning, reflection, critical analysis skills, insight, and logical thinking. Clearly, this task requires a range of critical and creative thinking skills.

***Advice and Ideas.*** Assign the specific concept-mapping task for your course or topic and provide the learners with the URLs (universal resource locators, or Web addresses) of available concept mapping tools. If a particular tool is preferred for use, let them know that. Share your assessment plans and criteria while providing examples from previous semesters or versions of the course or experience. Instructor or expert models are helpful. Offer students an opportunity to present and explain their concept maps either virtually (synchronously or asynchronously) or FTF, whichever is applicable. If possible, assign a peer evaluation and critique activity.

Be clear about the task, since this might be something that the students have never previously been assigned. Examples or models of low- and high-quality concept maps are often critical in nudging students into such a task and reducing their initial trepidations. Perhaps gather student testimonials related to how important this task was to their learning in the course. Keep in mind that any concept-mapping software employed for this activity may also be used for other learning purposes, such as brainstorming, analyzing decision-making charts, project management, or summarizing learning within a cooperative or collaborative task. Corporate trainers may find these functions especially attractive in online or blended training sessions.

***Variations and Extensions.*** Consider having learners generate concept maps at multiple points in the semester so that they can more readily perceive their knowledge growth. Or perhaps have them work with partners or in teams to discuss and then develop more elaborate conceptual structures. Instead of everyone coming up with the same displays, the learners might also be asked to design conceptual structures of their extra readings or online explorations. They could also embed within their work hotlinks that take the reader or browser on an online journey of his or her knowledge growth and explorations during the course. Of course, you should inform the learners of the grading scheme ahead of time or jointly produce the assessment criteria as a group activity. In addition, you might spotlight exemplary work from previous semesters.

## Key Instructional Considerations

*Risk index:* Medium to High

*Time index:* Medium (time for coordination and grading may vary)

*Cost index:* Low to High (depending on tool selected)

*Learner-centered index:* High

*Duration of the learning activity:* 1–4 weeks

## Activity 54. Videostreamed Lectures and Presentations

***Description and Purpose of Activity.*** Learning is enhanced when the learners can see their instructors' facial expressions and nonverbal cues during the delivery of course content. Sometimes students miss class for personal or professional reasons. And still other times scholars, educators, practitioners, and potential students learn from watching expert instructors or trainers present course content online. For all these cases, asking your media department or instructional support personnel to videostream your presentations or lectures would be advantageous. (*Note:* This may involve lecturing in a designated room or equipping a laptop or desktop computer with a Webcam and appropriate software such as Camtasia or Captivate to record and produce streamed videos. When done, instructors might assign students to watch these videostreamed lectures and summarize what they have learned. Instructors, across all types of educational settings, can relate to videostreaming since it approximates the expert telling approach of most class-room learning situations.

While some might perceive tasks with such content as boring and perhaps not cost justifiable, Bonk had a student who was two weeks late signing up for an eight-week course (since, as he put it, he signed up for the wrong class) who was able to catch up by watching the videostreamed lectures. In fact, he later excelled in that class!

***Skills and Objectives.*** Includes grasping visual cues, course content and declarative knowledge, and appreciation of instructor or expert viewpoints. Of course, a key goal here is convenience in allowing learners to access content nearly anywhere and any time.

***Advice and Ideas.*** Search Google Video, iTunes, TeacherTube, YouTube, CurrentTV, NomadsLand, SplashCast, and other online video repositories to determine whether preexisting content is available for your topic or course. Select and index one or more videostreamed talks for a particular course or unit. Perhaps start with one videostreamed talk or presentation and evaluate its effectiveness for your course content before spending extensive personal time developing such content for all course modules or lessons. Think about creative uses of this content beyond "talking head" videos, such as having students e-mail or engage in an online chat with the expert in the video. You might also require students to complete an associated form, write a reflection paper, engage in a discussion on a given series of questions, or complete some other activity after watching one or more online video lectures or presentations. Such videostreamed talks might also be optional content that can be chosen by learners when and where needed. After viewing the video, some instructors have their learners share their comments and thoughts in the course Web site, blog, or LMS/CMS to further stimulate collaborative learning.

***Variations and Extensions.*** This activity could be combined with Activity 53 by having students create concept maps of their learning from one or more streamed videos. In addition, students might create visual displays comparing two different experts presenting on roughly the same topic or issue. If you are using video materials developed by others, consider having students write reviews of such video content and send them to the developer for feedback.

## Key Instructional Considerations

*Risk index:* Medium

*Time index:* Medium to High

*Cost index:* Low to High (depending on whether free content is available)

*Learner-centered index:* Low

*Duration of the learning activity:* As needed

# Activity 55. Videostreamed Conferences and Events

***Description and Purpose of Activity.*** As conferences, seminars, and institutes are increasingly streaming session presentations and activities, instructors might use such content in their courses as a means to apprentice learners into a field of study. Professional conferences in business, education, law, or most any field provide opportunities for students to reflect on the content that they are learning and how others are currently using such knowledge, or perhaps how they might someday employ it as a practitioner in the field. Assignments might be structured around either archived conferences or live ones or both. Instructors might ask learners to watch such online conference videostreams and write reflection papers focusing on key course concepts that were mentioned or alluded to by keynote and plenary speakers.

***Skills and Objectives.*** Includes grasping visual cues, course content, and declarative knowledge, and appreciation of expert viewpoints. Another key goal is extending student content learning beyond the course instructor or text.

*Advice and Ideas.* Search the Web for archived conferences, institutes, and seminars related to the course or modules within it as well as for information on upcoming conferences that might be held during the course or semester. Assign students to watch (or at least listen to) a set number of hours of that conference or institute or to noteworthy talks or presentations you have selected. Next, depending on the type of content watched, require reflection papers, debates, or online discussions of key concepts. In addition, you might write to the conference organizers to find out if they can provide your class with additional information related to the conference (for example, copies of any papers, abstracts, or presentation notes related to conference presenters or keynotes).

*Variations and Extensions.* Students might watch a video of an author of a book related your class, such as Thomas Friedman explaining his widely acclaimed book *The World Is Flat* in a one-hour presentation at MIT, and then use an asynchronous forum to discuss and debate ideas heard in the video as well as compare them to those in the book. Or perhaps require students to write to one or more of the experts whom they watch in conference keynote or special event videos. Instructors might also write to the keynote presenters to solicit their feedback on their students' work or to invite one or more individuals for a synchronous chat before or after their conference session. If a synchronous session is not possible, such individuals could be invited to course-related asynchronous discussion forums or debates on their presentations. As an option, instructors might ask students to find conferences, institutes, workshops, and seminars relevant to the course that have been archived or that will occur later during the semester or course.

## Key Instructional Considerations

> *Risk index:* Medium
>
> *Time index:* Medium
>
> *Cost index:* Low (assuming the videostream is free)
>
> *Learner-centered index:* Medium
>
> *Duration of the learning activity:* 1–2 weeks

# Activity 56. Interactive News and Documentaries

*Description and Purpose of Activity.* Increasingly, online news agencies and services are offering text content mixed with pictures, videos, sound clips, animations, and other forms of media. As mentioned in the previous chapter, the

*New York Times, LA Times, Chicago Tribune,* the BBC, and other news services provide narratives, simulations, animations, and pictorial displays of news events (for example, a Flash timeline explaining global warming or interactive visuals demonstrating how tornados are formed during a major storm). Instructors might find an online news story that relates to course content (preferably something recent) and then embed interactive exercises with that story. Once designed, they might have learners watch those news stories and create linkages with course content in their online discussions, papers, presentations, or other tasks. Such current news story activities are ideal for language learning courses as well as courses in economics, business, and health care.

***Skills and Objectives.*** Includes linking new knowledge to current events in the news, encoding the news information both verbally and visually, observational skills, and critically analyzing instances of concept application.

***Advice and Ideas.*** Find interactive news sites related to your course content in popular online news services (for example, CNN.com, the *New York Times* online, Yahoo! News, BBC Online, MSNBC). Index or bookmark interactive news sites when you find them. Assign students to watch these interactive materials. Next, require tasks such as reflective writing, blogs, online discussions, or similar activities wherein students discuss key course concepts seen in one or more videos.

***Variations and Extensions.*** An instructor might have students explore the Web for interactive news clips related to the course or topic that they might present to the class or post linkages to in the online course Web resources page. Perhaps have students compare and contrast two or more different news resources covering the same or similar topics. Sometimes we give online learners bonus points in return for helping us find high-quality online content relevant to our classes. As an interesting enhancement to this activity, consider writing an e-mail to a reporter or editor who tends to write interactive news stories related to a particular field or topic and invite that person in for a synchronous chat.

## Key Instructional Considerations

> *Risk index:* Medium
>
> *Time index:* Medium
>
> *Cost index:* Low
>
> *Learner-centered index:* Medium
>
> *Duration of the learning activity:* 1–3 weeks

## Activity 57. Interactive Online Performances

*Description and Purpose of Activity.* With the emergence and continued evolution of the Internet2, involving higher speeds of data transfer, there are increasing ways to engage in high-quality videoconferencing over the Internet (Olsen, 2003). Music instructors can demonstrate how to play different instruments or specific songs or notes to distant learners. Disciplines such as theater and dance might also be taught from a distance by having students observe expert performances via videoconferencing. And, of course, businesses can take advantage of such technology to provide timely mentoring for employees on a wide range of blue-collar manufacturing jobs as well as an array of white-collar tasks and competencies. Instructors might also ask learners to reflect on online performances in discussion forums, expert chats, or personal reflection papers.

Keep in mind that this task is also highly related to the observational learning discussed in Phase 2 of R2D2. With interactive online performances, therefore, you can easily link Phase 2 and 3 activities into the same assignment.

*Skills and Objectives.* Includes observational skills, skill discrimination and analysis, feedback, coaching, and internalization of a visual of successful performance. This task employs coaching and modeling, which are key aspects of cognitive apprenticeship (Brown et al., 1989; Collins, Brown, & Newman, 1990).

*Advice and Ideas.* Be sure that you (and your students) have broadband access before attempting online performance activities; otherwise, the performance may appear choppy and distractive, thereby losing needed visual cues or required synchronicity as in dueling violins, online musicals, or theatrical performances. If you are a technology pioneer, find out whether special resources exist that you might pilot or experiment with; you might search journal articles, conference papers, books, or simply conduct an open-ended Google or Yahoo! search. In addition, explore emerging technologies and announcements from professional organizations (for example, Global Nomads Group) or conferences for live performances or demonstrations related to your course content. Use the search tools that may be provided at the Web site of each professional organization. Given the monotony of such tasks, consider hiring a student to conduct some of this searching for you. If you find or hear about a successful event, write to the designers for advice or suggestions. As noted in Chapter Three, you might create Webcasts with tools such as ePresence TV, Polycom, Tegrity, Webcast Group, or MediaSite Live. After exploring your options, choose the technologies you'll use for producing and recording the live performance task.

Next, using your creative talents or borrowing ideas from existing performances you might have found, write a tentative script for the event. Ask learners to be involved in script writing as appropriate. When a script has been drafted, prepare performers or participants with appropriate training and access to the technology as needed. For instance, if it is a live violin performance, be sure to have musicians practice ahead of time. If it is a fashion show, perhaps conduct a dry run of the event. Test the producing and recording systems at least once prior to the live event.

Invite colleagues, the media, or other guests to the live event. Facilitate the live event with technical support available as necessary. When the event is over, be sure to gather feedback and evaluations from participants and guests and archive a recording of the live event. Learners can choose to watch the event live or later on when time permits. They might also listen to a podcast of it on the go. Review the archived event with learners for further reflection on how the performance or demonstration has related to course learning objectives.

*Variations and Extensions.* Students can design their own video performances to display a skill that they have learned related to the course. They might post these to YouTube, and bonus points could be assigned for the video that obtains the most viewers or highest ratings at the end of the course. (Such activities link to the fourth phase of R2D2, discussed in Chapters Eight and Nine.)

## Key Instructional Considerations

> *Risk index:* High
>
> *Time index:* Medium to High
>
> *Cost index:* Low to High (depending on the form of videoconferencing)
>
> *Learner-centered index:* Medium
>
> *Duration of the learning activity:* As needed

# Activity 58. Design Evaluation

*Description and Purpose of Activity.* It is vital for learners to be able to compare high- and low-quality examples, products, or other course results in nearly every area of learning. The Web offers unique opportunities for showcasing student or vendor product designs. For instance, in courses in which design is a key element or topic (for example, art, engineering, Web design, architecture, marketing), the instructor might call up an array of preexisting designs and have students critique them in a synchronous session.

***Skills and Objectives.*** Includes concept analysis, application, and discrimination, exposure to low- and high-quality examples or cases, perspective taking, feedback, interactivity, and student interaction.

***Advice and Ideas.*** Assume, for example, you are teaching a course in Web design and want to emphasize different layouts, features, and critical issues. Find Web site designs, good and bad, that you wish to highlight, analyze, or compare. The Web browsing capabilities of most synchronous conferencing tools will enable you to call up a series of Web sites for comparison and contrast. In addition, you can embed lecture notes related to key points of the process or the sites being reviewed by using presentation tools. For instance, you might focus your students on the layout of Web sites of different companies in the same industry such as those offering social networking capabilities like MySpace, Friendster, and Facebook. Ask your students about where certain tools are placed (for example, sign up, login, profile, groups, and so on). Have them look for ways to add friends as well as send messages to existing friends. They might note features such as visual layout, text font sizes, key button locations and navigation features, and help systems.

In such activities, it is crucial to provide students with templates or other guidance on how to proceed. For instance, exemplary designs from prior years or semesters might be made available. In addition, a weekly discussion thread related to best designs might be generated each week.

There are several synchronous conferencing tools (for example, Centra, Elluminate, Interwise, and Adobe Connect Pro) that can be employed to carry out course-related tasks. For instance, you can use the polling feature to gather student opinions about the design. Ask students to discuss these designs in the online chat tool within the system. You can also use drawing or paint tools to point to different features of the design that you would like students to notice. When the design review is complete, you might assign students various critical thinking or evaluation tasks related to the designs or have them complete a checklist of key features in Web design as a means to review each design that was discussed. Such tasks will prompt their thinking while allowing rehearsal of and expansion on their newly learned skills.

***Variations and Extensions.*** Perhaps assign each student a different design-related object or example and have them critique or evaluate it in a synchronous situation or asynchronous discussion forum. Alternatively, students might find designs that they resonate with and present them to the class, while pointing out course principles, concepts, and ideas. Similarly, in an asynchronous course, instructors or students might upload different designs to a CMS or LMS and engage in discussions about their inherent quality.

### Key Instructional Considerations

*Risk index:* Medium

*Time index:* Medium

*Cost index:* Medium to High (depending on the synchronous conference system selected; pricing varies widely)

*Learner-centered index:* Medium

*Duration of the learning activity:* 1–2 weeks as needed

# Activity 59. Design Generation

***Description and Purpose of Activity.*** Instead of critiquing preexisting designs within a field of study or topic, learners might create their own designs in such classes as Web design, advertising, civil engineering, or art and post them to the course Web site. Instructors might ask students to post a portfolio of their design work for others in the class to observe, evaluate, and compare and contrast.

***Skills and Objectives.*** Includes design and creativity skills, product-based learning, comparison and contrast skills, audience analysis, feedback, application of course content, and analysis skills.

***Advice and Ideas.*** Provide necessary training or tutorials on the selected design tools relevant to your field. For instance, for Web design, technology tools that might prove useful include Authorware, Flash, Dreamweaver, FrontPage, and Adobe Creative Suite Web Premium. Give the learners sufficient guidelines and evaluation criteria when you assign the design task. Create a virtual space in which learners can present their drafts, designs, supporting documents, reflections, and justifications related to the critical design decisions that they make during the design process. Incorporate suitable peer review activities in the design-generation process as well as afterward.

Consider providing as examples exemplary work that you have saved from previous course offerings. If you did not save any, ask learners from previous semesters if their designs can be saved and posted as models for new students. You might also ask them for personal testimonials regarding the design-generation task. If there was a sense of course community or genuine interest in reconnecting with the class, prior students might be asked to provide feedback to current students as part of an apprenticeship process.

*Variations and Extensions.* Learner designs might be posted to a designated course Web site or CMS or LMS for peer or expert review and commentary. Such designs and associated reviews might then be archived for learners in later versions of the course.

## Key Instructional Considerations

> *Risk index:* Medium
>
> *Time index:* Medium
>
> *Cost index:* Medium to High (depends on the synchronous conference system selected; pricing varies widely)
>
> *Learner-centered index:* Medium
>
> *Duration of the learning activity:* 1–2 weeks as needed

# Activity 60. Design Reviews and Expert Commentary

*Description and Purpose of Activity.* To further apprentice or support learners in a course, a local or international group of individuals with expertise in designs related to your area or topic might provide feedback on student design efforts. Such experts might judge student designs, ask questions, or provide stories related to their own design efforts. The ability to quickly and cost-effectively bring high levels of expertise and alternative perspectives to a class is a distinct advantage of fully online and blended learning environments across different age groups and populations. In fact, as is probably evident, accessing online expertise ranks among our top reasons for promoting online learning environments. We believe that online learning offers educational opportunities for perspective taking and mentoring that the world vastly needs today.

*Skills and Objectives.* Includes skill discrimination, appreciation of multiple perspectives, feedback, coaching, and expert insights.

*Advice and Ideas.* Keep a list of potential mentors or tutors with expertise related to your online class. Contact international experts in your field and ask for their help in mentoring your students. Assign mentors to student teams, groups, or individuals. Supply mentors with sample statements, tips, or other advice that they might provide to students. Consider allowing mentors to rotate to other individuals or groups as key tasks are accomplished or the semester unfolds.

If connecting with such individuals is exciting, consider developing a community of such experts. For incentives that can be offered to experts, you might check whether there are internal or external funds that can be used to reward the mentors for their online course assistance. We have found that informing others of our online collaborative activities and international mentoring efforts often results in free marketing of our projects as well as small amounts of funding for continuing them (including paying our mentors small stipends). Be sure to thank all experts and mentors for their support and keep them posted on the progress of your students.

*Variations and Extensions.* If collaborative teams are used, assign experts to monitor different groups for at least a portion of their group activity. Templates or scaffolds for the types of advice and coaching expected should be made available, especially for experts new to such an activity.

## Key Instructional Considerations

> *Risk index:* Medium
>
> *Time index:* Medium
>
> *Cost index:* Low to High (depending on honoraria paid to your mentors)
>
> *Learner-centered index:* Medium
>
> *Duration of the learning activity:* As needed

# Activity 61. Online Timeline Explorations and Safaris

*Description and Purpose of Activity.* A timeline is a way to visually display data and information that helps learners remember key factual knowledge as well as discover underlying themes and patterns within it. When you guide learners to an online timeline exploration or safari related to key content areas or concepts in a course, it can extend their learning beyond traditional instruction in interesting ways. For example, students reading the book *The Lord of the Rings* can explore a timeline of J.R.R. Tolkien's life (including 360-degree panoramic views of places he lived in Oxford, where he resided for more than fifty years) as well as a virtual tour of the city of Oxford itself (see Figure 7.2). While a static timeline can enhance the learning situation by visually organizing content, an interactive timeline that allows you to visit points selected or expand on content within particular dates or time periods is even more engaging for learners. Interactive timelines empower learners by encouraging greater self-directed learning. As tools

## FIGURE 7.2. WEB SITE FOR VIRTUAL TOUR OF OXFORD.

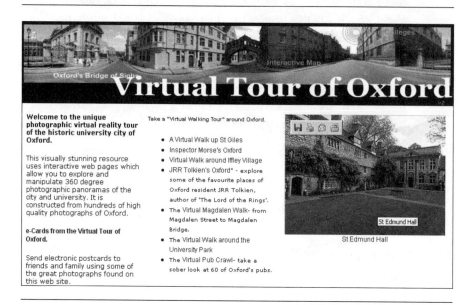

Welcome to the unique photographic virtual reality tour of the historic university city of Oxford.

This visually stunning resource uses interactive web pages which allow you to explore and manipulate 360 degree photographic panoramas of the city and university. It is constructed from hundreds of high quality photographs of Oxford.

**e-Cards from the Virtual Tour of Oxford.**

Send electronic postcards to friends and family using some of the great photographs found on this web site.

Take a "Virtual Walking Tour" around Oxford.

- A Virtual Walk up St Giles
- Inspector Morse's Oxford
- Virtual Walk around Iffley Village
- JRR Tolkien's Oxford" - explore some of the favourite places of Oxford resident JRR Tolkien, author of 'The Lord of the Rings'.
- The Virtual Magdalen Walk- from Magdalen Street to Magdalen Bridge.
- The Virtual Walk around the University Park
- The Virtual Pub Crawl- take a sober look at 60 of Oxford's pubs.

St Edmund Hall

for creating and using interactive timelines become more pervasive and user-friendly, they will increasingly be used in online courses.

While we see this technique primarily used in K–12 and higher education, online timelines are also employed in many types of training environments—for example, to illustrate product life cycles, such as that of the videocassette recorder (VCR) from its initial development in the 1970s to its pending demise today. Interactive online timelines often are valuable for detailing changes in military tactics in wars and conflicts over time, such as a comparison of the U.S. Civil War in the 1860s and the Vietnam War in the 1950s, 1960s, and 1970s. Such tools are also highly effective at demonstrating the impact of cultural or social intervention such as AIDS awareness or family planning in certain African countries.

You can ask your learners to explore objects and artifacts, dates, and key historical figures and events on the timeline. Students might also be asked to evaluate and present what they have discovered or compare what they have learned from the timeline to knowledge gained from other resources (for example, lectures, text, and so on) for that week or module. Experienced learners may be involved in the creation of such a timeline, individually or collaboratively, to visually represent their learning outcomes on a given topic (see Web resources for examples of online timeline tools).

***Skills and Objectives.*** Includes the visualization of facts, concepts, and events related to a course, logical thinking, insight, creative expression, product-based learning, and design skills.

***Advice and Ideas.*** Explore the Web for relevant timelines depicting concepts or data related to a key content area or unit within a course. Share the URLs of the relevant resources on the course Web site. Assign the exploration task with appropriate guides, scaffolds, and thought-stimulating questions. Require presentations and associated content critiques on what the learners have found.

If no high-quality timelines exist in your field, consider developing one or more of them for a course or topic within a course. Alternatively, assign students to develop such electronic timelines as part of an end-of-course assignment.

***Variations and Extensions.*** As a means to extend and connect their thinking, learners may be asked to present interesting and important resources that were linked within the timelines that they explored. Did any spontaneous or unexpected learning occur? In addition, students might be required to write reflective paper critiques on the timeline(s) of another student in the course and send that critique to the student, who must use it to redesign their timeline, or, alternatively, write a rebuttal.

## Key Instructional Considerations

> *Risk index:* Medium
>
> *Time index:* Medium to High
>
> *Cost index:* Low to High (depending on whether free timelines are available or need to be created)
>
> *Learner-centered index:* Medium to High
>
> *Duration of the learning activity:* 1–3 weeks

# Activity 62. Virtual Tours

***Description and Purpose of Activity.*** Similar to the previous activity, you might find an online tour corresponding to your course content or develop one of your own. Virtual tours might be especially relevant for displaying and engaging in content in fields such as geography, geology, archeology, religious studies, history, land management, forestry, space and aeronautics, natural resources, biology, anthropology, and zoology, though learners in many other content areas and disciplines can benefit from virtual tours. A virtual tour might be useful in military training, showing enemy terrain or simulated buildings. In addition, virtual tours can find use in health care settings when training information technology (IT) managers in complex operating systems, as well as in nonprofit organizations providing humanitarian relief training, governmental organizations charged with emergency preparedness training, or corporate situations involving employee relocations to a new plant or facility. In each of these situations, a chance to see the event, object, concept, or operation will enhance the learning process while reducing learner misconceptions or hesitancies.

***Skills and Objectives.*** Includes conceptual discrimination skills, coding information verbally as well as visually, identification and analysis of key concepts, and logical flow.

***Advice and Ideas.*** Search the Web for relevant virtual tours depicting concepts or data related to your class. If you find high-quality resources, consider writing to the original authors for additional information, or perhaps invite one or more experts into your online course for a synchronous chat. Virtual tour designers might also be asked for tour updates or information on other virtual tours in the area. If no high-quality tours exist, instructional designers, technology support services, or training department personnel might be solicited to develop one.

Post pertinent URLs to the course Web site. In addition, you might create a space for learners to post the links that they have found. Assign a virtual tour task with appropriate guides or scaffolds. Ask the learners for presentations or content critiques related to what they have found (for example, how would they restructure the virtual tour to make it more engaging and educationally valuable?).

***Variations and Extensions.*** Learners might be asked to find conceptual linkages or similarities between two or more online tours. Or, instead of using premade virtual tours, the learners might be asked to generate virtual tours for the class (*Note:* Such an activity links this task to Phase 4 of R2D2, where learners "do" something with their learning). After a virtual tour is used, instructors might conduct a discussion (online or FTF) related to concepts or ideas that became clearer as a result of the virtual tour.

## Key Instructional Considerations

*Risk index:* Medium

*Time index:* Medium

*Cost index:* Low to Medium (depends if online tours are available or if you need to build your own)

*Learner-centered index:* High

*Duration of the learning activity:* 1–2 weeks

# Activity 63. Visual Web Resource Explorations

*Description and Purpose of Activity.* As was mentioned in Chapter Six, there are many comprehensive Web sites that employ rich multimedia, such as the Valley of the Shadows and DNA from the Beginning (see Figure 7.3 for an example of the latter, showing animations, a picture gallery, video and audio files, links, and problems), freely available for anyone to use. Browse the Web for visual content related to your field or discipline. During this search, try to find and index high-quality databases of images, videos, and animations. Require learners to evaluate one or more of the visual resources discovered, or ask them to watch a videoclip interview or documentary related to a course topic and have them compare what they learned to their text-related knowledge. While the cost of such resources was often a deterrent for their use in the past, an amazing wealth of visual resources now exist online. At the time of this writing, there were more than 700,000 media files in Wikipedia alone (Wikipedia, 2007); these are all *free* to access and use in your classes. The times have certainly changed for teachers and trainers in all settings!

*Skills and Objectives.* Includes exploration skills, student autonomy and choice, visual discrimination skills, and analysis skills.

*Advice and Ideas.* Find an index of visually rich online resources related to your content area; perhaps explore open educational resources at the Multimedia Educational Resource for Learning and Online Teaching (MERLOT) or Connexions. Once sufficient online resources and materials are found, create a set of Web resource links related to each module or week in the course. Assign one or more such resources each week for learners to explore. Provide a job aid, scaffold, or guide sheet for student exploration. Require presentation, reflection, critique, concept mapping, visual representation, or some other capstone event.

## FIGURE 7.3.  DNA FROM THE BEGINNING WEB SITE.

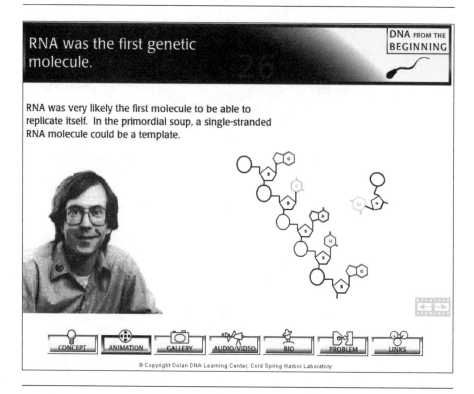

To extend your resource pool, ask experts and colleagues for advice on visually rich Web resources that they have used in similar courses. At the same time, index interesting sites when you learn about them in newsletters, at conferences, or from colleagues. Save any high-quality student and colleague submissions that might be mined for relevant resources later on.

*Variations and Extensions.*  Ask learners to submit one or two relevant Web resources or comprehensive Webliographies at key moments in the course. Students might also be asked to write reflection papers comparing the concepts that became clearer from exploring two or more online visual resources.

### Key Instructional Considerations

> *Risk index:* Low
> *Time index:* Low

*Cost index:* Low

*Learner-centered index:* Medium

*Duration of the learning activity:* 1–2 weeks as needed

## Activity 64. Animations

***Description and Purpose of Activity.*** As noted in Chapter Five, online educators, training organizations, and institutions are increasingly relying on animations as a tool for displaying complex content. The fact that costs for the storage of such animations have plummeted at the same time that the size of such files are shrinking has been a catalyst for growing acceptance and use of animations across all types of learning situations. While the use of animations may have been an infrequent or nonexistent event in our own schooling, the learner of today is coming to expect such opportunities. As such, instructors, trainers, or tutors can search the Web for animations relevant to their course content and embed them in the course or create their own. Once again, assign student reflections based on the content. When effectively used, such animations can provide visual anchors for later student learning.

***Skills and Objectives.*** Includes visual discrimination skills, student engagement, understanding logical sequence, and coding of information both verbally and visually.

***Advice and Ideas.*** Decide what topics or units may require or benefit from animations in the course. Find useful animations and categorize those you have found while noting which need permissions for use. Obtain permissions from copyright holders as necessary. Short animations can be powerful learning tools; however, be sure that they do not distract from key course goals and objectives. Embed animations at appropriate moments in the course and share what you have accomplished with colleagues both within and outside your organization. If possible, expand on the use of animations based on course results and positive learner feedback.

If no relevant animations exist, talk to your training department, instructional design staff, teaching and learning center personnel, or instructional consulting office about the possibilities of creating animation files related to your class. If you do not have technical support, consider writing a grant proposal or project plan for possible funding.

*Variations and Extensions.* If the learners possess adequate technological skills, provide an optional assignment to create course animations. If the course is a blended one, consider requiring students to use one or more animations in a class presentation. For example, one student or group of students might be assigned to present course concepts each week using a different animation resource or Web site; unless your students are technologically savvy or you teach in a technology-related field, this assumes premade materials.

## Key Instructional Considerations

> *Risk index:* Medium
>
> *Time index:* Medium
>
> *Cost index:* Medium to High
>
> *Learner-centered index:* Medium
>
> *Duration of the learning activity:* 1 week or as needed

## Activity 65. Advance Organizers: Models, Flowcharts, Diagrams, Systems, and Illustrations

*Description and Purpose of Activity.* Advance organizers were noted in Chapter Six as a means of helping students in an assortment of learning situations to connect new learning to their prior knowledge. The positive track record and relatively long history of advance organizers in education and training provides instructors with a powerful and highly familiar activity for learners in blended or fully online situations. For instance, instructors or learning designers might find that relevant online models, flowcharts, organizational charts, and illustrations can make highly abstract or novel content more understandable. Models can help learners elucidate complex behavior patterns, variable interactions, and flow processes (van Dam, Becker, & Simpson, 2005). Instructors might search for such models or organizational aids and explore their use as well as develop custom ones as needed.

*Skills and Objectives.* Includes critical thinking and analysis, comparison and contrast, priming knowledge, linking new knowledge to prior knowledge, and inferencing skills. A key goal of these types of activities relates to perceiving the macrostructure or big picture behind the concepts or ideas.

*Advice and Ideas.* Determine what organizational aids are available for your content area; you might find comparison and contrast charts, flowcharts, sequence chains, matrices, visual analogies of key terms, or some other visual representation or conceptual structure. Design advance organizers if none are readily available. Embed those found or created in your course learning materials. Another option would be to assign learners to construct their own advance organizers. When assignments are complete, evaluate the effectiveness of different types of organizational aids.

Test or evaluate the effectiveness of different organizational aids on learner memory. Certain aids may be better for different fields. If in K–12 education, find online lesson plan sites (for example, Teachers.net, the Lesson Plans Page, Discovery School, Education World; see Web resources) and explore these for advance organizers and other visual resources. If in higher education, explore MERLOT, Connexions, Jorum, and other learning portals or learning object repositories for such content. In addition, inquiries might be sent to book publishers and other resource providers about the types of supplemental aids or advance organizers they offer. Those in corporate training might explore internally indexed knowledge management resources.

*Variations and Extensions.* Consider alternating between instructor-developed advance organizers and those that require learners to complete part of them.

## Key Instructional Considerations

*Risk index:* Low

*Time index:* Medium

*Cost index:* Low to Medium

*Learner-centered index:* Medium

*Duration of the learning activity: 1 week or as needed*

# Activity 66. Virtual Field Trips

*Description and Purpose of Activity.* In addition to virtual tours, mentioned previously, the Web contains thousands of virtual field trips to different geographic places, historical events, and famous individuals. Many of these have been developed for K–12 education, though they could be used in an assortment of classes in higher education, including courses on geography, geology, education, history, political science, and the humanities. Teacher education students, for instance, might explore a virtual field trip designed to acquaint them with another country or locale prior to starting an overseas teaching experience there. In contrast, students in a geology course might be immersed in an aerial view of different land formations in a country or region of the world that can be redisplayed for different time periods or to highlight significant geological events. Students in a college course on ancient European history might be taken to specific landmarks or statues at the Acropolis in Athens, Greece, different views and points of interest at Stonehenge in the United Kingdom, or the remains of the Roman Coliseum in Italy.

There are myriad virtual field trips for younger learners as well. Virtual field trips to the Gettysburg National Military Park using online videoconferencing, for instance, allow high school students to view reenactments of this famous battle and turning point of the U.S. Civil War while simultaneously allowing them to ask questions of park rangers and other authorities and listen to storytelling experts. Other online resources on Gettysburg provide panoramic views of the many different battlefields there as well as the photos taken, monuments created, and books written.

Virtual field trips are so popular at the K–12 level, in fact, that the Florida Virtual School (FLVS) offers online virtual clubs and organizes many virtual field trips that connect online students with their peers (Brumfield, 2006). Students in the FLVS not only attend virtual field trips, they can use the knowledge gained to collaborate on national and international competitions (for example, the design of airplanes or bridges). Involvement in online field trips enlivens the content for students, and, if experts are part of the virtual field trip experience, lowers feelings of isolation.

***Skills and Objectives.*** Includes visual discrimination skills, conceptual analysis, and logical thinking. The virtual tour might be used for student review of concepts learned or to prime those they are about to encounter.

***Advice and Ideas.*** There are a wide range of virtual field trip portals categorized by grade and discipline; although most are designed for K–12 environments, many are available for higher education courses in such areas an anthropology, urban planning, archeology, geology, and geography. The University of Virginia and the University of California-Los Angeles have teamed up to create a virtual tour of ancient Rome in which the user can explore monuments, streets, aqueducts, bridges, buildings (for example, the Coliseum), and the overall typography and layout of the city itself. Field trips of different countries and regions of the world such as Chichen Itza in Mexico are now available in the highly popular virtual world, Second Life. In fact, exploring the wonders of the ancient and modern worlds takes on new meaning in Second Life. As tour companies make these virtual worlds available for exploration, instructors need to think creatively about how to use them in their teaching. They are typically *free*, so why not use them?

There are also tours of the world available in YouTube videos, such as the famous Where the Hell Is Matt? or Where in Google Earth Is Matt?, which showcase Matt Harding's explorations around the planet (he is known for his offbeat dancing at each stop). While Matt's initial journey was self-paid after he quit his job, he later received funding from Stride Gum as well as Google to dance around the world and document his adventures for others to view and learn from. From Angkor, Cambodia, to the Antarctic Peninsula to the Stratosphere Tower in Las Vegas to the streets of London to the Impenetrable Forest of Uganda to Bangkok, Thailand, to the Sydney Aquarium to ancient Mayan cities in Guatemala to Chuuk, Micronesia, to San Francisco to Cape Town to New York, Matt will lead your class on an exciting adventure around the world. With the emergence of Google Earth and other online mapping programs, virtual tours are becoming increasingly commonplace. Now is the time to begin experimenting with such exciting tools with which you can inspire learners into innovative learning quests and perhaps even new careers.

Explore virtual field trip activities and resources (for example, see the Web resources at the end of the book) and find ones that are relevant to your content area. Many virtual field trips also include teacher resources and advice. Advice for getting started (as well as templates or forms for student reflection and evaluation) is often provided. Explore such resources before reinventing the wheel. To add value to existing resources while contributing to the world bank of innovative uses of online technology in teaching, you can create interesting pedagogical activities around any virtual field trips you use. You might design novel debates, role plays, scavenger hunts, and interactive reflections around the virtual field trip; the exact nature of the activity will depend on your content area or discipline. When done, be sure to discuss and debrief the activity with your learners.

**Variations and Extensions.** In a blended course, students might use the virtual tours as a presentation tool or a means to arouse interest in a particular topic.

## Key Instructional Considerations

*Risk index:* Medium

*Time index:* Medium

*Cost index:* Low

*Learner-centered index:* Medium

*Duration of the learning activity:* As needed

## Activity 67. Video Modeling and Professional Development

*Description and Purpose of Activity.* Professional schools and corporate training organizations are increasingly employing online videos to demonstrate how skills are used in the real world or on the job. The Department of Psychiatry at Trinity College in Dublin, Ireland, for instance, has a virtual interview project through which students have opportunities to conduct interviews with virtual patients. When using these resources, the student decides what questions to ask and can then watch student responses to them.

Similarly, at Indiana University, teacher educators are using online video with preservice teachers, where they watch video lessons of exemplary math and science teachers. The lessons in this project (that is, "The Inquiry Learning Forum") are linked to the teacher lesson plans, teacher reflections, discipline-related standards, student work, and other relevant online resources. As shown in Figure 7.4, the E-Read Ohio program also effectively relies on expert videos for teacher professional development. In both cases, the online videos provide insights into skills and competencies needed within a profession. Such practice activities provide confidence for learners and are a safe harbor for practicing newly acquired skills before interacting with individuals in real-life situations. Video modeling can be used in nearly any discipline or profession. For instance, video resources are used by corporations and nonprofit organizations for training accountants, managers, sales agents, engineers, scientists, and call center personnel.

*Skills and Objectives.* Includes comparison and contrast, observational skills, enhanced reflection, inferencing, and evaluation. A key goal is to witness concepts in action and begin to internalize them. The videos are part of an apprenticeship or coaching process.

*Advice and Ideas.* Find or develop professional videos showcasing the real-world application of knowledge and skills related to your course or topic. Create a set of reflection questions or other learning activities around the video content. Be sure to provide students with feedback on their discussions and reflections. For instance, point out concepts and connections that are misunderstood, ignored, overlooked, or simply missed.

Professional development videos can be highly expensive. Find video materials and content that already exist in colleagues' offices, online learning repositories, and publishers' supplements. If possible, link any video selections to discipline standards, especially to recently changed or emerging standards. Such connections are highly effective in apprenticing students into a field of study or career.

## FIGURE 7.4. E-READ OHIO PROGRAM DISPLAYING VIDEO OF A TEACHER SCAFFOLDING A STUDENT IN READING.

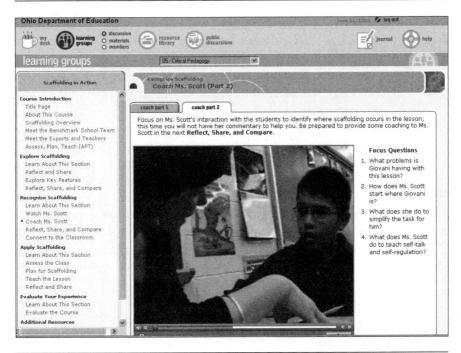

Used by permission of the University of Akron/Ohio Department of Education and by permission of Teachscape.

***Variations and Extensions.*** Assign students to watch two or more videos for a particular unit or module and write reflection papers in which they compare and contrast the skills applied or misapplied. Also, consider having students compare their reflections to their peers. For instance, partners might analyze their interpretations of different concepts and principles in the videos; they might note which ones they assessed the same or differently.

## Key Instructional Considerations

*Risk index:* Medium

*Time index:* Medium to High

*Cost index:* Low to High (depending on whether videos are freely available)

*Learner-centered index:* Medium

*Duration of the learning activity:* 3–5 weeks (or entire course)

---

# Activity 68. Movie Reviews for Professional Development

***Description and Purpose of Activity.*** Popular movies and television shows may also embed content related to your online class. We have used popular movies in our own online teaching activities. In Bonk's undergraduate as well as graduate educational psychology classes, he refers to dozens of different movies (for example, *Freedom Writers, Stand and Deliver, Dead Poets Society, Man Without a Face, Mr. Holland's Opus*) to display different instructional approaches, psychological concepts, and learning philosophies. Language instructors in both higher education and corporate training incorporate popular movies as a key activity in their courses. When selecting a movie, it should contain a multitude of relevant concepts and principles that link to your course content or that might provide the seeds for an online debate or discussion. Students can be assigned to watch and compare one or more movies (we typically assign two). When done, they might be asked to write reflection papers and create term glossaries based on the movies they watched.

In such tasks, we provide many movie options and allow students to suggest their own movies since those in different countries might not have access to all the movies that we list. And, by having the students rent, purchase, or borrow movies or watch them directly in a cinema or on television, we avoid copyright violations. (*Note:* Differences in copyright laws may make this assignment harder to conduct in certain countries or regions of the world.) We do not post movies to the Web, not even short clips or teasers. This is one case in which the primary content is not on the Web, but instead the Web is used for later interactive discussions as well as the posting of completed assignments. Of course, as with many of the 100+ activities we detail in this book, such an activity can also be used in traditional FTF classes.

***Skills and Objectives.*** Includes inferencing and evaluation skills, comparison and contrast, conceptual analysis and attainment, and observing skills or competencies used in alternative contexts.

***Advice and Ideas.*** We typically assign the movie review as a capstone activity in some of our online classes, although it could work effectively at other points in the course. Talk with colleagues about your movie selections, as most of them will have ideas and opinions as to what might or might not work.

Keep a running list of popular (and not so popular) movies or TV programs with annotations as to how they each relate to your profession or discipline. You might ask questions related to how concepts learned in a course are explicitly or implicitly seen in the movie. If you are in teacher education, for instance, learners might be asked to link different terms in the movie to create a learning model or theory. They also might be asked to compare and contrast views of learning and learners in each movie. In terms of such theories, just how are teachers portrayed in the movie? And what is the overall learning environment like? To help them process key principles and ideas related to different learning theories, we ask our learners to reflect on how their views changed or shifted while watching these movies. In their reflections, we require our students to explicitly include content from at least a few of the course topics or weeks.

Finding movies or TV shows in professional disciplines such as business, law, medicine, and education is not difficult. In addition, many movie trailers and short pieces of a movie are available in online resources such as YouTube. Again, be sure to abide by policies of your institution or organization when incorporating such video snippets into your courses. Such short clips can be shown in an FTF class setting prior to learners watching an entire movie as a means to excite them about their movie watching. There clearly is an abundance of teaching- and learning-related movies, with at least one popular teaching-related video appearing every year. When we employ them, psychological terms such as *instructional scaffolding, social modeling, negative* and *positive reinforcement, cueing,* and *achievement motivation* come alive.

Given the richness of these movies, it is important to design critique or analysis assignments with sufficient guidelines as well as to inform learners of all the key task procedures and evaluation criteria. For instance, we grade student papers for such criteria as insight and relationships or connections drawn, clear and logical flow, rich and novel information provided, clear understanding of course theories, thoroughness, and self-awareness. As a final step, we typically ask students if we can save their movie reviews and analyses for future classes and also share them with the current class. Finally, we encourage students to nominate movies and TV shows that we may have overlooked so as to make our courses learner centered while simultaneously enabling us to continue updating and adding to our movie lists.

***Variations and Extensions.*** Most students love this assignment. For some, it becomes an avenue for them to discuss their learning with their partners, peers, friends, and relatives since they can all watch the movie together and discuss course topics and principles. As a means to motivate them still further, you might inform students of your movie favorites or provide bonus points for hard to find but high-quality ones. An additional way to spice things up is to create two movie review lists—an A list and a B list. The A list should include movies that are directly related to course content; movies in the B list are less related. The use of movie lists can foster discussion of concepts that are more or less obvious or clear in different genres or types of movies. Movie list B might stretch student thinking or help them avoid overgeneralizing a concept. Such an assignment can foster deeper reflection on concepts that may be more implicitly embedded in such movies; that is, concepts that students may not have originally thought about (for example, cognitive apprenticeship, scaffolded learning, and modeling in *Star Wars* and *Lord of the Rings;* cognitive information processing and memory in *Finding Nemo;* Piagetian stages of cognitive development in the movie *Kindergarten Cop*). Such movie reviews might be linked to other activities in the course such as the discussion forums, debates, or expert chats.

### Key Instructional Considerations

> *Risk index:* Medium
>
> *Time index:* Medium
>
> *Cost index:* Low
>
> *Learner-centered index:* High
>
> *Duration of the learning activity:* 1–3 weeks

## Activity 69. Whiteboard Demonstrations

*Description and Purpose of Activity.* Instructors and trainers as well as their students might use interactive whiteboards during synchronous chats, Webinars, and other real-time online presentations. Statistics, chemistry, or mathematics professors might show derivations of formulas; language tutors might highlight correct grammar usage; sales trainers might display key components or features of a new product or promotional item; Internal Revenue agents might showcase new tax codes and policies; and computer science instructors might detail common (as well as not so common) code errors or mistakes. In all these situations, the whiteboard focuses learners on specific details or pieces of information.

*Skills and Objectives.* Includes concept attainment, visualization skills, design skills, inferencing, insight, and new conceptual linkages.

*Advice and Ideas.* Create a small-group learning activity related to your topic or course that may be best conducted with an interactive whiteboard. Given the novelty of such tools for most instructors, ask for help from instructional design staff or colleagues if needed and also test the system prior to use. (*Note:* Many course management systems come with an interactivity whiteboard tool or capability that is often connected to the chat system.) Coordinate times and dates for the virtual meeting. Ask learners to test the whiteboard tool on their own computers ahead of time. To initiate the actual session, select the whiteboard tool and use some of the features to demonstrate key concepts or processes. Perhaps allow students opportunities to assume control or modify or add to your ideas. When completed, gather feedback on how well the session went, and survey your learners on how the current activity might be improved or how a whiteboard might be used in the future course activities.

Experiment in a small way and see what works, perhaps with one group or small team and then perhaps with the entire class.

*Variations and Extensions.* Instead of using an online whiteboard as a one-way teaching device, for a more rich and interactive experience, require all class or group members to use the marking tools at some point in the activity. For instance, a small group might generate idea maps related to a key course concept or idea. Or the whiteboard might be used in small-group discussions to outline project steps or create agendas.

## Key Instructional Considerations

*Risk index:* Medium

*Time index:* Low

*Cost index:* Low

*Learner-centered index:* Low to High (depends on use)

*Duration of the learning activity:* As needed

# Activity 70. Online Visualization Tools

*Description and Purpose of Activity.* In response to the information explosion of the past few decades, information visualization and data-mining tools have definitely been on the rise. Visualization tools might be used for viewing and manipulating visuals, interpreting relationships, understanding abstract concepts, and clarifying difficult-to-understand text (Jonassen, 1996). At the same time, visualization tools can help learners express or communicate what they have learned.

For example, meteorology students have access to online tools for visualizing weather patterns across continents during particular weeks, months, or seasons of the year as well as analyzing storm formations during the hurricane season in the United States. Such weather-related visualization tools are critical for adventurers in dangerous situations, such as those climbing Mount Everest, since they can quickly realize when a storm is about to hit as well as access temperature and wind speed data by time and date during their tough climbs.

For younger learners, environmental and weather-related projects such as Kids as Global Scientists, the Global Learning and Observations to Benefit the Environment (GLOBE) program project, and Journey North enable middle and secondary students to learn the techniques of scientific inquiry and experimentation (Pea, 2002). Using online tools and maps, students might observe the stability of ocean temperatures in certain equatorial parts of the world as compared to polar regions, map out bird migration patterns across regions of a country or continent, or investigate changes in the ozone level.

In corporate training, online tools and resources might help learners visualize key business processes such as cash flow, supply chain management, customer service procedures, or innovative viral marketing techniques. As such, these tools can expedite training and significantly reduce learner time away from work.

Online visualization tools are often found in the hard sciences. Visualization tools exist in mathematics, chemistry, statistics, physics, and many other areas. Chemistry tools enable learners to view, rotate, and measure molecules, thereby helping them understand complex atomic interactions that would not have been visible with static graphs or pictures (Jonassen, 1996). Similarly, the Mathematics Visualization Toolkit (MVT) from the University of Colorado at Boulder enables students to visually see concepts in action and come to a deeper understanding of mathematical principles. This free resource won the Math-Classics and Editors' Choice award from MERLOT in 2005.

Another visualization tool for mathematical disciplines, Maple, is extensively used in myriad technical fields and industries including automotive, biotechnology, electronics, finance, aerospace, and mechanical systems. Although it is not free, Maple is extremely popular in higher education, governmental, and corporate settings. Maple's dynamic demonstrations and animations of complex mathematical concepts, principles, and properties in such areas as calculus, algebra, physics, and differential equations, foster student problem solving and knowledge representation.

***Skills and Objectives.*** Includes visualization skills, interpreting relationships, clarifying concepts, and knowledge flexibility. An objective of these tools is to build a visual track from which to recall or use course information later.

*Advice and Ideas.* Explore the Web, including useful knowledge repository sites (for example, MERLOT, Connexions, Jorum) for free and useful data visualization tools. Experiment with selected tools and perhaps pilot their use in a small way. Provide any necessary learner training on selected tools with tutorials, demonstrations, and examples. Create a group or individual project using one of the visualization tools mentioned above or found elsewhere. Share and showcase the visualization products within the class. Evaluate the learning outcomes and effectiveness of these tools.

E-mail or talk to colleagues about your plans and ask if they are interested in joining up. The original developer of the visualization might be e-mailed for advice or for information on usergroups or online communities related to that tool or product that your students might join or observe.

*Variations and Extensions.* Instructors or trainers might consider cross-class collaboration with different visualization tools and resources. Students may be more impressed if they begin to realize a particular visualization tool is deemed valuable by others.

## Key Instructional Considerations

> *Risk index:* Medium
>
> *Time index:* Medium to High (depending on whether relevant tools already exist or must be built)
>
> *Cost index:* Low to High
>
> *Learner-centered index:* Medium
>
> *Duration of the learning activity:* As needed

# Activity 71. Video Blogs and Adventure Learning

*Description and Purpose of Activity.* As indicated in Chapter Six, the ability to add videos to blogs will make them more appealing to visual learners. Adventurers and explorers have always attempted to include some visual data to enhance and add credibility to text-based diaries of their exciting journeys. As an example, Mark Fennell, a graphic designer from Sydney, Australia, often includes pictures, video documentaries, Flash animations, and audio clips to complement the highly captivating narratives surrounding his journeys. Fennell's blog contains an innovative interface with topographical maps to support his accounts and brilliant panoramic views (Bienias, 2004).

Similar blogs and stories are maintained by explorers such as Ben Saunders, who, at age twenty-six, was the youngest person to ski solo to the North Pole (see Figure 7.5). Through his 2004 expedition, Saunders raised awareness concerning global warming as he documented the thinning of the ice, open water, and temperatures up to 15 degrees higher than a similar trek he made in 2000. Learners and instructors in subject areas such as tourism, geography, history, telecommunications, outdoor education, environmental ethics, global warming, recreation, and world cultures might find such blogs highly informative and useful. Or, rather than simply accessing existing blog content, you might have students design "adventure" blogs or video blogs (vblogs) related to some aspect of your course content.

## FIGURE 7.5. ADVENTURE BLOG AND WEB SITE OF BRITISH EXPLORER BEN SAUNDERS.

***Skills and Objectives.*** Includes modeling, student motivation and excitement for learning, and awareness of concept use in the real world.

***Advice and Ideas.*** Search for video blogs that relate to course content; if appropriate, find those filled with actions and current events from adventure bloggers. Tools such as Technorati and Google Blog Search can help with such blog searches.

Given the newness of video blogs, be sure to view and review prospective video blogs carefully for validity and reliability before using in classes or training sessions. Beware of possible controversial topics and situations (for example, blogs with videos and eyewitness accounts of people being shot by government or military officials, blogs noting oil spills or environmental dilemmas related to potential drilling sites in the Arctic, blogs on stem cell research, and blogs with firsthand accounts documenting aspects of wars not covered in the popular media). Along these same lines, try to be sensitive to the diverse perspectives that global online educational resources may bring to your class as well the diverse views your learners may want to learn about and share.

Develop course-related activities around the video blogs you have chosen. If no relevant video blogs exist, consider having students create their own adventure blogs or other vblogs related to certain topics or aspects of the course and invite experts to provide feedback to these students on their vblogged events.

We need to caution the reader that, depending on the degree of student control and the connectedness with course content, this could be considered a high-risk activity. Keep searching—while adventure blogs and video blogs may not exist in your discipline today, there may be dozens in a year or two. Pedagogical use of such tools is still at an extremely formative stage, which makes creative use, documentation, and dissemination essential.

***Variations and Extensions.*** Contact a famed adventure blogger (or expert) for a class chat or asynchronous discussion, or ask one or more authors of adventure blogs to answer a few class questions.

## Key Instructional Considerations

*Risk index:* High

*Time index:* Medium

*Cost index:* Low to Medium (depending on task and equipment required)

*Learner-centered index:* Medium

*Duration of the learning activity:* 1–4 weeks

## Activity 72. Charts and Graph Tools

*Description and Purpose of Activity.* Embedding figures, charts, and graphs in content is not only visually appealing and engaging, it also allows learners to dual code information in both a visual and verbal manner. If a chart or graph is provided as an advance organizer (see Activity 65 in this chapter), it helps learners link new learning to existing learning or what is called "prior knowledge." As indicated previously, the considerable reductions in online storage costs during the past decade have paved the way for increasing use of charts, figures, graphs, and related content in any type of learning environment or situation, both formal and informal. Increasingly, instructional designers have allowed for such charts and graphs to be manipulable or have built activities that require the learner to complete partially filled-in visuals. Such activities link Phase 4 of R2D2 to Phase 4 (when the learner does something with the new learning).

*Skills and Objectives.* Includes visualization skills, motivation, inferencing, analysis, and perceiving relationships. A typical goal behind the use of charts, graphs, and figures is to grasp a theme or pattern or see the big picture.

*Advice and Ideas.* Determine where charts and graphs will enhance learning in your class. You might specifically ask students in both formative and summative course evaluations where in the course charts and graphs learning might be better enhanced. Contact publishers for supplemental online resources such as charts, figures, and graphs that they may maintain in a supplemental Web site for a textbook. Or correspond with other instructors in your department, program, or field for examples of online charts and graphs that they employ in similar courses.

Create a few pilot charts and graphs and ask for learner feedback and revise accordingly. Embed final charts and graphs in your learning materials. Encourage and demonstrate uses of these charts and graphics as cognitive tools for knowledge construction, representation, and restructuring or interlinking of ideas across members of the class.

*Variations and Extensions.* Assign students to build visuals for three or more chapters, units, weeks, or modules of the course. Perhaps have the class vote on their favorites, which receive bonus points and are reused in the following semesters or versions of the course.

### Key Instructional Considerations

*Risk index:* Low

*Time index:* Low to Medium

*Cost index:* Low

*Learner-centered index:* High

*Duration of the learning activity:* 1–2 weeks or as needed

# Activity 73. Mashups of Google Maps

***Description and Purpose of Activity.*** With so many visual resources and tools being developed for the Web, it is not surprising that some e-learning innovators and pioneers are suggesting *mashups,* in which a Web site or application combines information from multiple sources. For example, when using the tool Earthquakes in the Last Week, Google Maps can be "mashuped" with various types of content, such as data on earthquakes above a 2.5 magnitude from the U.S. Geological Survey (Branzburg, 2006). With such tools, your learners will not only be able to read about earthquake concepts and principles in their textbooks, but visually grasp where earthquakes have been occurring, including ones mentioned in recent news stories.

Besides locating earthquakes, Google Maps are helping people find transportation routes in dense cities such as London or New York. In addition, the Google Planimeter tool is a fantastic visual aid for geometry courses since it allows learners to measure the area between three or more points on Google Maps. And for those who like to walk, Gmaps Pedometer can be used with Google Maps to visually plot different routes for running or walking and then calculate how far one has traveled. And, finally, YourGMap allows learners to create tours of actual neighborhoods while marking key landmarks with comments and other identifiers, and then make the selected neighborhood available for others to explore on the Internet (Branzberg, 2006). While elementary students might designate city landmarks and places of interest such as grocery stores, police stations, parks, schools, and rivers, those in a college-level course on urban planning can take note of historical monuments, traffic flows, population densities, and recent areas of city growth. Those majoring in architecture might compare unique building designs and styles.

While most of these tools have taken initial root in K–12 education, the coming decade will witness a proliferation of mashups of different types of visuals— maps, timelines, concept maps, Venn diagrams, graphs, and so on—across all learning sectors. As such online visualization devices emerge, it could lead to new types of learning and levels of insight within a course, as well as to entirely new learning styles. Undoubtedly, such techniques will foster discussions of what it means to be visually literate that perhaps will lead to new forms of literacy assessments related to twenty-first-century skills.

*Skills and Objectives.* Includes insight, pattern recognition, perceiving unique concept connections, and visualization.

*Advice and Ideas.* Decide on an activity for which you might use Google Maps or other maps provided via the Web. Alternatively, think of other online tools or resources that you might mashup. For example, create an activity in a geometry class that mashups Google Maps and Google Planimeter. Using the Google Planimeter tool, students can estimate the area of a state, province, country, or geographic region. Geometry students might be asked to calculate the square miles of Lake Michigan by clicking three points on a map and then having Google Planimeter connect them in a triangle and compute the area, which is then compared to student estimates. As more data points are added for accuracy, such triangles created with the Planimeter automatically expand outward into a polygon with many sides, thereby increasing the accuracy of such calculations. Students might continue to plot more points to obtain still greater accuracy. If you experiment with this task, be sure to have your students predict the square miles that will be estimated from the points selected. After each round, you might then have students compare and discuss results.

Mashups make learning more alive and meaningful. Experiment with them where possible; perhaps have students suggest new activities. And keep in mind that they are just one option for creative use of the plethora of online visualization tools and resources available today.

*Variations and Extensions.* Show one example of a mashup to your learners and then conduct a brainstorming session in which they suggest interesting online resources that might be mashuped.

## Key Instructional Considerations

> *Risk index:* High
>
> *Time index:* Medium
>
> *Cost index:* Low
>
> *Learner-centered index:* High
>
> *Duration of the learning activity:* 1–3 weeks or as needed

---

# Activity 74. Broadcast Events

*Description and Purpose of Activity.* Many professional fields and disciplines have benefited from the recent explosion of visual data, especially as the Internet2 has enabled greater bandwidth or throughput over the Web. In the medical field, for instance, it is possible to access large databases of images as well as video-streams of live surgeries, while simultaneously connecting learners and instructors across different sites to highly esteemed medical experts. With the Internet2, it is becoming increasingly common to view real-time streaming videos of surgical and other medical procedures as they occur. Expert surgeons might augment views of the surgical procedure being displayed with their insights and commentaries as well as virtual images related to the body area on which the surgery is taking place (Dev et al., 2004–2005).

The combined use of video, static images, audio, and other resources creates a highly rich learning environment. While multisite demonstrations with expert commentaries are relatively new and still evolving, they are a powerful instructional delivery method. Keep in mind that such live events are not restricted to medical schools—this type of online professional development is occurring in many fields. For instance, future K–12 teachers observe live classrooms, law students watch live court hearings, and political science students remotely view Senate hearings online.

***Skills and Objectives.*** Includes visual discrimination skills, reflection skills, and observing skills used in real-world contexts.

***Advice and Ideas.*** Determine where virtual surgeries and other visually rich medical resources may play a role in a medical curriculum. Coordinate the broadcast of such events, including the recipients, instructional activities, expert opinions, and associated commentary. When complete, be sure to archive the events for future educational uses.

While powerful as a learning tool, live demonstrations of surgical procedures can be extremely expensive and complicated to coordinate. Consequently, it is vital to conduct several rehearsals or dry runs of the event with any camera, lighting, sound, and other production personnel, if possible. Given the novelty, complexity, and potential expense of such demonstrations, this is one activity in which the advice from those who have attempted it in the past would be extremely valuable. In a few years, such activities will likely be more common and less expensive; hence, there will be more examples to read and experts from whom to seek advice.

The medical area is not the only one in which such visually rich, live events might enhance learning. Broadcast events might also take place related to historical reenactments, anthropological digs and ancient discoveries, space shuttle transmissions of significant events and exercises, and political debates. Recently the use of embedded journalists in wars and conflicts has brought significant news events live into classrooms years before they might appear in books and curriculum objectives. In these cases, however, there is far less pre-scripting of the activity. Since the instructor cannot preplan many instructional activities in such situations, traits such as creative spontaneity, flexibility, patience, and persistence might be required for those venturing into this area. At the same time, the sheer excitement of the live event should be enough to motivate student participation and engagement—thereby elevating student learning—despite the ill structured nature of the event.

*Variations and Extensions.* Wrap a series of activities around the broadcast event such as discussion groups, chats, reflection papers, and student generated visual analyses (for example, Venn diagrams, charts).

## Key Instructional Considerations

*Risk index:* High

*Time index:* Medium

*Cost index:* High

*Learner-centered index:* Medium

*Duration of the learning activity:* As needed

---

# Activity 75. Online Multimedia and Visually Rich Cases

*Description and Purpose of Activity.* In addition to videos of live surgeries, as in the previous activity, students can learn from multimedia and from visually rich cases. For instance, several anatomy sites allow you to explore rich case information; some even contain virtual autopsies of patients as well as many types of medical cases. While not necessarily the most appealing learning activity mentioned in this book, virtual autopsies provide authentic data that can hook or captivate previously absent or aloof learners and promote their learning journeys.

The University of Leicester in the United Kingdom has a number of freely available autopsy cases (see Figure 7.6, as well as Web resources). Anatomy students might be asked to search such virtual autopsies for specific information or data. Although each emerging technology (for example, videodiscs, compact discs (CDs), Internet, and so on) usually promotes its benefits for medical cases, media rich cases now exist on the Web for most any professional discipline—engineering, business, education, law—and this availability will undoubtedly increase in complexity, quality, and ease of use during the next few years.

## FIGURE 7.6. VIRTUAL AUTOPSY CASE LEARNING EXAMPLE FROM THE UNIVERSITY OF LEICESTER.

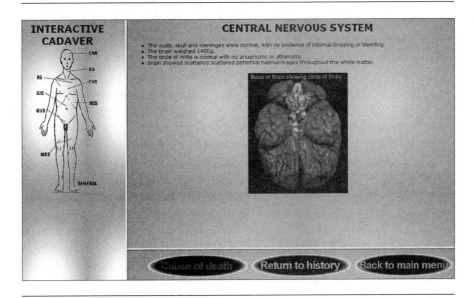

In education, for instance, a case of a teacher facing a problem might have links to classroom footage, teacher lesson plans and objectives, student portfolios, curriculum standards, teacher reflections on how the lesson went and what could be done differently, and online discussions about the case. Preservice and inservice teachers might access a databank of such rich cases and compare their solutions or ideas to those of dozens of previous learners. Videostreams from actual schools provide live cases for preservice teachers to reflect on. In business, a rich case might include a video of the case situation, links to implications of alternative solutions, interviews with key participants, decision making questions or guides, final products or solution tasks, and expert evaluations of user solutions. Business students might compare their ideas to each other or across teams that the instructor has set up to solve the case problems. As with schools, live video feeds can provide real-time case problems for a class to reflect on and solve.

Clearly, such learning approaches bode well not only for professional training in a college or university setting but also for recertification and skill upgrades when practicing in the real world. As dual-coding principles and theories of human motivation contend (see Chapter Two), online multimedia cases are more engaging and powerful than typical text-based cases.

*Skills and Objectives.* Includes concept discrimination, critical analyses, visualization, comparison and contrast, inferencing, and evaluation skills. A key goal is to facilitate the encoding of information both visually and verbally.

*Advice and Ideas.* Review the online cases available in your discipline or field of study. If available online cases are inadequate, consider developing cases with support from instructional design staff, personnel in one's teaching and learning center, or training department staff and resources. Alternatively, one might author innovative grant proposals earmarked for such resources or partner with other organizations or institutions to create them.

When multimedia cases have been procured, assign learners to different cases to analyze individually or in small groups. Have learners share and compare their analyses and solutions either online or in FTF meetings. Debate and reflect upon the findings and solutions.

Write to the designers of any excellent available cases to ask how they use them.

*Variations and Extensions.* Hold case solution competitions between groups, or create collaborations with students at other universities in which students discuss and debate online case problems.

## Key Instructional Considerations

*Risk index:* Medium

*Time index:* Medium

*Cost index:* Low to High (depending on cases available)

*Learner-centered index:* Medium

*Duration of the learning activity:* As needed

# Use and Outlook for Phase 3 Strategies

As shown in the activities in this chapter, there are multiple ways to incorporate visual learning in online activities and course experiences. Some organizations and institutions may, in fact, want to mandate the inclusion of visual components in any online course as a way of forcing pedagogical experimentation. Others may simply provide internal or external examples of visual learning as a way to gently shift instructors from text-only courses toward more multimedia-rich ones. Still others may decide to reward innovation in visual learning as a means of promoting online risk taking. In the midst of such visual learning experimentations, both formative and summative evaluation might be employed to determine what types of display activities learners prefer and benefit from.

As the activities outlined here for Phase 3 of R2D2 indicate, there are amazing opportunities to display objects and artifacts visually in online environments. However, these visual display tools and resources have arrived so rapidly that there has been scant time or training opportunities to consider more than just a few ways to incorporate them. Suffice to say, the untapped reservoir of educational opportunities in the Web of Learning is perhaps most salient here in the land of visual displays.

## Final Reflections

The creative pedagogical minds of the twenty-first century will be the ones who grasp the power of the visual learning resources described in this chapter as well as many of the innumerable tools and resources that will continue to emerge. Many of these tools can be thoughtfully embedded in preassigned curricula as well as in more experimental and nontraditional teaching venues. The activities here can inspire learners and bring them beyond the mundane aspects of reading yet another chapter, or writing another research report, white paper, or journal article. With visual displays, learning comes to life; one's internal power plant for learning is recharged.

Initially it may take some courage to look beyond popular and widely accepted textbooks and canned instructor lectures as the basis for student learning. However, there are now many exciting ways for this to happen. Instructors might experiment with new forms of online collaboration, exploration, and self-paced learning pursuits. Without a doubt, many of the most talented instructors of the twenty-first century will be those who ferret out creative and engaging educational applications of emerging tools and resources found in the Web of Learning and then, after their passionate experimentations and pedagogical refinements, find still other uses that no one previously contemplated. Of course, such talented people will need to be recognized for exercising their risk muscle and putting it on display for others to learn from, emulate, and perhaps even stretch light years beyond with R2D2.

For many educational professionals and students, visual learning might be deemed more exciting and glamorous than reflective or verbal learning. While the other two phases of R2D2 are no less important, visual representations provide a way to focus learner attention as well as a social space for reevaluation of one's learning. A videoclip or animation sequence can offer a common experience for all learners that can be replayed, compared and contrasted, and interactively discussed. And as will become increasingly obvious in Chapters Eight and Nine, some of these visuals are manipulable as part of a simulation or game that the learner enters into and controls in some manner. When this occurs, such activities extend the learner into Phase 4 of R2D2, which relates to hands-on or kinesthetic learning. The next two chapters address an assortment of Phase 4 learning opportunities, after which, in Chapter Ten, we reflect on the implications of the R2D2 model and this book.

# CHAPTER EIGHT

# PHASE 4 OF THE R2D2 MODEL

## Hands-On Learners

Once learners have read or listened to new content, reflected upon it, and displayed their learning, what else do they need to do? *Do* is the operative word here—of course, they want to try out that knowledge in various settings or contexts. Practice runs can take place in either simulated worlds or real ones. Or such trials might be located somewhere between these electronic and physical worlds, with videoclips of problems faced by expert practitioners that learners are asked to solve.

Are you a doer? Are your learners or trainees doers? Are they excited to test their knowledge within complex and time-restricted real-life problems, scenarios, and vignettes? If so, you might whet their appetites with raw data available in the Web of Learning. Using such data, students might track whale movements in the Pacific Ocean, analyze financial statements of a Fortune 500 company, calculate calories in different food groups, or diagnose a series of patient cases while in medical school. Or, if in a corporate situation, learners might respond to salary requests as a departmental supervisor, use newly learned product-related skills with virtual customers, respond to simulated customer service requests, or handle a typical business meeting. And, if in military training, you might watch trainees interpret battle maps signaling enemy movements or lead a squadron through enemy terrain. Across these situations, learners are *doing* something with their newly learned skills and information; it is no longer the fragile, inert knowledge of most formal learning situations.

In all these situations, the learner is making decisions about some action to take by using new skills and competencies acquired or in the process of being acquired. This is simultaneously the final step in the problem-solving process delineated in the Read, Reflect, Display, Do (R2D2) model as well the starting point for new education and training. It is the place to determine what was mastered as well as what was not sufficiently learned or internalized. Keep in mind, however, that while Phase 4 of the R2D2 model transports us to this land of knowledge and skill application, experimenting with acquired knowledge is a part of any phase; there is no need to wait until Phase 4 to begin to test or practice your newly learned skills and competencies.

Of course, a learner could enter an online learning experience with an immediate problem or issue to solve. For example, in a problem-based learning (PBL) environment, students may be introduced to a complex problem or project at the beginning of a learning cycle and be asked to accomplish a series of learning goals in the problem-solving process whereby they begin acquiring the necessary content knowledge. Asking for skill application prior to learning all of the content places the learner in a challenging and somewhat tense situation. Of course, such perceived pressure may be even more intense in an unfamiliar online learning environment. At the same time, it may be less stressful in online situations, where you get repeated practice or simulated opportunities to test your learning.

In general, however, Phase 4 learning is where learners' mettle is tested. Can they perform well? And, if so, can they effectively perform without external supports or guidance? How about when they are members of teams? In effect, are they ready to handle real-world situations? While most Phase 4 activities discussed in the next chapter are safe harbors for testing new skills and competencies, since they do not take place in real-world settings, some do push the envelope by having the learner immediately apply new skills and knowledge in a job setting. That is the direction of learning in the twenty-first century—toward on-demand learning or on the job training (OJT) in real-world environments where learners ideally can apply their knowledge directly on the job.

The tools and activities for Phase 4 learning are certainly on the rise. In terms of activities, online cases are prominent in many disciplines, including education, business, medicine, law, and engineering. They are also used in the corporate world for compliance training, sales training, and management and leadership executive programs. There are also many tools and technologies to promote hands-on learning. For example, learners using a wiki tool (software for quickly creating, editing, or linking Web pages) can collaboratively write a book or procedure manual, discuss and debate class assignments, plan training events, or document the functioning of a group involved in an online course or training program.

## Phase 4 of R2D2

Many individuals will immediately resonate with the ideas listed in the fourth phase of R2D2 (see Figure 8.1). This is the place where all gears shift to hyperspeed and where a galaxy of new and exciting opportunities await. It is here in the fourth phase that learners actually apply what they have read about, listened to, reflected upon, and seen displayed. Now such multimedia knowledge (that is, content that has been effectively dual coded; see Chapter Two) can be applied or used in multiple situations. Hands-on or kinesthetic learners are the ones who prefer to try things out. They need to touch, experience, imitate, and practice what they have learned. Fortunately, the Web of Learning offers such learners

**FIGURE 8.1. PHASE 4 OF R2D2.**

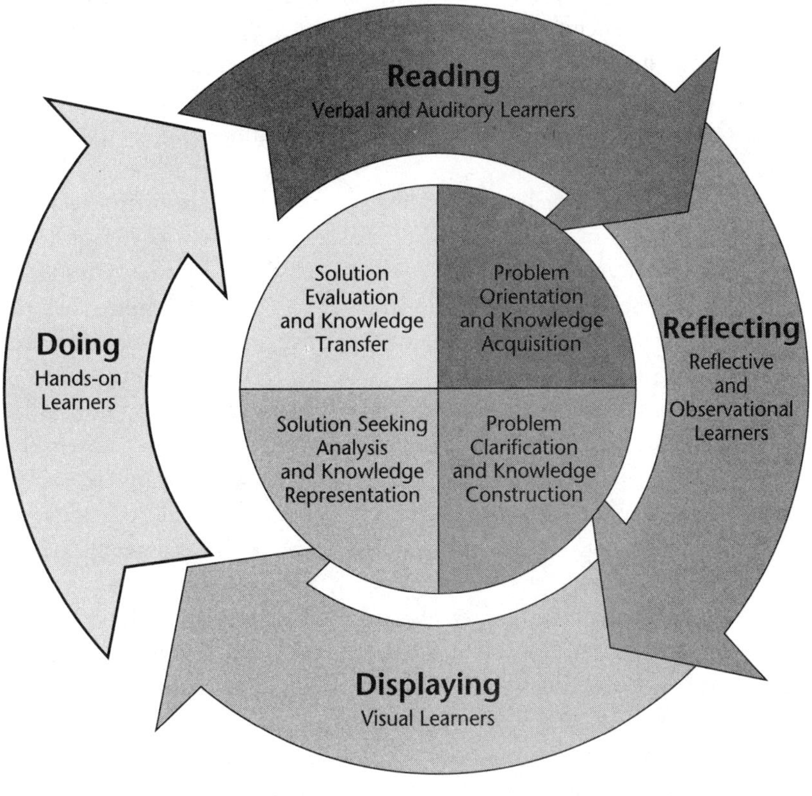

hands-on activities and experiences that can help them grasp content more fully and build self-confidence in their growing skills and abilities.

Before outlining these activities in Chapter Nine, we highlight some of the technologies and instructional approaches that enable learners to apply or test out newly formed skills, including simulations and games, online cases and scenarios, and wikis. Such technologies and approaches for "doing" will undoubtedly expand during the coming decades.

## Simulations and Games

As noted in the Preface to this book, enrollments in online courses are surging, and today's students—immersed in an increasingly digital world—are seeking richer and more engaging learning experiences. As part of such trends, Oblinger (2003) claims that recent generations of learners are accustomed to ubiquitous computing environments in which multitasking and staying connected are the norms. She further notes that students who are active participants in the information age want to engage in meaningful tasks rather than just complete worksheets and accumulate knowledge. Amid this rising tide of expectations, instructors, organizations, and institutions are exploring innovative ways to use popular and emerging technology to foster interaction, collaboration, and excitement for learning. Some are recommending the use of simulation and gaming technology.

Simulations facilitate learning by presenting an environment that attempts to represent or mimic reality. Simulations are built to engage learners in situations or events that would be far too costly, dangerous, complex, difficult, or time-consuming to replicate in the real world (for example, a chemistry experiment) or that may be problematic for moral, ethical, or societal reasons (strategic bombing missions, human brain surgeries, frog dissections, and so on). Because of these and other issues, many types of simulations are now available online. Simulations can help learners understand how to run a business, build a town, create an empire, or save an environment. Learners can also watch changes in work flow processes, explore different assumptions in key military battles, and create alternative worlds and histories (Rickard & Oblinger, 2004).

Simulations can find use in nearly any discipline or course. They not only ask the learner to employ facts and information learned, but they require strategic thinking and problem solving. They might also move the learner through increasingly complex and evolving situations or relationships. And as anyone who enjoys playing games knows, progressing through levels of difficulty in a simulation or game is personally rewarding and motivational. The problems, issues, and situations presented are engaging, at least in part, because they are dependent on participant decisions and successes (Gredler, 1996).

In addition to individualizing the learning process through these progressive stages and challenges and promptly reacting to participant decision making, simulations and games contain elements of play, fun, and fantasy as well as goal setting, rule following, and competition (Prensky, 2001). The motivation to play them comes from the goals and challenges that the learner needs to accomplish as well as the incentives that are provided for solutions along the way (Malone, 1981). And, unlike in traditional forms of training and education, there are multiple paths or routes to success in games and simulations.

***Simulations in K–12 Education.*** Simulations are increasingly available for elementary and high school students. For instance, in biology classes, there are free online simulations for frog dissection, so that real frogs (real dead ones, anyway) are no longer needed. For learning support, a young learner can watch a video to determine where to cut the virtual frog. Or at a different time he might explore the Cells alive! Web site, where he might observe what happens when magnifying the head of a pin with a dust mite on it. Next, he might watch a Flash animation of the complex steps of mitosis or meiosis. There are online chemistry and physics simulations the student might be assigned to explore or use in other classes or perhaps even use to help prepare for advanced placement college examinations.

If she were in a U.S. history or economics course, she might be assigned to complete an eye-opening simulation of the U.S. national budget. In fact, the National Budget Simulation allows learners to make specific decisions related to budgets for education, transportation, the military, agriculture, education and training, and other areas. And, for advanced classes or opportunities for deeper learning, there is a more detailed budget simulation available. This in-depth simulation requires learners to make decisions about subcategories within the area of education, such as (1) elementary, secondary, and vocational education, (2) higher education, and (3) research and general education. In contrast, the category of transportation includes budgetary decisions for highways, air, water, railroads, mass transit, and other forms of transportation.

A primary goal of each of these simulations is to get the learner more engaged in the content, to the point that she is physically manipulating content or variables and observing the results of those manipulations.

***Simulations in Higher Education.*** Without a doubt, simulations are playing key roles in online courses within higher education. For instance, the graduate nursing program at Monash University in Australia uses the Virtual Patient multimedia resource as a major part of its training (Kiegaldie & White, 2006). In this system, a series of critical incidents with a patient are demonstrated using text, videos, animations, sound, and pictures. Various patient vital signs are available via chest

X-rays, breath and heart sounds, and an electrocardiograph. Similarly, Stanford University has designed a three-dimensional (3D) virtual emergency room where users control onscreen avatars who are dressed in medical scrubs (Raths, 2006). There are six different trauma scenarios in this simulation; you might assume the role of nurse, x-ray technician, or emergency room physician. For instance, as an emergency room physician, you might have the avatar clear a patient's airway or check a patient's vital signs.

These are just a few examples of the many potential uses of simulations in the medical field. Simulations available today, for instance, can help explain diseases and medical conditions (for example, osteoporosis, hypothermia, spinal cord injuries, Alzheimer's disease), bodily functions (for example, the muscular system, how the brain works), and how to consult with patients. Similar simulation possibilities exist across other professional disciplines in higher education (for example, education, safety management, marketing, engineering) as well as in arts and science courses.

***Simulations in Business.*** In addition to secondary and college learning environments, simulations are highly useful in business and training environments (Bonk & Dennen, 2005). Managerial simulations are often used in business schools and corporate training department to teach decision making and leadership for individuals in executive and high-level management positions (Leemkuil, de Jong, & Ootes, 2000). In a managerial simulation, a learner might be asked to allocate resources to different parts of a plant or operation in order to produce and sell products (Ju & Wagner, 1997). These types of simulations—in which the learner plans production schedules, forecasts product demand, and develops marketing plans—can be played alone or in groups.

While the focus for the learner is often on maximizing points, beating the system, or outperforming other individuals (Leemkuil et al., 2000), the goal of the simulation designer or course instructor might be to maximize return on investment or corporate market share. Clearly, such systems have opportunities to promote student collaboration, ability to take multiple perspectives, and selection of relevant resources, while helping them avoid misconceptions as well as premature withdrawal from the simulation. And while peers, instructors, and experts may help learners solve problems presented, online agents and tutors are designed into many of these systems to help clarify a task and guide learners through critical stages of the activity.

Such business and training simulations are highly valued, since they provide a sense of consistency to the training, address wide audiences, and reduce the time required for learner competency (Clark, Gjerde, & Skinner, 2003). While prevailing reports on the impact of online simulations predict a significant increase in use in the coming years, such reports also indicate that many significant barriers or obstacles remain; most notably, high development and implementation costs, limited infrastructure, insufficient management commitment, low instructional value, complexity in measuring impact, and low employee motivation (Brennan & Kao, 2004).

***Simulations in the Military.*** The military is also highly involved in the simulation and gaming field. As an example, America's Army, a popular simulation of life in the U.S. Army, is free to download from the Internet. During the past few years, millions of potential recruits have survived its "basic training" modules. Recruitment has been enhanced as a result.

Other military simulations such as Full Spectrum Warrior include opportunities for quick decision making, planning, and collaboration by a squad leader in both urban combat as well as in peacekeeping missions (Stevenson, 2003). Here, the goal is not simply responding to threats but how the player devises and implements a strategy or plan (DiMascio, 2004). Such games have been used by the Afghan National Army, for instance, to help it fight alongside U.S. troops. As these military games and simulations become more complex, they require players to recognize real threats, fine-tune their organizational and analysis skills, and, generally, be able to lead (Wired News, 2003).

Many military games have the motivational appeal of Hollywood movies. In fact, the gaming industry has become increasingly linked to Hollywood, since most blockbuster movies have a coinciding video, and now many popular games have been made into movies (Snider, 2004).

Thanks to their motivational power, these types of games are vital recruitment tools (Jayakanthan, 2002). To continue to foster such career-related motivation, there is a push for more realistic simulation experiences that bring the recruit as close as possible to see, hear, smell, and touch the actual environment as well as for realistic computer-generated characters to interact with. Across such experiences, some of the key motivational features built into such games include a sense of challenge, conflict, curiosity, control, and fantasy. For instance, the focus is not on learning to fire a weapon but on the challenges and obstacles faced when leading one's squad, unit, or larger force.

Simulations are becoming increasingly complex, collaborative, and globally interactive. As Bonk and Dennen's (2005) report on massive multiplayer online gaming (MMOG) indicates, the U.S. military would like to teach planning, management, leadership, and other high-level skills through MMOGs rather than just enhancing response times in violent situations. In fact, the U.S. military is investing in gaming technology that eventually will host thousands of networked computers. In such games, players could participate for months or years in different roles and later reflect on the consequences of their decisions and actions (Harmon, 2003).

At the time of this writing, there are many highly popular MMOGs with millions of worldwide users, including Star Wars Galaxies, The Sims, Ultima Online, Lineage, Online, EverQuest, and Asherton's Call. With MMOGs, learners might be matched up in teams and play against other teams. Working in virtual teams, learners can learn effective communication skills while building trusting relationships and integrity (Roebuck, Brock, & Moodie, 2004). As is apparent from anyone watching high school youth play a game such as Halo, violent military and fantasy types of games currently dominate the MMOG marketplace; however MMOGs are expected to soon move toward more social and educational purposes as seen in the game Civilization. As this occurs, educators and trainers must be ready to embed them in their online courses.

## Online Cases and Scenarios

In addition to simulations, online case studies and scenarios offer ways to apply your learning, either as individuals or in teams. These types of learning methods allow learners to be immersed in a situation or problem in which they must test their knowledge against model answers or outcomes of experts, instructors, or peers. Cases, for instance, can be found on the Web of Learning in nearly any discipline or content area within higher education or corporate training. Cases can be short (for example, one paragraph) or long, with extended sets of online and paper-based resources. They might embed expert commentary or sets of questions and issues to respond to. Cases can also link to countercases or situations that have a somewhat different flavor or problem but contain similar knowledge (that is, Case A and Case B format). And cases might be part of online competitions for groups of learners to solve.

***Real-Time Cases.*** Imagine if learners were electronically planted in real company settings and solving real-world problems instead of reading and reacting to standard Harvard Business School cases. That is exactly what Professor James Theroux at the University of Massachusetts at Amherst does with his real-time case method (RTCM) approach in his entrepreneurship course. In the RTCM approach, a full-time case writer is located in an existing company, thereby allowing the learners in a course to experience and discuss actual events (for example, the start-up of a company, budgetary crises, the requirements of an initial public stock offering) as these events unfold.

No one technology is relied upon. Instead, the students and instructors might employ any tool or system that can help them learn better, including real-time chatting with company managers, teleconferencing, threaded discussion forums, Internet access to company data, and videoconferencing. The real-time chats with company officials overcome some of the key problems of most case-based learning by providing current updates and emerging data to the case situations; in effect, there is more depth and currency to the cases than usual.

Research from Theroux, Carpenter, and Kilbane (2004) reveals that such authentic, challenging, and multidisciplinary tasks are highly motivating and engaging. Interestingly, Theroux and his colleagues have experimented with multi-institutional delivery of these real-time cases that enables instructors to provide each other with guidelines and tips about their use as well as support in preparing pedagogical materials and sharing teaching responsibility.

***Medical Cases.*** In the medical field, cases allow you to obtain key information, order lab tests, make diagnoses, call up resources for decision making, and compare your solution to that of experts. Cases might be presented asynchronously with text, video, or animation formats or some combination of these. Alternatively, medical cases might be presented in a synchronous presentation session with online resources or activities wrapped around them. The proliferating use of learning objects will increase the cost-effectiveness of developing elaborate case situations involving rich multimedia as well as efforts to create extensive and thoughtful pedagogical resources.

***Teacher Education Cases.*** Medicine is but one application area for online case learning. The enormous and often beleaguered field of teacher education has incorporated case situations and simulations as a means of professionalizing the field (Bonk, Daytner, Daytner, Dennen, & Malikowski, 2001). Online cases or scenarios can also be linked to prominent theories in teacher education, such as constructivism and apprenticeship learning. In an online educational simulation, preservice teachers might interview for jobs in a simulated school, talk to school counselors, librarians, custodians, and principals about particular students or common problems, or explore case solutions of their peers. The learner might also decide to have an informal chat with a virtual technology coordinator or special education director about the school. While engaged in the simulation, you might use learning support tools to outline, map out, or compare what you have uncovered prior to making key decisions as well as for reflecting on those already made.

***Business School Cases.*** Case use is common in business schools as well as corporate training. For example, Biz/ed is a comprehensive United Kingdom-based Web site that includes cases, lesson plans, activities, and current events for students and instructors in areas such as business studies, economics, accounting, leisure, sports and recreation, and travel and tourism. For finance or accounting courses, Biz/ed offers profiles of real-world companies with an extensive database of facts and figures students can use to calculate financial ratios (for example, liquidity ratios, return on fixed assets, dividend yields, gross profit margins). Biz/ed also contains a slew of virtual resources, including a virtual farm game in which users run a farm for five years and attempt to make a profit, as well as a virtual developing country, virtual factory, virtual bank, and virtual economy.

*Corporate Training Cases.* In corporate training situations, designers are increasingly using scenarios in their online courses and environments. One company specializing in the use of scenario learning is WisdomTools. Dr. Marty Siegel, the founder of WisdomTools, points out that a key aspect of scenarios is in their storytelling power, which places learners in authentic learning settings and into the life situations of believable people. As such, scenarios are contextually rich and highly memorable for learners. In using time-revealed types of scenarios, WisdomTools relies on releasing information over time with the learners studying the material in cohort groups. In corporate training, the scenario of a company moving a plant or office to another city or country might be used. Scenario learning activities and training modules could prepare employees for such a move.

Clearly, there are varying levels or degrees of believability and authenticity in online cases and scenarios. As instructor and trainer use of the Web of Learning becomes more pervasive, there will be increased experimentation and risk taking. For example, instead of using prepackaged simulations, cases, or scenarios on a course Web site, the learners might enter a real-world setting wherein problem situations are placed in their laps by chief information officers, chief operating officers, and directors of human resources or training departments. As with other Phase 4 learning opportunities detailed in this chapter, online cases and scenarios present instructors and students with many exciting pedagogical possibilities.

## Wikis

Although emerging technologies such as podcasting (see Chapter Two) and blogging (see Chapter Four) can be easily linked to the hands-on activities of Phase 4 of R2D2, we emphasize a different emerging technology in this chapter, namely, wikis. We believe wikis offer exciting Phase 4 learning opportunities in both education and training environments. In wiki environments, learners participate in their own learning rather than passively receive it.

Ward Cunningham, who invented the first wiki, came up with the name for it from the Hawaiian term *wiki wiki,* meaning "quick" (Wikipedia, 2006).

Some people point out that it can simultaneously mean "what I know is," since this phrase captures the role of a wiki in knowledge collaboration, contribution, storage, and sharing or exchange of information.

Brandon Hall (2006), well known in the corporate training field for his annual e-learning awards as well as his extensive research in the field, recently defined a *wiki* as "a collection of Web pages that can be easily viewed and modified by anyone, providing a means for sharing learning and collaboration" (p. 13). He further pointed out that wikis can be used to design content "on the fly" as well as for generating a repository of information or summarizing progress of a group or team. A team can use a wiki not only to track the progress of team members but also to discuss that progress, share knowledge, and identify roadblocks as well as insights that they have. Hall notes that the benefits of wiki technology include speed of updating, ease of editing and collaboration, and overall simplicity.

A wiki, which can be public or private, is a Web site that allows visitors to change, edit, delete, or add to the content, sometimes freely without a password or account registration. Since wikis can also link to other online objects or resources, wikis, in effect, are similar to the Hypercard and hypermedia environments that were pervasive in the 1980s. However, unlike the days of Hypercard, in most wiki environments there is no programming expertise required. Also important, wiki systems create historical records of changes to the site, thereby allowing a user to roll back a page to a previous version or state at any time. In addition to tools for monitoring the constantly changing state of a wiki, such systems also typically include places for discussing issues or disagreements. This ease of use and updating has turned wiki tools into a growing means for online collaborative work and knowledge exchange. Wikis are still evolving; many useful add-on features include capabilities for spell checking, blogging, using emoticons, controlling access, editing, polling, and calendaring.

***Wikipedia.*** Among the more popular wiki sites is Wikipedia, which was founded by Jimmy Wales and Larry Sanger. Wikipedia, which was started in 2001, is currently one of the top twenty Web sites searched in the United States. As of May 22, 2007, the English-language version of Wikipedia had nearly 1,800,000 articles in it, with pages being edited an average of more than fifteen times since 2002 (Wikipedia, 2007). It was also available in more than 200 languages and offered a simple English version specifically created for those learning English.

Of course, the ease of editing (and using) a wiki as well as the general lack of review or approval processes for modifications can lead to accidentally inserted or intentionally placed incorrect information. For instance, Wikipedia was in serious trouble when journalist John Seigenthaler Sr. was falsely accused in Wikipedia of a pair of assassinations, namely, Robert and John F. Kennedy

(Seigenthaler, 2005). However, at roughly the same time, a December 15, 2005, news article in *Nature* compared the quality of *Encyclopedia Britannica* and Wikipedia and found them to be similar in the number of errors, omissions, and misleading statements (Giles, 2005; Lombardi, 2006). As would be expected, *Encyclopedia Britannica* issued a rebuttal report about how such errors were calculated (Encyclopedia Britannica, 2006).

Jumping into the debate, Jimmy Wales admitted to many shortcomings in Wikipedia (Read, 2006). Wales also agreed with educators who do not believe that Wikipedia should be cited as a primary source of data for their papers. Such shortcomings and problems, of course, should not be entirely unexpected given that Wikipedia is written entirely by unpaid volunteers.

***Other Wiki Sites.*** Wikipedia has become so popular that sister projects at the Wikimedia Foundation, such as Wikibooks, Wiktionary, Wikiversity, Wikispecies, Wikiquote, Wikimedia Commons, and Wikinews, have materialized. Wiktionary, for instance, is a free multilingual dictionary in which students can look up word definitions, pronunciations, spellings, synonyms, antonyms, and translations. Wikimedia Commons is a shared repository of images, sounds, videos, and other information focusing on areas of science, nature, and society. Wikisource is a vault or online repository of free content including biographies, speeches, fiction books, nonfiction, and other works. Both Commons and Wikisource link to Phase 1 of R2D2, as they provide extensive and searchable free content that can be referred to or used in online classes. And, of course, the image and video resource materials found in any of these Wikimedia Foundation projects relate to Phase 3.

Given our positions in higher education, we would be remiss if we did not mention Wikiversity. Wikiversity also offers free online learning materials and resources. The stated objective of Wikiversity is to create a multidimensional community dedicated to learning, teaching, research, and service. It intends to host free learning-related materials for all ages of learners and all languages as well as collaborative projects and communities wrapped around such materials. If the Wikimedia Foundation can nurture credible resources and communities within Wikiversity, it will send serious shock waves throughout higher education.

***Educational Applications of Wikis.*** From an educational standpoint, a wiki is a socially shared free space (Schrage, 1990) in which a community of individuals (that is, minds) can collaboratively write and debate ideas. Not only do such sites promote highly collaborative composing and communication (Emigh & Herring, 2005), but also a sense of design, originality, and creativity. Wikis are a highly constructivistic online space wherein one can generate new knowledge and negotiate meaning with peers. They are an exemplary form of participatory learning. Here, the power or responsibility is with the community of users, not necessarily with the individual.

In education and training courses, students might be asked to create or revise Wikipedia pages. Learners might also engage in cross-class projects or international exchange projects. In addition, teams might use a wiki to record their progress on final projects. And instructors might have their learners debate terms or ideas in a wiki. Moreover, learners might build course glossaries and other types of course resources in a wiki. And in journalism and English classes, a wiki might become a place to share creative writing. For instance, an English teacher might require a group or class essay in a wiki or have students build a set of resource links around famous poems. In corporations and nonprofit training settings, wikis might be used for project management and communication among learners in a course as well as for important course announcements from trainers.

At the higher end of the risk continuum, learners might jointly write a wikibook and share it online as a small group or class project. As an example, in the spring of 2006, Bonk launched a wikibook project in one of his graduate classes at Indiana University. This project involved students collaborating with Dr. Mimi Lee's class in the College of Education at the University of Houston. Student pairs were assigned—one person from each university—to provide feedback on each other's work or to jointly write a chapter (it was their choice). Such an activity, though just a pilot and with many limitations, demonstrated that wikis offer opportunities to extend student authorship and audience well beyond a single class and instructor. A wikibook is a marvelous online tool for learner collaboration and interaction.

## Collecting Real-World Data

We have noted numerous times in this book that the Internet is a gold mine for collecting, analyzing, and reporting information across disciplines, grade levels, and economic sectors. The content area does not really matter; there undoubtedly is online data to support learners in their learning quests.

In the previous simulation examples, students are typically manipulating and making decisions about data that someone else provided or prerecorded. However, learners might not only manipulate existing data; they might also collect their own raw data and analyze and report on it. Bonk has designed his own free, Web-based survey tool called SurveyShare that his students and many others use to collect real-world data. Students at places such as the University of California at Berkeley are using SurveyShare to conduct market research for companies in the Silicon Valley. Using such online survey tools, learners can collect data for their research projects and course activities. They are engaged in active learning!

When involved in such online data-gathering activities, students are placed at the center of real-world research rather than on the periphery. Some educators are using such tools for interesting research (including action research), while others use them for formative as well as summative course evaluations. There are dozens of Web-based tools available for collecting online survey and polling data (for example, SurveyShare, SurveyMonkey, Zoomerang, WebSurveyor, SurveyPro, SurveyConsole, and others); some are free, while others are definitely not.

Real-world research using online survey tools such as SurveyShare or Zoomerang provide a vehicle for students not only to explore concepts and principles that they are learning in real-life settings but to discover and share new knowledge. It is the apparent discovery of something unique that can excite and engage the learner. Some may even refer to this as a "peak learning experience."

After a learner has had such an *aha!* experience, he or she must then interpret it, put his or her own spin on it, and present it to others in an intellectually understandable and engaging way. When effective, a small pilot research study can evolve into a senior honor's paper, master's thesis, company vision statement, conference presentation, or doctoral dissertation. Equally important, it might lead to a summer internship experience, full-time employment, or paid consulting opportunities. And, of course, the presentation and publication of such work often results in unique networking opportunities, collaborative projects, and professional development endeavors. It is incumbent on instructors and course designers, therefore, to create avenues for primary data collection, analysis, reporting, and presentation in online courses or course components.

There are many other online tools and resources learners can use to collect, evaluate, or present real-world information. For example, learners might use Skype or Google Talk to interview a famous individual online or document a certain historical period or incident. Using such tools, learners can electronically interview people who lived through different historical events (for example, protests of the Vietnam War in the late 1960s, the U.S. stock market crash of 1987, the toppling of the Berlin Wall in 1989, the 1992 summer Olympic games in Barcelona, or the bloodless overthrow of the president of Thailand in 2006) and post those oral histories in an online podcast or digital movie for others to listen to, download, or comment on.

One tool that might be used during oral history activities is called the VideoPaper Builder. The VideoPaper Builder is a free multimedia tool that enables users to juxtapose a digital movie against a paper that they have written. The VideoPaper Builder tool helps the learner organize information in different formats, including text, PowerPoint files, and digital movies. Final videopapers can be uploaded to the Web for others to browse or download. As noted in previous chapters, such a tool is extremely powerful since it allows learners to dual code information in both verbal and visual formats.

The VideoPaper Builder is one of the few tools we have seen that makes this obvious. When Bonk visited Tufts University in the greater Boston area a few years back, university officials indicated that they were using such a tool in their Education Department. They noted that with the VideoPaper Builder, a learner might back up key points in a paper with video snippets of real-world events. In the teacher training program at Tufts, preservice teachers were reflecting on how performances that they observed (as seen in the video) compared to state or national teaching standards.

Learners can also juxtapose text and video in learning documentaries with vodcasts (video-based podcasts) and vblogs (video blogs). Here, learners might back up their text with a videoclip or series of videos. Even without video, learners might produce a weekly or monthly podcast radio station or show. Once again, the key is that learners are doing something with their knowledge or doing something to acquire still additional knowledge. When this occurs, students are designers instead of receptors of knowledge. They are participating in the learning process.

## Learning by Doing Galleries

The focus of Phase 4 learning on "doing" may prompt you to think about capstone or ending course experiences. How might learners at the end of an activity, module, or course showcase their learning? Phase 2 reflective learning emphasizes papers and reports, while Phase 3 visual learning highlights the importance of timelines, taxonomies, and concept maps. Phase 4 learning includes such reflection papers and visual displays, but it also includes any situation wherein the learner produces or generates something using her knowledge (that is, creativity) as well as when she employs it to evaluate or solve problems or controversial situations (that is, critical thinking).

Phase 4 learning examples might be made available for fellow learners as well as future enrollees of a course. Often, online instructors or course designers create a course Web site or project gallery where previously completed student work is placed on display. As was discussed with the Omnium project in Chapter Six, a project gallery extends a course experience to other experts, instructors, peers, and interested parties around the planet, directly or indirectly inviting their evaluation and feedback.

We have used such an approach in our own online teaching. As an example, in a five-year professional development program for teacher technology integration called TICKIT, Bonk and his colleagues had practicing teachers post their final projects to an evolving project gallery each semester with the details of the project, including a URL link to it as well as information related to audience, reflections on how it went, and general advice (see Ehman, Bonk, & Yamagata-Lynch, 2005). This gallery of final projects served both as a display to peers of what others had accomplished as well as a mechanism for future teachers and interested educators and scholars to browse and learn from. Not only did the online project gallery help to share ideas from the program, but additionally, it established task expectations for newcomers and offered them a layer of scaffolding to overcome personal fears about the amount and type of work required in the class.

The key issue here is to have a target goal or final product on which to center student energies. A production-based focus or tangible goal is a means to apprentice students into a discipline. When complete, they also have something to place on their resumes as well as an engaging experience to reflect on. In addition, individuals or groups of students might enter local, regional, national, or perhaps even international competitions with their productions. They might present some aspect of their work at conferences, seminars, or institutes. Or perhaps learners might hold an online press conference or symposium in a synchronous forum wherein they sell or present their ideas to others in their class or beyond.

An opportunity to produce real-world products is vital for motivating human learning. As we detail in one of the twenty-five strategies in the next chapter, a learner or small team within a class might produce something as part of a course-related consulting arrangement with a local business or organization. We have seen such techniques used by instructors of business, education, and computer science courses. In computer science, for instance, we have observed teams of students from a software engineering course consulting with local businesses to design innovative software solutions for them. Teams of students from a business course in entrepreneurship might help local small businesses create business or marketing plans (Groth & Robertson, 1999). We have also seen younger learners using their mathematical skills for analyzing online as well as print data for a local business.

Such approaches are employed in our respective education departments. For instance, we have observed learners in a Web design and evaluation class use their new and emerging talents to conduct usability tests aimed at redesigning key aspects of a Web site. In addition, in a course on e-learning pedagogy and evaluation, we have had students review e-learning plans and white papers found on the Web of Learning from universities, businesses, nonprofit organizations, and entire countries and make recommendations to the authors of such reports regarding possible updates or modifications. These are just a few examples of how to foster knowledge use as well as support students doing something with their knowledge.

## Recap

As discussed earlier, the fourth phase of the R2D2 model involves learners doing something with the content knowledge and strategies that they have acquired through the first three phases. Problem solving, decision making, evaluation, and so on are tests to determine whether the learner has sufficiently internalized the content knowledge, skills, and strategies of a course or unit. It is here in Phase 4 that learners make judgments about case situations, engage in debates with colleagues, conduct scientific experiments (both virtual and physical), and collect and analyze real-world data and artifacts.

As emphasized throughout this chapter, Phase 4 learning pursuits are focused on *doing* something or putting newly learned skills into practice. Such active learning avenues help learners personally interpret any new content based on their prior knowledge and prevailing needs and internalize or appropriate such content for their own purposes. Some course experiences may be somewhat limited in their Phase 4 opportunities and activities when learners use predefined resources and materials for their decision making. Other learning experiences push the envelope of learner control and active learning by granting sufficient control over the curriculum so that learners can design their own products or brainstorm unique projects and ideas. In either case—using existing resources or creating new ones—the learner is testing the knowledge he or she has obtained in the first three phases of R2D2.

As with each of the first three phases of R2D2, there are myriad tools and strategies for Phase 4. Scenario learning as well as learning via simulations and gaming is on the rise in training environments. At the same time, higher education instructors and institutions have spent much effort in the area of online cases. Cases also are extensively used in businesses such as International Business Machines (IBM) (Lewis & Orton, 2006) as well as the military (Kirkley & Kirkley, 2006; Wisher, 2006). And the collection and interpretation of raw data is increasingly evident in K–12 settings; witness many of the intriguing pedagogical examples listed at the Edutopia homepage from the George Lucas Education Foundation (GLEF).

Next-generation systems built for the Web of Learning will increasingly offer interactive tasks that place the learner in situations of knowledge use instead of only acquisition. Web 2.0 technology such as podcasts, wikis, blogs, and social networking software provide mechanisms for feedback and interactivity that previously were not possible. It will prove interesting to see how instructors and institutions take advantage of such interactivity. It will also be illuminating to watch learner reactions.

Stakeholders in both training and education environments have increasingly called for the ability to view the results of learning. What are the outcomes? Can they be documented in learning portfolios? Phase 4 learning does just that; it provides situations or contexts for testing the acquisition, application, evaluation, and transfer of knowledge. And, equally important, it helps to certify or place a stamp on learner ability to use that knowledge. In addition, success in this phase is not only personally rewarding but also motivates learners to push their learning-related limits and strive to achieve even higher goals in the future. Each of us needs such stamps. Each of us needs such goals.

CHAPTER NINE

## ACTIVITIES FOR PHASE 4

### Hands-On Learners

Following are twenty-five ideas for implementing Phase 4 of the Reading, Reflecting, Displaying, Doing (R2D2) model in online and blended learning experiences. Many ideas expressed in previous chapters, especially those related to displaying your learning (Chapters Six and Seven), could have been discussed in Chapters Eight and Nine and vice versa. Keep in mind that, while many of these ideas are exciting, some of them require that you download specific software or use a particular technology platform to implement them.

Keeping abreast of all the hands-on options and opportunities today is extremely difficult if not impossible. If you are in higher education, focus on reports from the Sloan Consortium (Sloan-C), EDUCAUSE, the Hewlett Foundation's program in Open Educational Resources, or many of the free online journals in e-learning. If you are in corporate training, we recommend reading reports from the eLearning Guild, the American Society for Training and Development (ASTD), or Brandon Hall Research on custom content development, online simulations, and emerging e-learning. And, if you are in K–12 education, you might explore reports found on the Edutopia Web site from the George Lucas Educational Foundation (GLEF) or reports from the Pew Internet and American Life Project. Many of the ideas presented in this chapter were inspired by one or more of these reports.

## Activity 76. Web-Based Survey Research

*Description and Purpose of Activity.* As indicated in Chapter Eight, there are numerous Web-based survey tools for collecting data (for example, SurveyShare, Survey Pro, Key Survey, and so on). Learners can collect online data that might inform nearly any type of course experience, though it is especially pertinent in courses on research methods, politics, marketing, entrepreneurship, and sociology. When learners collect primary data, it puts the onus on them to create clear survey instruments and obtain access to a relevant sample. Self-determined learners, especially adult learners who can link the data collection to their own jobs, will likely excel at such a task. And the results of any survey might be shared with audiences beyond the class to scholars in that field of study as well as to business and industry officials who might offer compensation for such work. Before conducting any primary research, be sure to determine the "human subjects" requirements or rules for conducting research of your school, organization, or institution; in a nutshell, if you plan to publish or present any of your research findings, you will need the permission of survey participants.

*Skills and Objectives.* Includes motivation and engagement in a real-world task, data analysis skills, recognizing patterns and themes, problem- and product-based learning, presentation and communication skills, and grasping how key concepts and principles are applied in the real world.

*Advice and Ideas.* Search for clients in your city or local community who are in need of survey research that members of your class might help with or respond to. You might call your local chamber of commerce or, if at a university, talk to someone in your business school or entrepreneurship center, if available. If no opportunities are found, design sample survey tasks that apply to your course or topic or allow students to generate their own. They might research motivational factors in YouTube videos, political interests of students before an election, or nutrition habits of classmates. If you need to obtain survey software, consider contacting a survey tool vendor (for example, SurveyShare) and asking for an educational discount or free trial.

Inform students of the survey task and demonstrate the use of the selected survey tools. Since Web-based survey tools have a multitude of features, a list or demonstration of the key features might prove helpful in gathering, analyzing, and reporting data. You might show them a few online survey tools that have scaled down or temporary use free versions that might fit the requirements of a course task or activity.

Participants or survey samples might come from interested clients, professional organizations, online user groups, social groups in MySpace or Facebook, or from your own institution or organization. If appropriate, discuss human subjects review board requirements and data collection ethics procedures. At all times, follow institutional guidelines when conducting research on human subjects.

In providing survey guidance to learners, offer hints on how to increase survey response rates (for example, keep the survey short, make the URL (universal resource locater, or Web address) easy for survey respondents to remember or link to, state the purpose of the survey, send reminders, and so on). If a project is deemed potentially publishable but requires extensive work, students might be encouraged to work in teams or with a partner.

Monitor student work during the survey collection and analysis stages. Provide pertinent survey guide sheets and timely feedback. Some guidesheets might have advice on creating survey questions, increasing survey respondents, and analyzing data. Require students to present their results (even if preliminary) either face to face (FTF) or online, or employ some combination of online and FTF presentations.

*Variations and Extensions.* Structure the task for the students by providing a few required questions, a template for the online survey, or a set of survey guidelines or procedures to follow. Such scaffolds might be eliminated as students become more familiar with the online survey tool or activity.

## Key Instructional Considerations

*Risk index:* Medium

*Time index:* Medium

*Cost index:* Low to High (depending on availability of free survey tools)

*Learner-centered index:* High

*Duration of the learning activity:* 3–4 weeks

# Activity 77. Video Scenario Learning

*Description and Purpose of Activity.* Scenario learning typically transports learners to a specific place and time (for example, December 16, 1944, during the famous Battle of the Bulge in World War II, a hospital waiting room in the midst of treating a patient with chest pains, a fourth-grade classroom on a new teacher's very first day, or a shareholder meeting of a Fortune 500 company at the exact moment when significant financial misreportings (that is, incidents of fraud) that were uncovered in an annual audit are announced. The scenario activity provides a series of challenges for learners to address in which they must make choices and decisions. Scenario activities can be brief or long and might entail many practice exercises.

Option Six in Bloomington, Indiana, develops e-learning courseware for dozens of corporate clients. One of the primary techniques they rely on is called "video scenario learning." In video scenario learning, you explore a video or set of slides with adjoining audio that describes a problem or situation in the form of a story (for example, a salesperson interacting with a client, a medical receptionist receiving a phone call during which someone asks for sensitive patient data while others are in the room, a fitness trainer giving advice to someone starting a new training program, and so on) (see Figure 9.1). After the story has been completed or at key decision-making moments, there are typically a set of questions that you must answer.

### FIGURE 9.1. SCENARIO LEARNING EXAMPLE DESIGNED BY OPTION SIX.

***Skills and Objectives.*** Includes concept recognition and application, visual discrimination skills, inferencing, perceptual cues, coaching, feedback, and evaluation. In effect, through narratives or stories, students can more powerfully learn the material.

***Advice and Ideas.*** Determine the content in your course or topic that would benefit from scenario learning, as well as the technologies that will most effectively deliver it. If course development budgets are thin or nonexistent, you can create video scenario learning activities using a set of still pictures or PowerPoint slides; it does not have to cost lots of money. Instead, the use of video scenario learning simply requires some imagination and creativity.

If you decide to create a more technologically sophisticated presentation or set of resources, conduct formative and summative evaluations to be sure that any additional costs incurred are beneficial and can be justified. Given that Generation X and Y learners are often technologically savvy, perhaps test a couple of different scenarios and delivery technologies with your students before deciding on the ultimate design of your scenario activities.

Although we typically see the more cost-intensive video scenarios in large-section college classes and in corporate training settings, there are various levels of media richness and sophistication. The main component is always the realistic nature of the story and forms of interaction and reflection wrapped around it.

The scenario might come from areas in which students have exhibited difficulties in mastering the content or from areas that are rich with terms and concepts. Write and storyboard any necessary scripts. Subject matter experts might be colleagues, former students, or local business leaders who are willing to give their time and services. With any subject matter experts who might be involved, design a prototype or mock-up of the video scenario and test it out with a few student volunteers or colleagues by having them think aloud as they try out the scenario. Create the video scenario with graphic artists, instructional designers, and other required personnel. Tools like Macromedia Flash, Camtasia, or CamStudio (CamStudio is free) might be employed.

Implement video scenario learning activities in your course. Continue usability testing and other forms of evaluation. For instance, if it is a sales training scenario, you might evaluate the impact on company sales. Remember that the scenarios may need to be updated in a few years.

***Variations and Extensions.*** Post scenario solutions to an asynchronous discussion thread. Perhaps have competitions between groups for best solutions and create a "Best of" solution Web site.

## Key Instructional Considerations

*Risk index:* Medium

*Time index:* Medium to High

*Cost index:* High

*Learner-centered index:* Medium

*Duration of the learning activity:* Use as needed

---

# Activity 78. Content Review Games

***Description and Purpose of Activity.*** As mentioned in Chapter Four when discussing the Cisco Networking Academy and Sun Microsystems' Java training, corporate, government, and military training departments often use e-learning for self-paced types of activities. Such training typically relies on a great deal of learner-content interaction. Option Six, mentioned in Activity 77, has developed a group of such learner-content interaction exercises, in which the learner tests out her new or emerging content knowledge while playing a game or completing an interactive task. E-learning content might be tested in such game formats as Bingo, *Wheel of Fortune*, Monopoly, *Jeopardy, Who Wants to Be a Millionaire?*, *The Weakest Link*, and Hangman as well as through crossword puzzles, mazes, hidden messages, word searches, double puzzles, and cryptograms.

For those organizations and institutions preferring training at the lower end of the risk continuum, traditional types of games embedded with multiple-choice test questions might be more appropriate. An important point to remember is that e-learning games can be packed with content and designed for different levels of learning (for example, beginner, intermediate, and advanced). While common in corporate e-learning, increasingly interactive puzzle and game sites as well as software programs are available for higher education and K–12 education (for example, Puzzlemaker from Discovery School). Many such sites and resources, in fact, have free puzzle templates that anyone can use. Of course, creative design of an online content review game might be costly and require significant course enrollments to justify it.

***Skills and Objectives.*** Includes student motivation and engagement, basic skill assessments, knowledge recognition skills, and overall content review.

***Advice and Ideas.*** Review the content of your course or lesson for terms, concepts, and topics that learners typically have trouble with or that are critical to their later learning. Next, create simple educational games, targeting this content with internal resources and software such as Flash or StudyMate, or use the free ones found on the Web. Once developed, test these games with one or two learners, perhaps from previous semesters or offerings of the course. Make relevant assessment decisions, including issues related to how learner scores on these games will be used in the course assessment system, if at all. After modifying the games where necessary, make these review games available to learners. Gather user formative and summative feedback for future use and improvement.

Experiment with different types of games and game formats. Some will be highly successful, and some may not work so well. Games might engage Gen X and Y learners, but they will not appeal to all learners. As with many other methods mentioned in this book, you should attempt to obtain formative and summative feedback on games used in online courses. In addition, you must keep the content in the games up to date, perhaps using student volunteers or providing them with bonus points for such updates. In addition to utilizing student or staff support in game development and associated updates, look to online learning portals and learning object repositories for free games. Be sure to share any noteworthy gaming resources you discover with your colleagues and technology support staff.

***Variations and Extensions.*** Find a game or puzzle (for example, Puzzlemaker) in which students can create the test or challenge for other students. Have all students design one challenge during the course.

## Key Instructional Considerations

> *Risk index:* Low to Medium (depending on game selected)
>
> *Time index:* Medium
>
> *Cost index:* Low to High (depends on tool selected)
>
> *Learner-centered index:* Medium
>
> *Duration of the learning activity:* 1 week as needed

# Activity 79. Online Review and Practice Exercises

***Description and Purpose of Activity.*** When online learning became fashionable in the late 1990s, many instructors, trainers, and instructional designers in both higher education and corporate training relied on online course resources for content review and practice. Even after a decade of experience and vast changes in online teaching and training environments, a common activity for testing recently learned knowledge and information is the review or practice exercise. Such online tests can entail much more than simple multiple choice, true-false, or matching questions. Instead, as discussed in Activity 77, there may be a scenario or vignette that a learner must watch and then respond to. Or perhaps a concept is displayed visually and the learner must then make a series of decisions. In some cases, a situation is presented, with a set of questions or activities following it to determine whether the learner understands the concept. For instance, the University of Calgary and Concordia University in Montreal both use the Lyryx Interactive Financial Accounting software, which scores user accounting work and decisions immediately, instead of the days or weeks an instructor would need to score such work (see Figure 9.2).

With software such as Captivate, the development of drill-and-practice types of tests becomes really easy for online courses. Software training sessions

## FIGURE 9.2. SCREEN FROM LYRYX INTERACTIVE FINANCIAL ACCOUNTING ONLINE PROGRAM.

**Your solution was:**

| Income Statement Items | Case A | Case B |
|---|---|---|
| Gross sales revenue | 150,000 | 170,000 |
| Sales returns and allowances | 18,000 | 17,000 |
| Net sales revenue | 132,000 | 153,000 |
| Cost of goods sold | 110,400 | 114,500 |
| Gross profit | 39,600 | 38,250 |
| Operating expenses | 17,000 | 18,500 |
| Income before income taxes | 22,600 | 19,750 |
| Income tax expense (20%) | 4,520 | 39,500 |
| Income before extraodinary items | 18,080 | 15,800 |
| Extraordinary items | (1,680) | 9,100 |
| Net income | 16,400 | 24,900 |
| EPS (10,000 shares outstanding) | 1.64 | 2.49 |

**Marking:**

**Case A:**
The cost of goods sold value should be $92,400, but you have not entered this. This amount can be calculated using the formula: 'Net sales revenue (132,000)-Gross profit (39,600)'. This will cost you 2 marks.

**Case B:**
The cost of goods sold value should be $114,750, but you have not entered this. This amount can be calculated using the formula: 'Net sales revenue (153,000) $\times$ 0.75'. This will cost you 2 marks.
The Income tax expense (20%) value should be $3,950, but you have not entered this. This amount can be calculated using the formula: 'Income before income taxes (19,750) $\times$ 0.2'. This will cost you 2 marks.

**Total marks for this question: 24**

**Overall Mark: 24/30**
**Your mark of 24/30 is your best mark so far and is recorded.**
**Your previous best mark was 12/30**

Used by permission of Lyryx Learning Inc.

for instructors or course developers can easily incorporate activities on how to develop such testing components. And the software can contain cues or branching procedures that come into play if a learner does not respond with the right action within a given time frame (3 seconds or 1 minute, however predefined by the test designer). When such software is well designed, the test results are dynamically updated with feedback to learners based on the testing results. In other cases, hands-on review exercises might involve learners plotting graphs and then interpreting the data, comparing expert statements, analyzing the credibility of sources, searching for evidence, checking assumptions, and other critical thinking skills.

***Skills and Objectives.*** Includes trying out concepts, gaining skills in practice, reviewing concepts and principles learned, reflection on knowledge acquired, knowledge recognition and application, and skill internalization.

***Advice and Ideas.*** Review the type and level of learning outcomes you expect in your course and then reflect on the content interactivity that would help students to achieve such goals. Use existing e-learning materials that can meet your goals and objectives for your course or module. If you must design such activities from scratch, be sure to pilot test them with a few students and revise accordingly.

If you use a series of online review or practice exercises in a course, you might toss out students' lowest online quiz scores or provide them with a "Floating A" that any student can use one time if needed. Such flexibility and options will reduce course tension and help motivate students.

For those in corporate or other types of training environments, check out the various interactive review activities used by companies such as Option Six and Allen Interactions. Ask them for free sample exercises; Allen Interactions has a free compact disc featuring more than twenty e-learning activities from projects they have developed. At the same time, gather recommendations from colleagues in training departments of other companies that make available examples of interactive online activities.

***Variations and Extensions.*** A variation on this task would be to have students discuss their answers with a critical friend or partner before submitting them. Each person would submit individual responses, but they would first have the chance to discuss their answers with a peer. If this activity is used in a FTF class or students are geographically close to each other, you might have teammates or critical friends sit next to each other in a computer lab or some other convenient setting when completing their online review exams. If this is possible, they could discuss their answers prior to submission.

### Key Instructional Considerations

*Risk index:* Medium

*Time index:* Medium to High

*Cost index:* Low to High (depending on whether content is free)

*Learner-centered index:* Medium

*Duration of the learning activity:* 1 week or as needed

## Activity 80. Mock Trial or Fictional Situations

***Description and Purpose of Activity.*** One way to enable learners to begin to internalize the content that they are learning is to engage them in a mock trial or fictional situation. For instance, professors at the University of Glamorgan in Wales have their business students enter a boardroom in which they are furnished with a case problem that they must solve (see Figure 9.3). In this virtual boardroom, students have access to resources and an online chat tool for debating points.

### FIGURE 9.3. ONLINE BOARD ROOM CASE SITUATION.

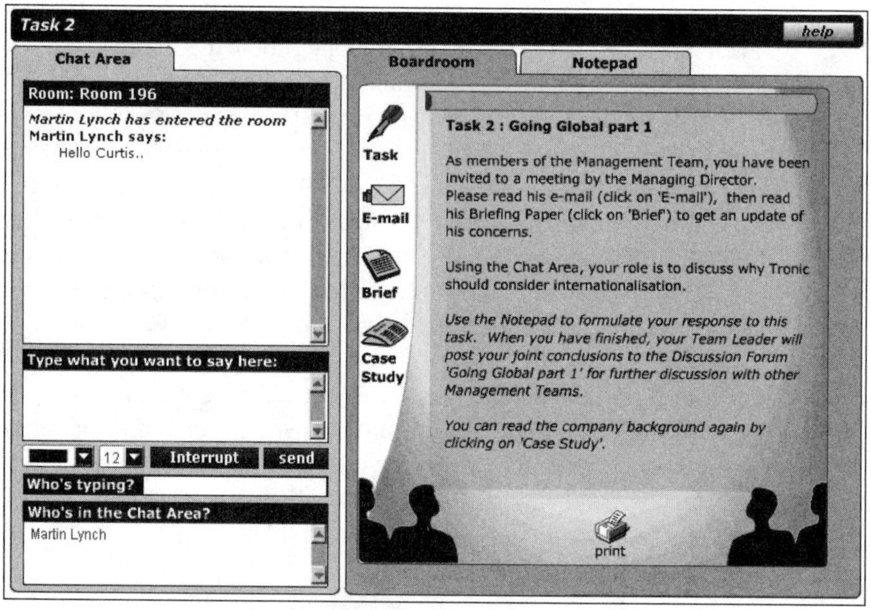

Used by permission of University of Glamorgan.

While the virtual boardroom may have been a novelty when developed in Wales a few years ago, such mock trial and fictional simulation tools are now expected in prominent business school training programs as well as most other professional schools. In fact, many M.B.A. programs, such as Massachusetts Institute of Technology's Sloan School of Business, have mock stock exchange centers, where students trade stocks, bonds, or even "ideas" (Feder, 2002). At the present time, dozens of mock stock exchange software programs are available for simulated financial analyses and portfolio management.

Mock trials are certainly applicable to many fields outside business. In our own education classes, for example, we have had students in mock trial situations in which each student has a role within a trial (for example, attorney, defendant, bailiff, prosecutor, witness, judge, jury, and so on). While such techniques are extremely captivating and effective in both online as well as in traditional classroom situations, they are perhaps most powerful in blended learning situations, such as FTF courses with videoconferencing to multiple sites or a FTF mock trial with a follow-up online discussion and debate.

***Skills and Objectives.*** Includes appreciation of multiple perspectives and perspective taking, content review, and application of concepts in a realistic situation.

***Advice and Ideas.*** Brainstorm ways in which a mock trial or fictional situation might be employed in your course. You might ask colleagues if they have tried something like this in their classes. Is there a person or controversial case in your field that you might put on trial to help foster deeper student learning? Decide upon and create the mock trial situation, and then assign student roles within it (be sure to follow the role play advice offered next in Activity 81). The first time you use it, you might tell your students it is just an experiment. When you have enacted the mock trial and experienced success, ask other instructors for their feedback on improvements or variations that they might employ.

***Variations and Extensions.*** Hold a debriefing session on the role play task (perhaps in an asynchronous discussion thread) in which students reflect on the activity and skills gained. They might also provide formative and summative feedback on the effectiveness of the task.

## Key Instructional Considerations

*Risk index:* High

*Time index:* High

*Cost index:* Low

*Learner-centered index:* High

*Duration of the learning activity:* 1–2 weeks

# Activity 81. Online Role Play of Personalities

***Description and Purpose of Activity.*** In addition to a mock trial presented in Activity 80, students can engage in online role plays. Role plays typically ask participants to assume or act out different perspectives, personalities, characters, or attitudes. Role play situations can be tightly structured by the instructor or instructional designer or more loosely structured, where the participants might assume multiple roles or suggest fully new ones. One popular online role play simulation platform that was developed in Australia is called Flabusi.

In our own teaching, we have conducted role plays using both asynchronous and synchronous conferencing technology. As noted in Chapter Five, we have done this in many different ways, including assigning students specific personalities to play in the online environment (for example, pessimist, questioner, protestor, comic, summarizer, and so on). In fact, we have designed twenty-eight different personality roles. Sometimes we assign students to one of these twenty-eight roles and other times they sign up for those that are of most interest to them. To add spice to the activity, we often attach names of real individuals to the personality role; for example, Mother Teresa might be assigned to someone in the humanitarian role, Sir Edmund Hillary to someone in the adventurer role, and Attila the Hun to someone who is the warrior. The warrior, pessimist, or devil's advocate role is usually central to student interaction and resulting learning; we find that without such role assumption, students are hesitant to be critical of their peers online. These roles give them license to be critical or negative in their feedback.

Such role play activities may be used in online or blended settings to promote critical thinking, awareness and sensitivity to diversity, problem solving, decision making, and other higher-order thinking skills. In K–12 settings, role plays can be fun and rewarding, such as the replaying of historical events that are being taught or current news stories that relate to the course content. And, in teacher education programs, role plays can foster a comprehensive understanding of the dynamic social system of education. For example, teacher education students might act out the roles of different parties or stakeholders involved in a technology integration project, the sharing of high-risk technology ideas and initiatives with the local community, or events aimed at creating technology-related policies for a school district or community. Learners in a customer service training situation in the corporate world may play various types of customers with their different problems or complaints. Here, participants may need to choose and defend different responses and solutions for customer satisfaction.

***Skills and Objectives.*** Includes critical thinking, appreciation of multiple perspectives and perspective taking, application of skills learned, feedback, problem solving and problem identification, and overall flexible application of learned concepts and principles.

***Advice and Ideas.*** Carefully select the content or topic for which an online role play would be useful. If funding allows, purchase a prepackaged role play from a publisher. If you do not have significant resources, find a free or less expensive program online or design your own creative role play activity that captures the material being taught in the class. Set up the role play platform in the learning management system (LMS) or course management system (CMS) using the discussion forum or conference to post an initial thread or arrange for a synchronous conferencing meeting in which all participants act out their roles live. We have done that for our own classes and found much success without spending money on software packages.

Define student online roles with sufficient detail and provide guidelines as necessary. Such guidelines may relate to when to post, how much to post, and how to respond to peers. Assign learners to specific roles or have students sign up for them. Give learners as much control over this task as possible, including signing up for roles and perhaps even designing or suggesting new roles. If students do not like a role that they selected or were assigned, allow them to change roles. Typically, we maintain roles over multiple weeks of an activity but change them when the activity changes. Be careful to train those in any negative type of role (for example, devil's advocate, pessimist, idea squelcher, and so on) on how to critique ideas instead of attacking people.

Facilitate the online role play activity with prompts, questions, and task structuring. The latter might involve reminding learners of participation dates, expectations for interaction, and, of course, their roles (whether they are participating as expected). At some point in the process, provide an opportunity for learners to address the conflicts or disagreements between their assigned roles and their own thoughts or viewpoints. In the end, any debriefing with reflections and discussions on the role play activity will reinforce and extend their learning.

*Variations and Extensions.* One variation of this activity would be to use a small set of preselected key roles (for example, summarizer, questioner, coach, starter, optimist, and pessimist) that students sign up for weekly. Then allow the students who have not signed up for one of the preselected roles to pick any other open or unassigned role each week, or, if none are appealing, allow students simply to be themselves. Reflections after the completion of the role play activity can be encouraged to further promote critical thinking.

## Key Instructional Considerations

*Risk index:* High

*Time index:* Medium

*Cost index:* Low (assumes use of free or existing resources)

*Learner-centered index:* High

*Duration of the learning activity:* 1–2 weeks

# Activity 82. Action Research

*Description and Purpose of Activity.* One way to personalize learning is to assign an action research project using students' new learning acquisitions. In action research, an individual or a team conducts field research to examine one or more questions or issues. While used in real-world settings such as training environments, action research tends to be found more often in higher education classes. Of course, data collected during this field research may serve to alter or advance the original set of learner questions. And the learners will likely learn additional principles and concepts beyond the instruction.

We have used action research in our professional development classes with practicing teachers. At the start of such courses, we provide these experienced teachers with a guide sheet and ask them to brainstorm action research ideas and then to reflect on how they will accomplish the idea that they selected. Next they design a technology integration project while collecting student surveys and other data about its effectiveness. At the end of the semester they present not only their curriculum innovations but also student satisfaction findings and any student learning achievement data available.

Similar action research projects could be developed in any discipline when students who are working full or part-time are in the course. Businesspeople in a leadership training course, for instance, might collect data from their employees on their management practices. School counselors might collect survey data from students whom they have helped or worked with. Dentists might have customer satisfaction forms for customers to complete. Of course, if this research is being reported beyond the class, there are usually human subject and ethical considerations to keep in mind.

***Skills and Objectives.*** Includes application of skills in a real-world context, evaluation skills, inferencing, presentation and communication skills, critical thinking, design skills, insight, and problem- and product-based learning.

***Advice and Ideas.*** Action research, and research of any kind, is often a highly stressful experience for learners who have never conducted research before. As a result, the more examples, testimonials, and supports students are offered, the better. To help overcome misconceptions about the task as well as reduce anxiety, ask former students who succeeded in this task to present testimonials, either in FTF settings or online. In addition, you can provide students with guide sheets for brainstorming action research plans and reflecting on resources and goals.

Develop an action research assignment for learners in your course. Consult necessary books on this topic, as appropriate. Offer support and direct feedback on student action research plans as well as on their progress reports as activities and problems unfold. Of course, monitor action research processes and provide online moderation and coaching as needed.

When done, create a format in which students present their results to peers in the class and possibly to online experts as well. Save high-quality research as examples for future course offerings.

***Variations and Extensions.*** Require students to present the results of their action research projects to local community members, fellow employees, or others who might benefit from their findings. In addition, establish a project gallery of action research success stories.

## Key Instructional Considerations

> *Risk index:* High
>
> *Time index:* Medium
>
> *Cost index:* Medium
>
> *Learner-centered index:* High
>
> *Duration of the learning activity:* 3–6 weeks

## Activity 83. Interactive Fiction and Continuous Stories

*Description and Purpose of Activity.* Our colleague Sivasailam Thiagarajan from the Thiagi Group (known to most simply as "Thiagi") once showed us a Web site he developed in which anyone coming to the site could add to a particular story that others had started. Thiagi called the technique "interactive fiction." In using his interactive fiction site, we found it amusing to add to a story and then observe the creative insights and ideas of other individuals from around the planet as they shaped its evolution.

While Thiagi works mainly with adult learners in corporate and higher education settings, an effective strategy for those focused on creativity in K–12 settings is the use of interactive and continuous online stories. Using tools such as Writer's Window, for instance, young learners can post their poems, short stories, reports, and book reviews as well as help write a "continuous story." As with Thiagi's interactive fiction site, a continuous story is started by one student and then others add to it. The online stories generated might be used as starter text from which learners can write their own personal stories or as examples of different writing genres for English teachers to share and discuss. Stories are not only an excellent way for students to learn from others but for them to summarize their learning as well.

*Skills and Objectives.* Includes creative expression, communication, logical sequencing and chains of reasoning, text coherence, insight, knowledge transfer, and appreciation of multiple perspectives.

*Advice and Ideas.* Consider conducting an online session in which students present their stories or summaries. Perhaps discuss or debate issues from the stories or summaries in an asynchronous discussion forum. Peer assessment and awards for best stories might enhance this task.

Select an appropriate technology tool that your level of learners may use to write their online stories. In you are in the K–12 field, you might employ Writer's Window, mentioned earlier. If you are in higher education or corporate training, your learners might be familiar with using MSWord for their online collaborative efforts with peers. They can use MSWord to share and extend stories through e-mail document attachments or by uploading to the course CMS/LMS. If you want more efficient document management instead of multiple versions of a text (which is what happens when relying on e-mail-based collaboration), you might use Google Spreadsheets and Documents or a wiki tool (for example, MediaWiki, Wikispaces, Socialtext, and so on) for collaborative creation of a story. With such tools there will be only one document that everyone will work from.

For even more sophisticated document collaboration, you might test out tools such as Collanos or LetsPowwow Collaboration Software; both can currently be downloaded free of charge (see Web resources). Even more powerful, in terms of the sheer number of collaborative features and functions, is Groove from Microsoft. In fact, since Groove is embedded with the Enterprise and Ultimate editions of Microsoft Office 2007, you may already have it available. Groove is also available as a standalone application. Several Web conferencing tools such as WebEx, Elluminate, and Interwise combine document sharing with online collaborative meetings. And if online group brainstorming of stories is vital, ThinkTank from GroupSystems is available. Clearly, there are myriad options for your collaborative efforts.

No matter what tool or system you employ, you should assign the task with sufficient guidelines and examples. Creativity starts with awareness that everyone can be creative. Therefore, discuss creativity and the creative process with your learners prior to the start of the interactive writing task and perhaps show your students creative products from previous semesters. At the same time, you need to make your assessment plans clearly understood by learners. Moderate any creative and collaborative processes as necessary. When done, be sure to collect and share the stories.

*Variations and Extensions.* Such a technique can not only be used for fictional stories; it might also be employed to summarize class sessions or modules as well as brainstorm key points. In effect, this activity combines both creative as well as evaluative skills of the participants.

## Key Instructional Considerations

> *Risk index:* Medium
>
> *Time index:* Medium
>
> *Cost index:* Low (assumes free tools are used)
>
> *Learner-centered index:* High
>
> *Duration of the learning activity:* 1–2 weeks

# Activity 84. Real-Time Cases

*Description and Purpose of Activity.* As was mentioned in Chapter Eight, a recently popular online activity involves the use of real-time case studies. In real-time cases, business students address real-world problems and issues as they occur.

To facilitate this process, in agreement with company officials, a student is planted in a company or government setting and writes up the case situation. Correspondence with the class or institution happens in a variety of formats, including synchronous chats, blogs, asynchronous discussion, videoconferencing, Webcams, and so on.

Such a technique enables students to witness course concepts, principles, and ideas in action in real-world settings. Incorporating real-time cases not only legitimizes the course content but extends the class beyond it. At the same time, this high-risk strategy might expose the instructor to criticisms of the class content from those in executive-level positions in the real world. Those implementing this technique in K–12 settings might rely on local experts, community members, or parents for such real-world problems and case situations. Be aware that there may be legal or ethical issues you and your class would face in such situations that may require the advice of your legal department and the development of special procedures. Human subjects forms may need to be completed.

***Skills and Objectives.*** Includes application of knowledge and skills in a real-world context, flexible application of knowledge, appreciation of multiple perspectives, problem-based learning, and critical thinking.

***Advice and Ideas.*** Working with real-time cases can be a highly novel activity. If you are not familiar with it, start with a small pilot case or activity that is drafted by the instructor or found in your textbook and reflect on the process as well as the results. Read articles by Professor James Theroux at the University of Massachusetts at Amherst on the use of the real-time case method (Theroux et al., 2004) and perhaps write to experts like him seeking additional advice or with specific questions. Contact government agencies, schools, nonprofit organizations, or businesses about the use of real-time cases and solicit their interest in participating.

As an example of a real-time case, assume you have a marketing class that is working with a new Web 2.0 company called Social Networking Agents for Interactive Language Exchanges (SNAIL-E). SNAIL-E has created a new system for users of social networking services that employs intelligent agents to automatically translate transactions or comments within a social networking site (for example, Facebook, Friendster, MySpace, and so on) to any of thirty-five different languages (say, Japanese, English, Spanish, Dutch, Polish, Russian). Using these special language agents, SNAIL-E software helps friendships grow across languages and cultures. In addition, if you are planning a trip, the SNAIL-E tool searches for people with interests in the countries and cultures you are visiting and establishes an initial link between parties for potential meetings. The SNAIL-E president, Victor Speed, is a highly experienced and creative computer programmer but has limited marketing skills. Although many Web 2.0 companies rely on viral marketing and word-of-mouth instead of direct marketing or sales personnel, SNAIL-E's revenues have been nominal for two years and monies from angel investments and venture capital have been used exclusively for software design and testing. The SNAIL-E usergroup is growing at a tremendous pace, but revenues remain minimal.

You brief your students on the situation and then plant one of your students, Jennifer, in the day-to-day operations of the SNAIL-E company as part of an internship experience. Jennifer assumes the role of case writer who reports back to your class about the company in daily e-mail exchanges as well as in her blog posts, which are open only to your class. In addition, you arrange a thirty-minute chat session or videoconference each week with Mr. Speed. Jennifer describes the marketing (as well as management) situation at SNAIL-E, and your students reflect on it and offer their advice, either as individuals or as teams that compete against each other for solutions that the SNAIL-E president rates and might implement. Such forms of authentic learning are highly engaging and motivating for learners.

In your course, create a real-time case task for the class with one of the companies or organizations you contacted previously. The student embedded in the company may be a prior student of the class who is now in an internship or practicum experience. The remaining tasks and activities may be divided based on previous experience, interest, personality, time available, or instructor preferences. Decide on the technologies that might be employed (for example, chat tools, videoconferencing, Web cams, asynchronous discussion forums, and so on). Enact the task. When complete, save the resulting case situation and final products for future use. You might archive a summary of the event on your course Web site.

***Variations and Extensions.*** Ask your students to post to an asynchronous discussion forum themes that they notice in two or more real-time cases used during your course.

## Key Instructional Considerations

> *Risk index:* High
>
> *Time index:* High
>
> *Cost index:* Medium to High
>
> *Learner-centered index:* Medium
>
> *Duration of the learning activity:* 1–2 weeks as needed

## Activity 85. Course Resource Wiki Site

*Description and Purpose of Activity.*  Wiki tools allow members of a community to record events, activities, news, and other information. In an online or blended class, a wiki can serve similar purposes. In a course wiki site, an instructor might post key course advice and assignment reminder information or provide feedback on student projects in individual student wiki pages, and students might add to such notes and reminders. In a course on romantic poetry, for instance, students might use a wiki to link poems to pictures, music, expert commentaries, blog postings, and word definitions or interpretations (Read, 2005).

One of our colleagues, Dr. Ted Frick, teaches a course at Indiana University in computer-mediated learning using a wiki as a learning support tool. In this course, students use the wiki to select specific course task options or sign up for final presentation timeslots. In addition, Dr. Frick lists useful external resources that the learners may need. Because Dr. Frick's course is a truly blended course, the wiki is not the main course Web site; it is one of several supplemental course resources. For participatory learning, Frick's students create personal wiki pages with Web links to their course products or deliverables. As a result, students can see each other's products and comment on them. In summary, embedding a wiki in a course can enable instructors to coordinate their course more effectively as well as allow students to take charge of their own learning and become self-directed learners.

Keep in mind that it is the communal aspects of wiki tools that relate to Phase 4 of R2D2. The instructor might have students add information to a community wiki for the course, with sections on Web resources, course advice, task examples, team members or groups, peer or expert contact details, progress reports, relevant conferences or seminars, job information, news related to the course, and so on. As such, a class wiki is a way to communicate about important resources from instructors to students. It simultaneously is a collaboration and student empowerment tool, since anyone in the course can add, modify, delete, or enhance any information or resource found there.

*Skills and Objectives.*  Includes collaboration, interactivity, student participatory learning, problem- and project-based learning, and assignment feedback.

*Advice and Ideas.*  Talk to colleagues for their advice on where you might use wikis in your instruction or where they have seen them used. For instance, you might incorporate wiki tools into your course for sharing resources, papers, course announcements, procedures, advice, and so on. Colleagues might have ideas about motivating students to use a course wiki on a regular basis. Simply put, some students will actively contribute to such a site and others will be more hesitant because they are not familiar with wiki projects. Given that a wiki is a community portal or document, students might not be clear on how their contributions will be evaluated. As a result, many of them will simply follow the lead of others. It is important, therefore, that you model posting behaviors in the wiki resource site. In addition, assessment criteria as well as task structuring is vital information for the learners. And, as part of the task structuring, clear project deadlines should be established.

Talk to the training department or instructional support office about free and open source wiki tools that are available for your organization or institution. If the Wiki tool chosen has sophisticated or unusual features, ask for someone to provide training for both you and your students.

There are a maze of alternatives and options here. For instance, you might decide not to allow students to delete the work of peers and require them to post under their real names or designated usernames instead of anonymously. You might also open up your course site to the world community for advice and feedback. As you use course wikis for different tasks or functions, discuss and debrief with your students so that the task can continually be updated and enhanced. In fact, when the semester or course ends, consider holding a brainstorming session related to how the wiki site might be reused or changed next time.

***Variations and Extensions.*** Students might generate products in a course wiki based on their course readings and work, such as a class-generated list of task deadlines and procedures, lists of key findings from the readings, or a course glossary. Using the wiki tool in Moodle (an open source CMS system), our colleague, Dr. Ron Owston at York University, had his students negotiate their entire course syllabus during the summer of 2007. This course, Digital Technology in Education, was organized around weekly thematic topics (simulations and games, the design of e-learning, blended learning, and so on). While Owston had a set of notes and article readings for each week, small groups of students were required to add to those notes, readings, and associated commentaries. Given the newness of the technology, initial discussion and continual scaffolding of such a task is vital.

## Key Instructional Considerations

*Risk index:* High

*Time index:* Medium to High

*Cost index:* Low or Medium

*Learner-centered index:* High

*Duration of the learning activity:* Throughout course or as needed

## Activity 86. Wikibook Projects

*Description and Purpose of Activity.* A wiki is a community-developed resource. A wikibook, therefore, is developed by a community interested in a particular topic or idea. In a class, students might be assigned to create a wikibook (or multiple wikibooks if the class is large enough) based on their interests. A wikibook project is appropriate for adult learning or K–12 students; in fact, there is a special section of junior wikibooks for elementary youth at the wikibook Web site. A wikibook project requires learners to work with other students who are developing chapters while simultaneously pushing them to individually explore ideas for their own chapters or modules. Such a project extends the audience of the course to anyone with Web access. While a wikibook project can be highly motivating, it can also be stressful, since students may not want others to view their work. Fortunately, you can use simple user control menu options to make the wikibook open to the general public, password protected, or entirely private.

*Skills and Objectives.* Includes active learning, creative expression and insight, student motivation and engagement, student-generated or participatory learning, knowledge construction and negotiation, collaboration and interaction, and appreciation of multiple perspectives. Of course, writing is a tool for fostering thinking and the growth of new thoughts and connections.

*Advice and Ideas.* Before attempting such a project, explore existing wikibooks for examples and ideas of possible books your class could write or help write. Once comfortable with the format, you should design the wikibook task with sufficient learner structure and guidance. For instance, you might demonstrate how to use the wikibook tool and provide a training or trial period as needed prior to the wikibook project. Assign feedback partners for different sections or modules of the book. Monitor the progress carefully and provide feedback in a timely fashion. When the book is complete (or near completion—some argue that a wikibook is never complete), consider holding an online press conference for the class or the world at large. Be sure to also ask for student reflections on what they have learned in the wikibook process and what they would do differently in the future and why.

Unless the class size is large, avoid making this task optional. Our experience indicates that making it optional will not create enough momentum to complete the book. In addition, be sure to provide learners with training on how to use the wikibook site while clarifying the goals of the project before commencing with it. It is also crucial to create job aids or support templates for each phase of the project. To foster interaction, collaboration, and timely feedback, you might designate small teams for particular wikibook activities and require peer feedback on each completed task. We have found cross-institutional wikibook projects to be highly engaging and valuable to learners as well as instructors.

*Variations and Extensions.* Hold competitions between students for different chapters by having the same chapters written by two or more students and then asking the class to vote on them according to certain guidelines. The chapters with the highest ratings could be included in the wikibook.

## Key Instructional Considerations

*Risk index:* High

*Time index:* High

*Cost index:* Low (depending on the wiki tools selected)

*Learner-centered index:* High

*Duration of the learning activity:* 4–5 weeks

# Activity 87. Online Glossary and Resource Links Projects

*Description and Purpose of Activity.* Some courses include options through which learners create extensive yet practical final projects that benefit both current students as well as those taking the course later. An online glossary is one such project. Here, a learner or a group of learners designs an interactive online glossary that summarizes key concepts and ideas for the course. Web links might be generated that connect terms and definitions to articles, well-known individuals in the field, and media elements (audioclips, videoclips, animations, and so on). One variation of this activity is to assign individual learners to different letters of the alphabet for the wiki glossary while having one or two volunteers accumulate all the work and make it available online. This forces each learner to have responsibility for different aspects of the glossary or problem situation, thereby establishing meeting group goals and associated expertise.

*Skills and Objectives.* Includes concept review and extension, application of concepts, concept discrimination, insight, exploration, and evaluation.

*Advice and Ideas.* Assign the online glossary task as an individual, small team, or class activity. If this is a team activity, one team could work on the online glossary while another finds relevant Web resources to link it to. Given the complexity and possible novelty of the task, you should provide examples from previous semesters or a similar class, if available. In addition, create and share your evaluation criteria with the task assignment. During the task, your role is to coach and mentor students in their efforts; without a doubt, at key moments in the process, your students will need timely encouragement and feedback. Offer advice and task structuring when and where needed (perhaps by reacting to glossary drafts and innovative ideas). Post the final products to the course Web site or blog. Given that this is a semester-long type of project with many people benefiting from the final product, it is vital to celebrate success and share final glossaries and other course products with colleagues.

If course content changes each semester or year, this activity could be repeated in the following semesters or versions of the course. It might also be used as a starting point for course lectures or other activities. In addition, you might find other online glossaries on the Web and index them as guides for student work.

*Variations and Extensions.* Sometimes we assign all students to create glossaries with definitions (in their own words) as well as pertinent stories or examples. In addition, you might design review games, quizzes, and other activities from the online glossary with which students are tested on their knowledge of different terms. As an extrinsic motivator, high scores might be posted to the course Web site.

## Key Instructional Considerations

> *Risk index:* Medium
>
> *Time index:* High
>
> *Cost index:* Low
>
> *Learner-centered index:* High
>
> *Duration of the learning activity:* 3–4 weeks

# Activity 88. On-Demand and Workflow Learning

*Description and Purpose of Activity.* While instructor-led training will always exist, the pace of innovation and change in the twenty-first century mandates that learning opportunities be provided to learners in a more timely or rapid fashion. In response, workflow learning allows a person to complete a task or achieve desired goals using relevant resources immediately when needed. As an example, International Business Machines (IBM) employs work-embedded learning; they believe that the employee will be more motivated to learn at or near the very moment of need (DeViney & Lewis, 2006). In effect, this approach involves the fusing of learning and doing something with that learning.

Workflow learning occurs when learning "just in time." Electronic supports are provided to the employee or learner at the point of need or demand. For instance, when needed, a helicopter mechanic might call up special schematics and procedures on a handheld device, laptop computer, or augmented reality goggles or eyewear (Kirkley & Kirkley, 2006). Such resources allow her to learn how to fix or replace key parts of a helicopter and are available for review at any time, if necessary.

As higher education institutions adjust to fast-changing economies and the teaching of skills needed for workers in the twenty-first century, workflow learning becomes increasingly critical for administrators and instructors to consider. As part of these efforts, new forms of educational delivery systems are currently being tested. In the online M.B.A. program at Indiana University, for instance, instructors are often planted in work settings at places such as General Motors to deliver their instruction. The same is often now true in other professional disciplines, such as teacher education, engineering, and medicine. As the learning delivery formats are increasingly blended and varied, the options for workflow learning proliferate.

While e-learning courses may provide initial knowledge experiences and certifications, they fail to support the daily knowledge needs of most service technicians, repair personnel, and most anyone with a full-time job. However, using mobile devices on demand, the technician can pull up such information as required during the performance of a task (Singh, 2006). A tax accountant might call up new regulations related to stock options when working on an annual report rather than taking a class or seminar beforehand and then forgetting what was learned. A petroleum engineer might access stored data from subject matter experts as it is needed, engage in online sharing and reflection activities, and be guided through self-analysis activities in courses that update him on the rapid changes in technology related to oil production (Collis, 2006). When learning is embedded in authentic work-based tasks, workers can more quickly acquire the skills needed for the vast changes in knowledge taking place within a particular field or discipline. And workers can learn to solve everyday problems related to their job roles, not fictitious or contrived ones from a textbook. When this occurs, there is more of a direct match between knowledge acquisition and use.

As is evident, in these work-embedded learning environments—often referred to as "on-demand" and "workflow" learning—learners become increasingly empowered to shape and control their own learning experiences and paths.

As university-school-corporate types of partnerships increase, so, too, will the opportunities to embed as well as evaluate such new forms of learning. This may be an ultimate goal (and test) of a society attempting to train its citizenry in the midst of massive global economic and technological changes such as those faced today.

**Skills and Objectives.**  Includes concept application, awareness of knowledge use and implications, skill discrimination, interactivity with content, timely feedback on performance, and critical analysis.

**Advice and Ideas.**  If you are in a program with direct connections to real-world learning, brainstorm with learners or employees where just-in-time learning may be beneficial. Create content for a mobile and wireless learning environment in which learners can search, find, and use information as needed. Monitor learner use and completion of such resources by downloading computer log data and administering polls and surveys. Continually evaluate the effectiveness of such mobile learning environments and modify or adapt online materials and tasks as needed.

This is an important and fast-changing field. Keep abreast of new developments by reading recent reports related to on-demand and workflow learning or attending conferences or institutes on it. If you have limited time, perhaps attend a free 1–2 hour synchronous training session or Webinar on the topic. Read materials from workflow advocates and e-learning gurus such as Jay Cross (2007), Harvey Singh (2006), and Betty Collis (2006). When at conferences, talk to colleagues on how they are putting on-demand and workflow ideas into practice.

**Variations and Extensions.**  After designing a series of job aids and content for learners to use in their job settings or situations, ask learners (that is, trainees) to design the evaluations or ratings of their effectiveness. Next, have them put together a planning document or report making recommendations for changes as well as future directions in workflow learning.

## Key Instructional Considerations

> *Risk index:* High
>
> *Time index:* High
>
> *Cost index:* High
>
> *Learner-centered index:* High
>
> *Duration of the learning activity:* As needed

## Activity 89. Digital Storytelling

***Description and Purpose of Activity.*** As software used on the Web evolves, there is a continued explosion of ways for learners to embed multiple forms of media in their online learning projects. A recent trend, especially in K–12 education, is the use of digital storytelling. Professor Bernard Robin at the University of Houston has created a unique and highly valuable Web site indexing educational uses of digital storytelling with an assortment of interesting projects and ideas (see Figure 9.4).

Digital storytelling employs multimedia software to combine text, pictures, sound, graphics, and videos. Here, learners take control of their own learning

### FIGURE 9.4. EDUCATIONAL USES OF DIGITAL STORYTELLING FROM THE UNIVERSITY OF HOUSTON.

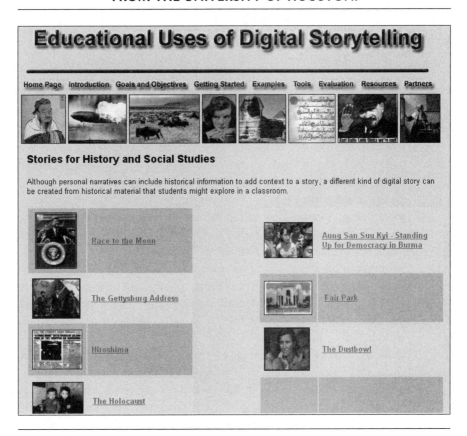

by writing scripts to tell their stories. Through digital storytelling, learner ideas come to life. Such an activity nurtures learner creativity as well as information filtering, synthesis, evaluation, and organization skills. Digital stories serve many purposes; they can be instructional, informational, historical, or autobiographical. In addition, they can raise serious environmental, scientific, or political questions and issues. In an online course, a digital story might document student learning in the course, add credibility to community-based research, or augment a final report or project presentation. In effect, digital storytelling requires students to synthesize a huge amount of content while learning important communication and technology skills. Additionally, students learn to present their ideas and insights in highly personal and meaningful ways.

In many ways, assigning students to create YouTube videos, as one instructor at Mohawk College in Ontario, Canada, recently did (and with a great deal of success) is a form of digital storytelling. The growth of sites such as YouTube and TeacherTube and the assignment of video blogging to students is evidence that video storytelling is infiltrating higher education as well as other educational settings today.

*Skills and Objectives.* Includes synthesis, communication, creative expression, collaboration, exploration, knowledge generation, and logical sequencing.

*Advice and Ideas.* Assign the digital storytelling task and provide sufficient guidelines. These guidelines might relate to length, subject matter, diversity of perspectives gathered, and questions or issues to raise. If possible, provide examples of final products from previous courses. Next, ask your learners (or teams) to select topics for digital stories as well as the underlying goals or purposes of the stories (to inform, document, persuade, account for, prove, and so on). Help students locate image resources such as pictures, drawings, photographs, maps, charts, and so on. In addition, locate audio resources such as music, speeches, interviews, and sound effects. Perhaps provide an annotated list of such media resources for learners. Require that students create their digital stories and scaffold the learning process. Some subtasks might relate to scripting the event, accessing experts, reserving equipment, recording the event(s), and editing and polishing the product. Post digital stories to the course Web site (with permission) and share them with the rest of the class. Assign appropriate reflective activities. Instructors might share final products with colleagues or enter them in competitions (with the appropriate student permissions, of course).

If this is a new task, ask for student volunteers to assist with this project. It is extremely important to provide specific and clear guidelines for students. Given the focus on creative design, instructors might simultaneously teach students about the creative process so that they are more self-aware of their own creativity.

***Variations and Extensions.*** When done, instructors might publish student work on the Web for peer and expert critique as well as for others around the globe to view. At the very least, the most intriguing or creative digital stories should be made available for students in the following semesters.

## Key Instructional Considerations

> *Risk index:* High
>
> *Time index:* High
>
> *Cost index:* Medium
>
> *Learner-centered index:* High
>
> *Duration of the learning activity:* 3–4 weeks

# Activity 90. Online Documentation of Internship, Field Placement, Practicum Knowledge Applications, and Experiences

***Description and Purpose of Activity.*** One way students can practice or do something with the knowledge they have acquired is to participate in a follow-up course or a real-world activity connected to the class, in which the learners put into practice the knowledge they have gained. For instance, an accounting major who has taken courses during the previous year in auditing and tax accounting might in a summer internship opportunity be given an assortment of auditing and tax-related tasks. A preservice teacher might be given opportunities to teach during her senior year of college while working with Native American school children in New Mexico or Arizona. A medical intern might interview a patient and record notes before the doctor arrives. A college student in a fitness training program might work at a summer sports camp or institute, helping camp participants with weight training, endurance, and overall conditioning plans. A manager in a training department might implement a new training evaluation method in accordance with a management course he is presently taking.

Earlier in this book, we discussed how such practicum or field-based observations could be reflected upon in online discussions or personal blogs. In this activity, we promote the use of online tools to document or display the use of different course-related skills on the job. One simple approach is to have students in internships or practica (and perhaps their supervisors) complete online forms indicating what they have accomplished related to their course or program requirements. These online forms might be as simple as checkboxes to indicate simple use of knowledge, or they might entail extensive evaluations or comprehensive papers summarizing the concepts and ideas encountered during the internship. These activity handouts as well as the student reflections might be posted online.

***Skills and Objectives.*** Includes application of concepts on the job, reflection skills, problem-based learning, coaching and mentoring, feedback on skill use, and skill discrimination.

***Advice and Ideas.*** Create a set of learning guides and reflections to be used by students doing internships. Communicate the task requirements and expectations with the onsite supervisor or contact person during the course. Be sure to gather learning outcomes in the form of portfolios, projects, products, designs, creative artifacts, and reflections from the learner upon completion of the internship or field work experience. In addition, obtain any onsite evaluations of learner performances and learning experiences. Provide comprehensive evaluation results and feedback to learners.

There are many interesting activities that can be performed in the workplace. The supervisor in the field might be required in advance to sign a form agreeing that students will be involved in certain prespecified tasks to use their knowledge. And when the course ends, you might interview students or their supervisors to determine what was most effective as well as what might be modified next time to facilitate skill use and internalization. In addition, instructors teaching this course might hold brainstorming sessions with each other during which they generate ideas about how to have students successfully try out their course-related knowledge when in a field placement, practicum, or internship situation.

***Variations and Extensions.*** There are numerous additional ways to document the use of concepts in action. For instance, students might post pictures to a special Web site or blog showing them using their ideas in the workplace. Or they might create a video documentary (for example, a YouTube video) or digital story documenting their work. Such videos could be taken from student mobile or handheld devices and placed in a designated course Web site for instructor and peer review and commentary. Alternatively, students might create a podcast episode or two detailing concepts and principles that they learned during the internship, field placement, or practicum that link to particular courses or their overall program.

Tools for documenting the use of skills learned during blended and fully online courses are proliferating. As a result, many pedagogically exciting and engaging activities await the creative online instructor and learner during the coming decades.

## Key Instructional Considerations

*Risk index:* Medium

*Time index:* Medium

*Cost index:* Low to Medium

*Learner-centered index:* Medium

*Duration of the learning activity:* 6–8 weeks

# Activity 91. Authentic Data Analysis

***Description and Purpose of Activity.*** Most learners love to get their hands dirty rather than listen to yet another boring lecture or read more dry content. One of our colleagues in the anthropology department at Indiana University collected important artifacts in Africa for many years. In the mid-1990s, she digitized much of her work and placed it online in an interactive timeline called the TimeWeb tool, from which her students called up artifacts in a virtual dig and performed realistic tests using online tools.

Fast-forward to a decade later, and there are dozens of such archaeology and anthropology sites available for students to access and manipulate. DiscoverBabylon.org is one that is being developed to handle vast resources from ancient Babylon, Egypt, and many other early civilizations. At other sites, students might virtually explore ancient Mayan ruins while asking questions of experts, exploring links to associated resources, making scientific predictions, and weeding through additional information related to current Mayan discoveries in the news.

Similarly, a wellspring of real-time, dynamic, project-based learning sites with real-world databases are available for K–12 education. Ou and Zhang (2006), for instance, specifically discuss an assortment of resources available on the Internet for K–12 teachers for database-related learning activities, including dynamic projects involving global collaboration. For example, projects like One Sky, Many Voices dynamically engage students in captivating projects to learn various subjects locally as well as through interactions with peers and experts from across the planet. Similarly the Globe Program connects students worldwide in hands-on science-related learning activities. Importantly, Ou and

Zhang (2006) provide a list of selected databases found on the Internet by subject and grade level in K–12 settings.

Besides these rich K–12 situations, authentic data is often fairly easily obtained in online professional development programs and corporate and government training. And, in such situations, there is typically a purpose or practical implication of such analyses. For instance, a small Web-based survey sample or online focus group interview might provide the kernel for a larger report or evaluation project. Here, the learning can be carried over into your job setting.

***Skills and Objectives.*** Includes motivation and engagement, problem- and product-based learning, goal setting, data analysis and evaluation, witnessing concepts in action, comparison and contrast, communication and presentation skills, and team collaboration.

***Advice and Ideas.*** Test out any online tools or systems that claim to allow for authentic data analysis before using it. Once relevant sites are located, you might create a task in which students virtually collect and analyze real-world artifacts, objects, and data. To help, search for Web sites with real-world data and materials. Ask colleagues for advice and suggestions and then post what you have found for your learners. Be sure to make known the assessment criteria and prepare learners with sufficient guidelines and resources. As with any novel online activity, you need to monitor the process and provide scaffolds and moderation as appropriate. In addition, have learners share milestone steps in the process and resulting findings via the LMS/ CMS, course Web site, or course blog. Perhaps involve guest experts to comment on the data collected and analyzed as well as the associated analysis results and reports. When done, involve learners in reflective activities on the processes and outcomes. If possible, have students rework final reports on such data into conference proposals or reports back to the organization that created or maintains the Web site.

***Variations and Extensions.*** Perhaps create a collaborative task that involves a final presentation or competition with students from another university or country.

## Key Instructional Considerations

*Risk index:* Medium

*Time index:* Medium

*Cost index:* Low to High (depending on software availability)

*Learner-centered index:* Medium

*Duration of the learning activity:* 1 week or as needed

# Activity 92. Online Science Labs and Simulations

***Description and Purpose of Activity.*** One recent online learning phenomenon is the shifting of live laboratory activities to virtual ones (see Figure 9.5). As the Web resources listed for this chapter indicate, there are countless simulation and lab resources in psychics, chemistry, economics, engineering, biology, psychology, and many other disciplines. Using these resources, students might complete a classical experiment in Gestalt psychology and compare their results to the posted norms. Or they might pose hypotheses and then determine if their predictions were accurate. Using the Learn Anywhere Anytime Physics (LAAP) curriculum, for instance, students might select equipment and instruments for different physics tests, set up and execute their own experiments, pose hypotheses, and report results.

## FIGURE 9.5. A VIRTUAL CHEMISTRY EXPERIMENT.

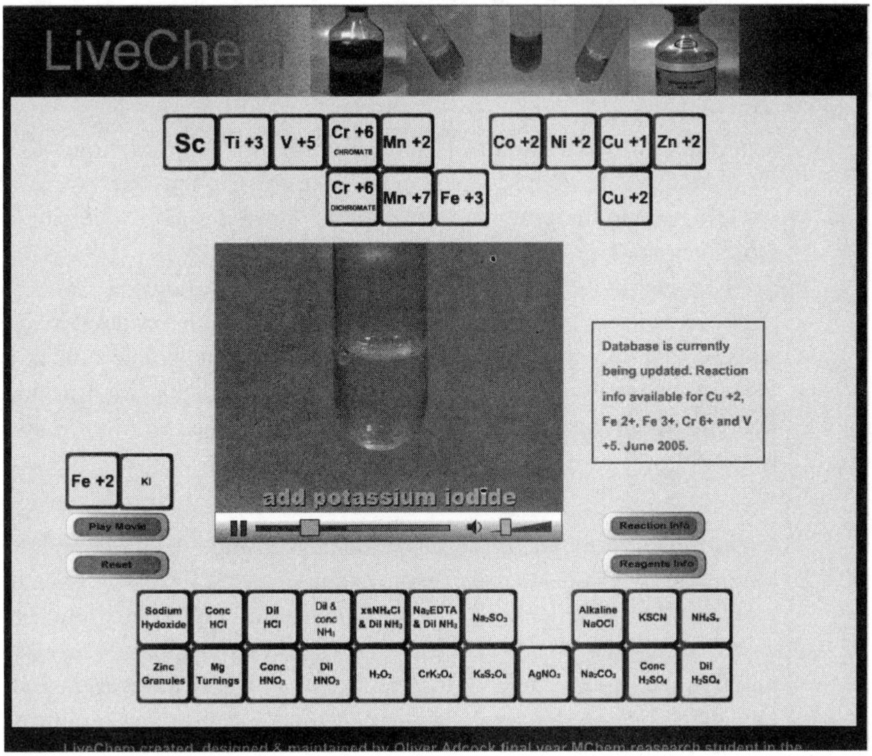

The goal, of course, is to construct a mental model or framework of the principles involved and to test it out. These simulations and online lab activities help students confront any misconceptions or conceptual difficulties that they have. Their online experimentations, therefore, allow them to observe what happens, reformulate their ideas and models, compare predictions or hypotheses against actuality, and analyze results with the tools and instruments that real-life scientists might use in their own lab settings. Online labs allow students to make mistakes that are not costly or dangerous. Such online explorations and investigations can take place prior to content delivery, during it, or after it, with each option having its own set of advantages and disadvantages.

**Skills and Objectives.** Includes reflection, motivation and engagement, insight, critical thinking, comprehension and application skills, decision making, problem solving, and analysis and evaluation. Key goals here are practice and feedback on that practice.

**Advice and Ideas.** Explore the Web for simulations and labs in your content areas or courses. Contact colleagues for suggestions and recommendations as well. When attending conferences, ask experts in your field what types of simulations and online labs they are using or have heard about.

Online labs and simulations often require special software tools to run effectively. As a result, double check any simulation or lab resources that may have worked great in the past; many are not maintained due to technology changes, funding limitations, or loss of personnel.

Consider embedding in the selected online simulation or lab general exploratory activities to spur student motivation and higher-order thinking. Assign tasks or experiments for students to conduct using the online simulation or lab. Provide learners with a set of guidelines or job aids for this learning activity. Perhaps assign final reflection papers or blog posts on what students have learned.

**Variations and Extensions.** Ask students to complete an online lab or simulation task that collects their results prior to an FTF class or have them post their results and reflections to an online forum or Web site. During the FTF class, use different means to address learner misconceptions or issues raised in online warm-up activities or forums. Another highly motivational alternative involves asking students to find their own online resources and present them to the class.

## Key Instructional Considerations

*Risk index:* Medium

*Time index:* Medium

*Cost index:* Low to High

*Learner-centered index:* Medium

*Duration of the learning activity:* As needed

# Activity 93. Simulation Games

***Description and Purpose of Activity.*** There are a number of manipulable online games that are used to explain concepts and principles to learners. Relatively brief and inexpensive online games and simulations can explain how television works, how ice melts, how Prozac functions in the human brain, or how avalanches happen. Many such simple games can be found for a variety of disciplines in higher education at the Multimedia Educational Resource for Learning and Online Teaching (MERLOT) and Connexions Web sites mentioned in earlier chapters.

Of course, there are more elaborate simulations, too, such as the free Virtual U Project, in which the user attempts to manage university or college resources (see Web resources for a link to this system). In the Virtual U Project, the user must make hiring and firing decisions, decide on pay raises, allocate resources, manage enrollments, and make other key decisions of a university administrator. Similarly, in the corporate training world, the free IT Manager Game from Intel can be played over a fairly lengthy period of time. In the IT Manager Game, the person playing it makes management-level decisions such as whom to hire or fire, how much to pay, and what technologies the company needs. She must also decide on many budget-related issues that concern an information technology (IT) department. Of course, the primary goal is a healthy and profitable company that is at least, in part, made possible by sound IT decisions.

In the K–12 arena, BrainPop is a popular resource with hundreds of short animated movies in different content areas (for example, science, social studies, English, math, and so on) with associated activities, timelines, and experiments. In the health section, for instance, BrainPop movies explain such topics as the circulatory system, asthma, AIDS, nutrition, and chicken pox. BrainPop and other simulation games are fun and interactive ways to help learners understand difficult concepts.

*Skills and Objectives.* Includes reflection, motivation and engagement, insight, critical thinking, comprehension and application skills, recognition of basic terminology, problem solving, trial-and-error testing, exploration, goal setting, and competition.

*Advice and Ideas.* Determine if simulation games are available in your content area. You might do this through literature reviews, searching MERLOT or Connexions, or writing to colleagues in your field who are known for innovative pedagogy. If no games are found, consider asking your media support personnel to help you locate or build one. Test any simulation games you are considering with your students; simulation games have different features that attract students to them. Incorporate these games in your course with a set of guiding questions and other learning activities. Be sure to provide your learners with assessment criteria and debrief the use of the simulation games when done.

*Variations and Extensions.* You might assign such a task prior to an FTF class as a warm-up activity that can lead to extensive discussion and greater insight. A game might also be a postclass activity for reflection and review of concepts learned. You might even make it an optional assignment in which students locate online simulations relevant to a course and post how the simulations might be best utilized in class.

## Key Instructional Considerations

*Risk index:* Medium

*Time index:* Medium

*Cost index:* Low to High (depending on whether freely available)

*Learner-centered index:* Medium

*Duration of the learning activity:* 1–2 weeks or as needed

# Activity 94. Simulations and Games for Higher-Level Skills

*Description and Purpose of Activity.* The U.S. military as well as many educational institutions teach higher-level skills such as planning, management, and leadership through simulations and gaming—in particular, with highly popular massive multiplayer online games (MMOGs) (see Bonk & Dennen, 2005). MMOGs allow thousands of individuals around the world to play the game—and, therefore, potentially interact with each other—simultaneously. Educators might review simulations and games such as Civilization, Star Wars Galaxies, or even Halo for the types of higher-order thinking and metacognitive skills that they could promote. They might also explore how to teach collaboration and teamwork using these games.

Some colleagues may make light of your use of simulations and games in teaching and learning. However, keep in mind that we remain at the dawn of such use in education and training settings. It has not yet been determined how best to assess the results of playing such games. Still, there are vast resources and huge budgets in the simulations and gaming industry. If some of these resources are used to build and promote high-quality educational games, online courses may soon be designed to teach specific skills such as planning and teamwork.

***Skills and Objectives.*** Includes reflection, teaming, motivation and engagement, decision making, perceptual skills, feedback, insight, critical thinking, comprehension and application skills, goal setting, problem solving, and analysis and evaluation.

***Advice and Ideas.*** Create a plan or vision for how simulations and games might be used in your organization or institution to teach high-level skills. If not sure, talk to experienced MMOG educators or trainers for their ideas, suggestions, and recommendations. Try out a pilot or experimental task with an online simulation or game with a class or small group of learners. After such experimentation, discuss other potential uses or enhancements with your learners.

Students in a history class, for instance, might be asked to play Civilization for a set period of time. When finished, instructors might assign reflection papers comparing concepts learned in the online game to those mentioned in course textbooks and lectures. Extensive discussion and debate will likely ensue.

***Variations and Extensions.*** Ask one student to play the game for 30 minutes while thinking out loud, and have a partner record her thinking and the strategies she used. Then switch roles for 30 minutes. When done, have students post their observations to an online forum or a blog for discussion and debate.

## Key Instructional Considerations

> *Risk index:* High
>
> *Time index:* High
>
> *Cost index:* Low to High
>
> *Learner-centered index:* High
>
> *Duration of the learning activity:* 4–5 weeks or as needed

## Activity 95. Client Consulting and Experiential Learning

*Description and Purpose of Activity.* In some courses, small groups of students might provide course-related consulting support to a local business, project, or institute. This shift toward placing student learning in real-world contexts is not surprising given that institutions and organizations are increasingly appreciating and advocating the use of experiential and problem-based learning in training and education (Bowlin, 2001; Edens, 2000; Groth & Robertson, 1999).

As a prime example, at the University of Northern Iowa, Dr. William Bowlin has witnessed students in his cost accounting classes develop real-world job-costing systems, analyze company pricing strategies, evaluate inventory control procedures and overhead rates, establish budgeting systems, investigate inventory variances, flowchart processes and activities, and prepare major pricing plans (Bowlin, 2001). In such projects, students can experience the typical problems associated with communicating with teammates, insufficient data, changing deadlines, and priority differences among management and staff as well as within management itself. These students also learn skills related to teamwork, critical thinking, planning, organization, scheduling, flexibility, assigning responsibilities, and succinct reporting.

Such experiential course experiences can be even more engaging and informative in blended and fully online courses. In blended courses, students can access the Web for up-to-date information, upload documents, engage in team chats, and e-mail the client, while also meeting with the instructor to learn strategies for analyzing and interpreting that content. In addition, a final presentation to the client (as well as the class) can take place using videoconferencing or with a synchronous conferencing system such as Breeze or Eluminate.

*Skills and Objectives.* Includes problem-based learning, decision making, authentic data analysis, problem solving, communication and presentation skills, data filtering and synthesis, and team collaboration. A key goal, of course, is the increased awareness of skills and concepts used in real-world settings.

*Advice and Ideas.* Contact local businesses that might be in need of products or services related to your course or module. Meet with officials from the business to design the task and associated requirements and expectations. A signed agreement may be required.

Inform learners of the different projects available and determine their respective interests, roles, and responsibilities. Create clear guidelines for each part of the project. Satisfying client needs is never easy, and it is even more difficult when done online. Given these difficulties, it is important to be clear with students as to the ramifications of not meeting the client's intended outcomes. For highest-quality results, the project may extend over an entire year or two semesters of a course sequence.

Consider grouping learners as needed. Bowlin (2001) notes that the optimal size of groups might be three or four students per team. In addition, Groth and Robertson (1999) recommend considering the heterogeneity of the consulting teams. They argue that one should avoid grouping together students who have language deficiencies or for whom English is clearly a second language, since they may encounter difficulties communicating with the client as well as the instructor. Along these same lines, instructors might pair more experienced with less experienced students.

Require learners to meet with clients (either online or FTF). In addition, ask them to present their project proposals and feasibility studies (either online or FTF). Have learners spec out project deliverables with agreements from both the instructor and the client, keeping in mind that timelines and deadlines for the deliverables are vital to project success.

During the ensuing weeks, learners continue to work with both you and the client (either online or FTF). Meet with the students periodically (online or FTF) to consult with them on their progress. Given the open-ended nature of this task, they will need extensive resource guidance and support to create viable products. When done, students implement, test, and verify their products and solutions. They deliver final products to the clients, while you communicate and gather client feedback and share such feedback with the learners. Require that students submit a final reflection paper on what they learned from this activity.

***Variations and Extensions.*** Class competitions might take place between groups for their solutions, with corporate-sponsored end-of-class awards and prizes.

## Key Instructional Considerations

*Risk index:* High

*Time index:* High

*Cost index:* Low (generally speaking)

*Learner-centered index:* High

*Duration of the learning activity:* As needed

## Activity 96. Online Tutoring and Mentoring

*Description and Purpose of Activity.* If we had a short list of the key advantages of online learning environments, the possibilities for virtual tutoring and mentoring would be near the top of that list. We have embedded online mentoring activities in our graduate and undergraduate courses for more than a decade, and the typical results are both intellectually exciting as well as personally fulfilling. There are many ways to establish and facilitate online tutoring and mentoring activities. When acting as online tutors and mentors, learners must use the skills that they are learning. They must quickly and flexibly interpret and respond to questions. Clearly, when the student becomes the teacher, course knowledge and information is more richly learned.

As an example of Web-based tutoring and mentoring, in May 2006, the *Chronicle of Higher Education* featured an article on the use of videoconferencing or Webcams as a means of tutoring hearing-impaired high school students on their homework (Kiernan, 2006). The people conducting the tutoring session were preservice teachers from Valdosta State University (VSU) in Georgia who had been learning sign language. Through videoconferencing, college instructors at VSU could observe their students when they were working with hearing-impaired students in a real classroom.

Of course, there are many ways to practice sign language. Students can act as interpreters for deaf students who use Webcams on their laptops to share lessons they are being taught. In this way, a deaf college student can learn the lesson better and more fully participate in a class. These examples epitomize notions of Phase 4 of R2D2; learners are putting their new skills to practice in real-world settings. Imagine what other innovative uses of the Web may help learners who have special needs.

*Skills and Objectives.* Includes coaching, feedback, motivation and engagement, comprehension skills, and overall skill internalization. Mentoring and tutoring should also reduce learner anxiety or trepidation regarding the course.

*Advice and Ideas.* Conduct a needs assessment for learners you plan on tutoring. Determine the technologies required. Compare to budget. Create a plan or vision statement to obtain the necessary funding or administrator buy-in. Conduct a pilot test of your plans and ideas. When deemed ready, implement these ideas more fully and continue to test them out.

Create a form or guidesheet for the tutors or mentors. In it, specify the types of help they might provide or questions they might ask the learners. At the end of each course, have the mentors and tutors update these guidesheets. Those being tutored might also evaluate the mentors. The mentors with the highest evaluations might be recognized in some fashion.

*Variations and Extensions.* Ask the instructor of an advanced-level class to include a mentoring assignment or task in which the advanced students mentor the students in your (less advanced) class. Reflection papers or activities posted to a CMS or LMS will allow students to compare mentoring experiences and knowledge gained from it.

## Key Instructional Considerations

*Risk index:* High

*Time index:* High

*Cost index:* Low to High (depending on system used)

*Learner-centered index:* High

*Duration of the learning activity:* As needed

# Activity 97. Cross-Class Product Development and Creativity

*Description and Purpose of Activity.* Before a visit to the University of Illinois at Urbana-Champaign (UIUC) for a speech in the spring of 2005, Bonk decided to explore the UIUC Web site for interesting online pedagogical activities and news. Though he found many innovative technology stories in computer science, education, and art and design, one piece of news that attracted his attention was about Professor Bruce Wicks' course in leisure studies on the Dynamics of Tourism (Mitchell, 2002). Students in this course teamed up with Korean students at the University of Dongguk in Kyongju to create mock tour packages. Here, the Illinois students used online resources to design eight- to ten-day tours for their Korean counterparts who were being trained to work as guides in English-speaking countries. The tours they designed included stops in Chicago area blues clubs, Las Vegas hot spots, and Disneyland, as well as whitewater rafting excursions. Despite various time and language barriers, this project was deemed highly successful and potentially expandable to many other countries.

Cross-class collaboration projects such as this one foster key twenty-first-century skills, including perspective taking and virtual teamwork. When required to think about the online learning avenues or journeys through the Web for a person from another culture or country, students begin to appreciate the diverse ways in which their course content knowledge can be applied. And they simultaneously begin to witness the nuances related to the application of that knowledge.

***Skills and Objectives.*** Includes perspective taking, collaboration, interaction, product-based learning, motivation and engagement, presentation skills, and decision making.

***Advice and Ideas.*** Brainstorm ideas for cross-class collaboration with colleagues. You might restrict brainstorming to course instructors or include the students in such idea-generation processes. The brainstorming event could take place using e-mail, asynchronous discussion, synchronous chat, videoconferencing, or some combination of such technologies. Be sure to coordinate schedules with an online clock since collaborators may be in many different time zones (see World Clock: Time Zones from timeanddate.com in Web resources). Share responsibilities in the development of the task selected and be sure that all parties agree to the task structure and associated timelines.

Do not make assumptions on what will or will not work. First, check on the existing technology infrastructure at the respective institutions. Next, conduct pilot tests of equipment and the general course activity. When those are completed satisfactorily, create help systems, job aids, guide sheets, and other learning scaffolds. When appropriate, begin cross-class collaboration with the instructor and among learners. Follow all procedures and division of labor in the process. At the end of the activity or course, debrief with your students and discuss enhancements or modifications to the task.

Sharing is a vital part of any new and exciting innovation in online pedagogy. You might share results with colleagues as a means to show what is now possible online. In addition, present at international conferences and other venues as a means to network with international colleagues. Consider conducting action research on possible international projects and presenting the results of such activity in the partnering country. You might even conduct such research with your new colleagues at the collaborating institutions. To be successful, you must be open and flexible as well as willing to experiment with new pedagogical approaches or ideas as the technologies change.

Those who take such risks often serve as role models for others. Professor Wicks, in the previous example, was the director of the Office of Recreation and Tourism Development and served as a role model for all instructors in his department and institution, especially for junior faculty members.

***Variations and Extensions.*** Perhaps bring in outside experts from other countries or locations (those who are unbiased toward a particular institution or country) to rate or evaluate the products produced. Team competitions and awards may fuel student interest and participation.

## Key Instructional Considerations

*Risk index:* High

*Time index:* High

*Cost index:* Low to Medium

*Learner-centered index:* High

*Duration of the learning activity:* 1–4 weeks

# Activity 98. Cross-Class Content Discussions, Analyses, Competitions, and Evaluations

***Description and Purpose of Activity.*** We have conducted online international case analyses on a number of occasions. In one project that ran from 1996 to 2000, Bonk had preservice teachers from Finland, Korea, the United Kingdom, Peru, and the United States write problematic case situations or vignettes in an asynchronous discussion forum on the Internet based on their field observations. Student colleagues in other countries attempted to solve the problems the others posted based on their content knowledge and previous experiences. During the five years of this project (The Intraplanetary Teacher Learning Exchange, or TITLE), Bonk conducted a series of research projects exploring the quality of cases, forms of feedback, assistance or mentoring provided online, and cross-cultural differences in student as well as teacher exchanges (Bonk, Angeli, Malikowski, & Supplee, 2001; Bonk, Hara, et al., 2000). Using the Web, these students generated the case vignettes and associated questions instead of reacting to ones provided by instructors or book publishers. As a result, they were more authentic than typical college cases.

More recently, Bonk's students were matched with students in Dr. Abtar Kaur's class at the Open University of Malaysia to solve short case problems that were posted online. Instead of solving cases individually, they had to negotiate a solution with peers from another region of the world. The instructors moderated or facilitated the process.

In both situations, students had to make decisions about a problem or vignette based upon their knowledge. Most important, they had to perform or do something with the knowledge they gained from the textbook, instructor lectures, field observations, or other course resources.

**Skills and Objectives.** Includes decision making, problem- and case-based learning, comparison and contrast, motivation and engagement, appreciation of multiple perspectives, creative expression, and critical thinking and evaluation.

**Advice and Ideas.** Brainstorm ideas for cross-class collaboration with colleagues, including possibilities for online discussions, analyses, evaluations, or competitions. Coordinate task development with instructors at the other locations—be sure each instructor agrees to the basic outline of the task and associated timeline. Check on technology access and familiarity at each location. An initial pilot test at each site might be advantageous. Try to hold a presession using synchronous chats, video conferencing, Webinars, or Webcams in which the goals and objectives of the project are explained.

Create any job aids, help systems, guide sheets, or learning aids that students might need. Provide examples of how to give feedback on online activities and model such feedback. Translate any guide sheets to the native languages of the participants. Have all online activities translated for student native tongues. Perhaps begin the cross-class collaboration with a social ice breaker or some type of easy task. Monitor the event and let students know how they are performing. When done, debrief with students on how they think the activity went. Perhaps have a final videoconference between the sites to share what each other has learned.

**Variations and Extensions.** During the activity, instructors might supply intermittent summaries of how the activity or event is going: examples of interesting cases and quotes from students, as well as data on the number of cases posted, number of participants, and average length of postings. Such updates are simultaneously motivational and instructional in providing reminders about the task.

## Key Instructional Considerations

> *Risk index:* Medium
>
> *Time index:* Medium to High
>
> *Cost index:* Low to Medium
>
> *Learner-centered index:* High
>
> *Duration of the learning activity:* 2–8 weeks

# Activity 99. Learner Podcast Activities, Events, and Shows

*Description and Purpose of Activity.* In addition to course-related podcasts from the instructor or course developers discussed in Chapters Two and Three, learners may develop their own podcasts. For instance, students in a middle school history course might design a special weekly radio show during which they focus on some aspect of their learning activities for that week (for example, a skit or role play recounting a famous battle of World War II, or someone reading Abraham Lincoln's Gettysburg Address during the U.S. Civil War). They might also podcast oral reports of their learning in a high school history or psychology course to supplement, extend, or replace written reports. Such podcasts might be accompanied by PowerPoint presentations, Web links, written reports, blog reflections, and associated references.

Learner-produced podcasts are particularly powerful in language learning courses. Students in a French language class, for instance, might practice their language lessons orally and post them online for later feedback from the instructor or from peers in Belgium, France, or Quebec. For those interested in using podcasts to display creativity, students in a music course or program might record their own music and put it on the Web for others to listen to. Learner creativity might also be displayed in podcasts of comedy routines, poetry readings, and news shows.

In corporate training settings, learners might create a set of podcasts for others in their department or unit related to the information learned during a particular class. Or a podcast production might be a component of a final learning assessment in which one or more learners relate aspects of their course content to their job setting.

Alternatively, the podcast might be a tool for showcasing critical thinking. For instance, online M.B.A. students might conduct interviews with experts or key industry figures and post them as podcasts to the course Web site. These M.B.A. students might each ask a set of similar questions of different leaders and then critically compare results, including evaluating the credibility of different arguments, checking assumptions, noting biases, and exploring the justification of reasoning. Similarly, students in an educational research course might record their interviews and observations as part of action research they are conducting as a means to back up the statements or claims in their reports. Others in their research team might download these audio files and help analyze them.

As these few brief examples indicate, there are myriad ways for students to display their learning via the podcast; some involve creative expression, while others help students hone their critical analysis and evaluation skills. Such activities are ideal for Phase 4 learning, since they set up goals and tangible products for students to strive to achieve. In addition, the audience for most of these podcasts is anyone with access to the content, including friends and relatives as well as outside experts.

**Skills and Objectives.** Includes student-generated learning, presentation and communication skills, concept review, creative expression, interaction, motivation and engagement, and critical reflection.

**Advice and Ideas.** Prepare learners for learner-generated podcast activities with appropriate instructions, job aids, resources, or training prior to the session. Typically, a podcast demonstration is all that is needed to hook students in. Perhaps start off by conducting an open brainstorming session of all the possible uses of podcasting. Then hand out resources discussing uses; compare the list with the uses your students have brainstormed and resume brainstorming activities. Eventually require students to narrow in and focus on activities that they might try out. Throughout these events, you must provide the necessary online supports for student podcasting activities.

Once students have committed to podcasting ideas and topics, be sure to require and review the podcast session outline or drafts of session narratives prior to podcasting. Conduct podcast sessions. During these sessions, instructors or trainers should act as guides for student podcast shows and events. To enhance motivation, showcase the podcasts within the class or to your department or the general public. Discuss final results with students.

**Variations and Extensions.** Consider competitions related to student final podcast products with possible awards or recognitions. As part of this, an exciting annual event might be designed to promote podcast competitions.

## Key Instructional Considerations

*Risk index:* High

*Time index:* Medium

*Cost index:* Low to Medium

*Learner-centered index:* High

*Duration of the learning activity:* 1–2 weeks or as needed

## Activity 100. Design Course Web Site

**Description and Purpose of Activity.** We want to mention here another participatory and active learning project. One of our ambitious colleagues, Dr. Jonathan

Plucker at Indiana University, teaches an amazing course on human intelligence. Not only is the content fascinating, but so is his pedagogy. As a prime example of Phase 4 or hands-on learning within the R2D2 model, Dr. Plucker has his students continually design and redesign the course Web site. And some students never want to leave—they continue to help with the course Web site long after they have received their grades. This comprehensive course has dozens of real-world case examples from the field of intelligence, information on key controversies within the field, a wealth of Web resources, an interactive map indicating an insightful array of influences in the field, a time period index, key biographical information (Plato, Edward Thorndike, J. P. Guilford, Lewis Terman, Robert Sternberg, Howard Gardner, and so on), hot topics within the field, and an interesting array of information, pictures, and important historical documents related to key individuals who have fashioned the field of intelligence.

Professor Plucker's students not only read about monumental figures in the area of human intelligence, they might correspond with them (assuming they are still living) or their descendants and ask for photos, visuals, papers, or vital documents. While his students are not necessarily experts in instructional design, their design work significantly influences their course-related learning. Simply put, they learn how to synthesize a vast amount of knowledge and communicate with an audience well beyond the instructor. Additionally, they obtain advanced levels of knowledge and insights within a field and become more self-aware of everyday changes or events related to the discipline. In effect, the goal-based learning aspects of such a task so engages these learners that they continue to be interested in the field throughout their lives.

***Skills and Objectives.*** Includes audience awareness, student knowledge construction and evaluation, problem- and product-based learning, goal setting, motivation and engagement, design skills, communication and presentation, feedback, creative expression, and knowledge filtering and synthesis.

***Advice and Ideas.*** There are many stages and substages in the design of a useful course Web site. First, you might challenge individual students or the entire class to build or enhance a course Web site or learning portal. To pique their interest, show students examples from other classes. Alternatively, if a course Web site has already been built, perhaps have one or more of the original student designers demonstrate the site and share their thoughts on how it might be improved.

Once the students are on board with the project idea, ask them to draft various Web site design or improvement plans and then apportion the work. Prior to implementation, require that students present mock-ups of design changes. When ready, implement the changes and check for accuracy. Share the new or remodeled site with colleagues, students, experts, and friends.

This is an exciting activity, but student excitement one semester may wane, thereby leaving the Web site with an array of dead links that are in serious need of updating. Keep in mind that even the most enthusiastic and supportive of students will someday graduate and need to attend to their own family responsibilities and career goals. As a result, instead of taking the approach of "Build it and they will come," instructors must have a long-range plan or vision for any site or learning portal they develop. Perhaps the plan will be to design important pedagogical activities for the field and share them. Perhaps it will be to serve as a historical marker for the field. Or perhaps the goal will be to collect and index vast resources for anyone taking a course in the area.

No matter what the plans or goals, consider writing a grant proposal to maintain, upgrade, and effectively share the site once an initial prototype is developed. And, as the semesters scroll by, you should continue to promote the course Web site or activity portal to colleagues and friends. As part of these efforts, a link to the site might be placed in a national or international knowledge repository such as MERLOT, Connexions, or Jorum. Never stop dreaming—a Web design activity in one course could evolve into an internationally designed and delivered master's program involving myriad well-known universities and instructors.

*Variations and Extensions.* Perhaps expand the project into a cross-institutional project in which students from two or more universities work jointly to create or enhance a Web site, or where they create separate Web resources or materials for related courses.

## Key Instructional Considerations

*Risk index:* High

*Time index:* High

*Cost index:* Medium to High

*Learner-centered index:* High

*Duration of the learning activity:* Semester long (continual)

# Use and Outlook for Phase 4 Strategies

Of all the phases in R2D2, Phase 4 is perhaps the most exciting for the field of online teaching and learning. It is here that you touch learning and learning touches you back. The learning activity tugs at the learner to try out a strategy, make a decision, or reflect on whether her current knowledge base is sufficient. But the learner can tug back at the system by requesting even more difficult problems or scenarios or by offering creative responses that cannot be electronically analyzed and evaluated; at least not at the present time. In addition, the learner may tug even harder by sharing her solutions with others who might use such an online tool or resource later on.

Questions abound here. For instance, must the act of "doing" something online be unique to be authentic? How can resources continue to enable learners to come up with creative ideas and content in an age when knowledge sharing and communication continues to proliferate? Can a wikibook developed one semester, for instance, be considered an exemplary form of participatory learning in later semesters when students are asked to build upon or redesign it? Is such learning an honest form of participatory learning only in the first instantiation of the book? Or are there variations in the degree of doing, in the levels of participation, or in the types of task authenticity? Despite these questions, there is no doubt that hands-on learning activities are exciting and exploding.

## Final Reflections

What does it mean to "do" something? Does it necessitate a physical space? Is a witness required? Must the act of doing be recorded for it to be authentic? Is an electronic record of completion sufficient or do pervasive plagiarism concerns necessitate gathering additional evidence?

In the twenty-first century, learners need to perform both in physical worlds as well as in electronic ones. If electronic, the paths for doing something with your new knowledge will be tracked and saved. Of course, the power of such virtual learning worlds is only starting to be understood and appreciated.

But just as we begin to tame and cultivate the learning possibilities of three-dimensional worlds, augmented reality, or simulation games, new technologies and experiences will undoubtedly spring forth. Perhaps they will involve headgear of some type or perhaps there will be a chip implanted in our brains or within the skin to create real-world sensations for learners. It is also plausible that memory cards or indices will take the learner to increasingly more difficult performance challenges or levels of knowledge. No matter what happens, what it means to "do something" will continually change. Part of the power of R2D2 will be in making sense of why such activities or experiences are powerful and where they can best be utilized.

Now that we have explored the four phases of R2D2, Chapter Ten attempts to bring the entire problem-solving cycle of this model into perspective with comprehensive instructional approaches and strategies that address all four phases to some degree. Again, as asserted earlier in this book, R2D2 is only one way of dividing or categorizing the endless resources found in the Web of Learning. The final chapter offers a means to pull together the four phases as well as to reflect on unique applications for and options within R2D2.

# CHAPTER TEN

# INTEGRATING R2D2 AND FINAL REFLECTIONS ON THE WEB OF LEARNING

By now, the four phases of R2D2—Read, Reflect, Display, and Do—should be fairly clear. We hope that you were able to gain from Chapters Two through Nine at least a couple of ideas that you can now use. As indicated throughout the book, the four phases of the R2D2 model overlap. In addition, each aspect is a significant component of a problem-solving cycle or wheel of learning. While one might employ any of the four spokes of this wheel at any given moment, it is their combined power to move the learner successfully through complex and difficult educational and training situations that this final chapter addresses. Sometimes task involvement in all four phases of the model is obvious, and other times it is more subtle.

In Chapters Three, Five, Seven, and Nine, we mapped out more than 100 activities that might be used across a range of online and blended learning situations. Table 10.1 provides an overall summary of them, including the key instructional considerations for each activity.

## Comprehensive Strategies for R2D2

### Phase 1: Reading (Chapters Two and Three)

Quite a few of the activities and ideas presented in Chapters Two and Three involve two or more phases of R2D2. For instance, the use of a podcast was

**TABLE 10.1. SUMMARY OF ACTIVITIES FOR R2D2 WITH KEY INSTRUCTIONAL CONSIDERATIONS.**

*Phase 1: Reading (Addressing Verbal and Auditory Learners)*

| Learning Activity | Risk | Time | Cost | Learner-Centeredness | Duration of Activity |
|---|---|---|---|---|---|
| 1. Online Scavenger Hunt | Low | Medium | Low | Medium | 1–2 weeks |
| 2. Web Tours and Safaris | Medium | Medium | Medium | Medium | 1 week as needed |
| 3. WebQuests | Low | Medium | Low | Medium | 1–4 weeks |
| 4. Guided Readings | Low | Medium | Low | Medium | 4–15 weeks |
| 5. Discovery Readings | Medium | Low | Low | High | 1–2 or 4–12 weeks |
| 6. Foreign Language Reading Activities and Online News | Medium | Medium | Low | Medium | 1–2 or 4–10 weeks |
| 7. FAQ and Course Announcement Feedback | Low | Medium | Low | Medium | Weekly or as needed |
| 8. Question-and-Answer Sessions with Instructor | Medium | Medium | Low | Medium | Weekly or as needed |
| 9. Online Expert Chats | Medium | Medium | Low | Medium | 1 week as needed |
| 10. Online Synchronous Testing | Medium | High | Low | Low to High | Weekly or as needed |
| 11. Synchronous or Virtual Classroom Instructor Presentations | Medium | Medium | High | Medium | Weekly or as needed |
| 12. Online Webinars | Medium | Medium | High | Medium | Weekly as needed |
| 13. Public Tutorials, Wizards, and Help Systems | Low | Low to High | Low to Medium | Medium | 1 week as needed |
| 14. Expert Lectures and Commentary | Low | High | Medium | Medium | Weekly as needed |

| Activity | | | | | Time |
|---|---|---|---|---|---|
| 15. Online Podcast Lectures or Podcast Shows | Medium | Medium | Medium | Medium | 1–2 weeks |
| 16. Audio Dramas | Medium | Medium | High | Medium | 1–2 weeks as needed |
| 17. Posting Video-Based Explanations and Demonstrations | Medium | Medium | High | Medium | Weekly as needed |
| 18. Online Sound or Music Training | Low | Medium | Low | Medium | Weekly as needed |
| 19. Online Literature Readings | Medium | Medium | Low | Medium | Weekly as needed |
| 20. Online Poetry Readings | Medium | Medium | Low | Medium | Weekly as needed |
| 21. Posting Webliographies or Web Resources | Medium | Medium | Low | High | 2–4 weeks |
| 22. Text Messaging Course Notes and Content | High | Medium | Medium | Medium | As needed |
| 23. Text Messaging Course Reminders and Activities | Medium | Medium | Medium | Medium | As needed |
| 24. Online Language Lessons | Medium | High | Low to high | Medium | As needed, perhaps for the entire course |
| 25. E-Book and Wikibook Reports and Critiques | High | High | Low | High | 4–8 weeks |

*Phase 2: Reflecting (Addressing Reflective and Observational Learners)*

| Activity | | | | | Time |
|---|---|---|---|---|---|
| 26. Post Model Answers | Low | Low | Low | Medium | As needed |
| 27. Reuse Chat Transcripts | Low | Medium | Low | Medium | 1–2 weeks for each activity |
| 28. Workplace, Internship, or Job Reflections | Medium | Medium | Low | Medium | 4–15 weeks |
| 29. Field and Lab Observations | Medium | Medium | Low | High | 4–10 weeks |
| 30. Self-Check Quizzes and Exams | Low | Medium to high | Low | Medium | As needed |
| 31. Online Discussion Forums and Group Discussions | Medium | High | Low | High | 10–15 weeks of course |

*(Continued)*

**TABLE 10.1.** *(Continued)*

| Learning Activity | Risk | Time | Cost | Learner-Centeredness | Duration of Activity |
|---|---|---|---|---|---|
| 32. Online Portal Explorations and Reflections | Medium | Medium | Low | Medium | As needed |
| 33. Lurker, Browser, or Observer in Online Groups | Medium | Medium | Low | High | 4–8 weeks |
| 34. Podcast Tours | Medium | Medium | Low | Medium | 1–2 weeks |
| 35. Personal Blogs | Medium | High | Low | High | 8–15 weeks |
| 36. Collaborative or Team Blogs | Medium | High | Low | High | 8–12 weeks |
| 37. Online Resource Libraries | Medium | High | Low | High | 1–2 weeks or 6–12 weeks |
| 38. Social Networking Linkages | High | Medium | Low | High | 1–3 weeks |
| 39. Online Role Play Reflections | High | High | Low | High | 1–2 weeks |
| 40. Synchronous and Asynchronous Discussion Combinations | Medium | Medium | Low | High | 1–2 weeks for each instance |
| 41. Self-Check Reflection Activities | Low | Low | Low | Medium | As needed |
| 42. Electronic Portfolios | Medium | High | Medium | High | 12–15 weeks (entire course typically) |
| 43. Individual Reflection Papers | Low | Medium to high | Low | High | As needed; perhaps 1–4 weeks for each writing activity |
| 44. Team or Group Reflective Writing Tasks | Medium | High | Low | Medium | 3–8 weeks |
| 45. Super-Summaries, Portfolio Reflections, and Personal Philosophy Papers | Medium | Medium to high | Low | High | 3–15 weeks (might be ongoing for entire semester) |

| Activity | | | | | |
|---|---|---|---|---|---|
| 46. Online Cases, Situations, and Vignettes | Medium | Medium to high | Medium to high | Medium | 1–4 weeks |
| 47. Satellite Discussion or Special Interest Groups | Medium | Medium | Low | High | 4–12 weeks |
| 48. Small-Group Case Creations and Analyses | Medium | High | Low to medium | High | 1–3 weeks |
| 49. Small-Group Exam Question Challenges | Medium | Medium | Low | High | 1–2 weeks |
| 50. Reaction or Position Papers | Medium | Medium | Low | Medium | 1–2 weeks |
| *Phase 3: Displaying (Addressing Visual Learners)* | | | | | |
| 51. Anchored Instruction with Online Video | Medium | Medium to high | Low to high | Medium | As needed |
| 52. Explore and Share Online Museums and Libraries | Medium | Medium | Low | Medium | 1–2 weeks |
| 53. Concept Mapping Key Information | Medium to high | Medium (time for coordination and grading may vary) | Low to high | High | 1–4 weeks |
| 54. Videostreamed Lectures and Presentations | Medium | Medium to high | Low to high | Low | As needed |
| 55. Videostreamed Conferences and Events | Medium | Medium | Low | Medium | 1–2 weeks |
| 56. Interactive News and Documentaries | Medium | Medium | Low | Medium | 1–3 weeks |
| 57. Interactive Online Performances | High | Medium to high | Low to high | Medium | As needed |
| 58. Design Evaluation | Medium | Medium | Medium to high | Medium | 1–2 weeks as needed |
| 59. Design Generation | Medium | Medium | Medium to high | Medium | 1–2 weeks as needed |

(Continued)

**TABLE 10.1.** *(Continued)*

| Learning Activity | Risk | Time | Cost | Learner-Centeredness | Duration of Activity |
|---|---|---|---|---|---|
| 60. Design Reviews and Expert Commentary | Medium | Medium | Low to medium | Medium | As needed |
| 61. Online Timeline Explorations and Safaris | Medium | Medium to high | Low to medium | Medium to high | 1–3 weeks |
| 62. Virtual Tours | Medium | Medium | Low to medium | High | 1–2 weeks |
| 63. Visual Web Resource Explorations | Low | Low | Low | Medium | 1–2 weeks as needed |
| 64. Animations | Medium | Medium | Medium to high | Medium | 1 week or as needed |
| 65. Advance Organizers: Models, Flowcharts, Diagrams, Systems, and Illustrations | Low | Medium | Low to medium | Medium | 1 week or as needed |
| 66. Virtual Field Trips | Medium | Medium | Low | Medium | As needed |
| 67. Video Modeling and Professional Development | Medium | Medium to high | Low to high | Medium | 3–5 weeks or entire course |
| 68. Movie Reviews for Professional Development | Medium | Medium | Low | High | 1–3 weeks |
| 69. Whiteboard Demonstrations | Medium | Low | Low | Low to high | As needed |
| 70. Online Visualization Tools | Medium | Medium to high | Low to high | Medium | As needed |
| 71. Video Blogs and Adventure Learning | High | Medium | Low to medium | Medium | 1–4 weeks |
| 72. Charts and Graph Tools | Low | Low to medium | Low | High | 1–2 weeks or as needed |

| | | | | | |
|---|---|---|---|---|---|
| 73. Mashups of Google Maps | High | Medium | Low | High | 1–3 weeks or as needed |
| 74. Broadcast Events | High | Medium | High | Medium | As needed |
| 75. Online Multimedia and Visually Rich Cases | Medium | Medium | Low to high | Medium | As needed |

### Phase 4: Doing (Addressing Hands-On Learners)

| | | | | | |
|---|---|---|---|---|---|
| 76. Web-Based Survey Research | Medium | Medium | Low to high | High | 3–4 weeks |
| 77. Video Scenario Learning | Medium | Medium to high | High | Medium | As needed |
| 78. Content Review Games | Low to medium | Medium | Low to high | Medium | 1 week as needed |
| 79. Online Review and Practice Exercises | Medium | Medium to high | Low to high | Medium | 1 week or as needed |
| 80. Mock Trial or Fictional Situations | High | High | Low | High | 1–2 weeks |
| 81. Online Role Play of Personalities | High | Medium | Low | High | 1–2 weeks |
| 82. Action Research | High | Medium | Medium | High | 3–6 weeks |
| 83. Interactive Fiction and Continuous Stories | Medium | Medium | Low (assuming free tools exist) | High | 1–2 weeks |
| 84. Real-Time Cases | High | High | Medium to high | Medium | 1–2 weeks as needed |
| 85. Course Resource Wiki Site | High | Medium to high | Low to medium | High | Throughout course or as needed |
| 86. Wikibook Projects | High | High | Low to medium | High | 4–5 weeks |
| 87. Online Glossary and Resource Links Projects | Medium | High | Low | High | 3–4 weeks |
| 88. On-Demand and Workflow Learning | High | High | High | High | As needed |

(Continued)

**TABLE 10.1.** *(Continued)*

| Learning Activity | Risk | Time | Cost | Learner-Centeredness | Duration of Activity |
|---|---|---|---|---|---|
| 89. Digital Storytelling | High | High | Medium | High | 3–4 weeks |
| 90. Online Documentation of internship, Field Placement, Practicum Knowledge Applications and Experiences | Medium | Medium | Low to medium | Medium | 6–8 weeks |
| 91. Authentic Data Analysis | Medium | Medium | Low to high | Medium | 1 week or as needed |
| 92. Online Science Labs and Simulations | Medium | Medium | Low to high | Medium | As needed |
| 93. Simulation Games | Medium | Medium | Low to high | Medium | 1–2 weeks or as needed |
| 94. Simulations and Games for Higher-Level Skills | High | High | Low to high | High | 4–5 weeks or as needed |
| 95. Client Consulting and Experiential Learning | High | High | Low | High | As needed |
| 96. Online Tutoring and Mentoring | High | High | Low to high | High | As needed |
| 97. Cross-Class Product Development and Creativity | High | High | Low to medium | High | 1–4 weeks |
| 98. Cross-Class Content Discussions, Analyses, Competitions, and Evaluations | Medium | Medium to high | Low to medium | High | 2–8 weeks |
| 99. Learner Podcast Activities, Events, and Shows | High | Medium | Low to medium | High | 1–2 weeks or as needed |
| 100. Design Course Web Site | High | High | Medium to high | High | Semester long (continual) |

highlighted in Chapters Two, Three, Five, Eight, and Nine, but the use of podcast technology can be linked to every chapter of this book. Learners can listen to the podcasts of their instructors, as noted in Chapter Two, or create their own podcasts, as detailed in Chapters Eight and Nine. As noted in Chapter Five, learners can take a podcast tour of a museum, park, or national monument. And with vodcasting, learners or instructors can add video components to podcasts, thereby linking to the material in Chapters Six and Seven as well. Furthermore, learners may be required to reflect on or summarize the learning that transpired in their podcast or vodcast, which links back to the second phase of R2D2, discussed in Chapters Four and Five.

Similarly, the use of WebQuests and Web safaris, presented in Chapter Three, can be linked to the content of many chapters. Such tasks might address multiple learning preferences by incorporating audioclips, video or image explorations, moments of reflection, and a final assignment at the end of the course.

Online language learning lessons, also addressed in Chapter Three, may require acts of listening and reading as well as reflecting, visualizing, and doing. Chinesepod is a first-rate example; it has announcements, podcasts to listen to, a blog for reflections, online discussions of language lessons, grammar and language use exercises, and even a wiki for copies of the lesson transcripts (see Figure 10.1). As further evidence, learners in such language learning systems might not only listen to actual language use, they can watch associated videos to witness how that language is actually used in the real world.

A Webinar or synchronous presentation is another activity presented in Chapter Three that addresses all aspects of R2D2. The activity might involve synchronous chats between participants, questions for instructors, use of drawing tools by the presenters to emphasize key points, polling and surveying of participants, and touring the Web of Learning. There are dozens of activities that are possible in a Webinar session: an audio conference only or possibly videoconferencing. The Webinar, therefore, while being mainly about the presentation of content to participants (that is, Phase 1 of R2D2), is a wonderful example of a technique that involves all phases.

## Phase 2: Reflecting (Chapters Four and Five)

Chapters Four and Five included many methods that cut across all phases of R2D2. The use of blogs (Web logs) and ORLs (online resource libraries) is highlighted in those chapters. For instance, in video blogging, there are text and visual components and considerable opportunities for learner reflection. In addition, you might take your blogs a step further to a report, white paper, or some other

### FIGURE 10.1. HOMEPAGE OF CHINESEPOD.

final product. In a successful video blogging task, the learner typically has read or listened to some content, reflected on it in the blog, embedded videos or picture files with the reflections, and shared it with other people for their reactions.

Another strategy discussed in Chapters Four and Five that relates to multiple phases of R2D2 is the use of the electronic portfolio. Electronic portfolios require learners to showcase their learning across a series of course activities, learning events, or course experiences. In most cases, they require learners to exhibit what they have learned and internalized. Additionally, such activities typically require personal reflections on the learner's pinnacle learning experiences as well as visual displays of that learning. Finally, e-portfolios often involve making salient instances or situations in which students applied their learning or did something with it, consistent with Phase 4 of R2D2.

### Phase 3: Displaying (Chapters Six and Seven)

Chapters Six and Seven, which present activities for Phase 3 of R2D2, are also loaded with comprehensive tasks. For example, the use of online timelines and concept maps is discussed. While the visual aspects of such tasks are quickly apparent, these tasks also relate to Phase 4 (Chapters Eight and Nine), since they involve the learner in completing a project and showing what he or she has learned. However, such learners would not likely be successful without sufficient background readings, reflections, and analyses, or ample Phase 1 and 2 activities (that is, links to Chapters Two through Five).

The various design evaluation tasks noted in Chapters Six and Seven engage many learning styles or preferences. Learners must find designs to critique and then bring those up for class review, or they might share their own designs for external review and feedback (Phases 1 and 2 types of activities). And they might transform sample designs into unique products that they create and showcase, as in Phase 4.

## Phase 4: Doing (Chapters Eight and Nine)

Not too surprisingly, most ideas mentioned in Chapters Eight and Nine address multiple phases of R2D2. For instance, the first activity in Chapter Nine, survey research, asks learners to grapple with real-world data, which might be better understood through visualization in figures and graphs. It might also cause the learner to reflect on exactly the types of relationships that are vital to emphasize. And in order to design an effective survey instrument, the learner, or assigned team of learners, will need to read the prevailing literature in an area.

Also mentioned in Chapters Eight and Nine is the use of simulation games, online science labs, real-time cases, and digital storytelling, where text, pictures, graphics, and sound are combined. Such techniques are often simultaneously complex and time-consuming to design and use effectively; however, they are exciting when successfully and thoughtfully integrated into online and blended learning courses.

Other ideas in Chapters Eight and Nine address more than one phase of R2D2. In scenario learning, such as a virtual crime scene, the learner must understand the content (perhaps by reading or listening to it; here, the evidence and autopsy reports), reflect on the knowledge obtained, view it being displayed in the online simulation or video scenario, and then make a decision (that is, who killed the woman). In effect, in an online analysis of a scenario or situation within a simulation, all four phases of R2D2 are addressed.

Similarly, a wikibook task, also extensively detailed in Chapters Eight and Nine, requires learners to read or learn in an area extensively so that they can write a chapter or module for the book. In addition, learners in a wikibook task will likely need to reflect on their chapters as well as provide feedback on the chapters of other contributors. As a team, these learners might sketch a visual outline of the content their chapter addresses or a model or overarching framework related to the content. And their final completed chapter or book is a testament to their doing something with their knowledge.

Clearly, dozens of the 100+ activities outlined in this book directly address multiple phases of R2D2, as will many activities that you might design or read about elsewhere. Nevertheless, the four distinct phases of R2D2 can serve as a viable tool for building, enhancing, transforming, and sharing online courses, programs, and experiences. We hope you agree.

## Reflections on R2D2

In the previous paragraphs we mentioned just a few examples of the types of activities that address all four phases of Reading, Reflecting, Displaying, and Doing. You might emphasize any one phase of R2D2 or sequence within it; there is no one central focus or order required to employ it. Some high-risk-taking instructors, in fact, might decide to assign activities in the opposite sequence of the four phases of R2D2 we laid out in this book. Such individuals might start with action-oriented or experiential learning tasks and end with learners reading or listening to materials that explain what they just did.

Another unique instructional approach might be to embed in your learning context many highly comprehensive strategies that touch all or most aspects of R2D2. What happens when learners are given tasks that address every aspect of the model? And if they can select from several comprehensive task options, which ones do the learners select? When given a choice among course tasks, do they choose activities that would be located primarily at Phase 1, 2, 3, or 4? As indicated earlier, many learners state that they prefer activities in the third phase (that is, visual tasks) as well as the fourth phase (that is, hands-on activities) of R2D2, but does their behavior match their attitudes and explicit expectations? Many such researchable issues and questions remain unaddressed for now.

Also open are concerns about what might be added to enhance the model. What is missing from it? Equally important, what instructional design models might effectively be used in conjunction with it? An additional and perhaps more critical question is whether R2D2 is philosophy neutral. Or is there a teaching and learning philosophy underlying it? If so, what might it be? As we alluded to in earlier chapters, instead of promoting a particular learning theory or philosophy, we take a more eclectic "learning environment" approach. So while we resonate with those in the constructivist movement as well as those promoting a learner-centered teaching and learning philosophy, it remains an open question as to what teaching philosophies and perspectives best align with R2D2. Perhaps even the behaviorists and direct instruction advocates will find much to use here—we hope so!

For some, the R2D2 model satisfies a need to address student learning styles. They recognize that some learners get excited by visual exercises, some prefer to listen to instructors or to read silently and reflect on their learning, and still others want to always try things out and see how they work. R2D2, however, is not a learning styles method. Instead, it is an approach for online teaching and learning that encourages multiple teaching and learning methods, enhances the learning process, adds variety to the learning experience, and addresses student learning preferences.

The R2D2 approach offers a mechanism for instructors, trainers, and designers to evaluate whether they are addressing diverse forms of learning in their online courses, certificates, degrees, and programs. Some organizations or institutions might use it to evaluate content or activities in particular courses. That would prove interesting indeed. As this occurs, it is not just the deficiencies and the means by which they are addressed that we would find historic; rather the opportunities for reflection on instructional approaches will likely prove momentous. If that occurs, R2D2 and frameworks like it will not only address online and blended learning activities and experiences but will resurface in traditional face-to-face (FTF) instructional settings as well as other educational situations.

Explicit use of R2D2 can benefit more people than just teachers, trainers, and instructional designers; more important, it can benefit the learner. If instructors mention their use of the R2D2 model (or some other similar model) in their online courses and activities, learners might begin to realize that many learning approaches or avenues are possible. They might become comfortable with multiple ways to learn and begin to demand such approaches of other instructors or learning situations. And in their informal or spontaneous learning journeys, they might pursue resources in the Web of Learning that match their learning preferences. They might also follow up a formal learning activity in which they were exposed to a simulation or online adventure and investigate it more deeply on their own or perhaps share it with others. And it is ultimately the learner who matters—R2D2 may explicitly or implicitly address online educator needs and decisions, but the true test is whether it empowers learners.

## Using R2D2 in the Web of Learning

During the coming decades, frameworks like R2D2 will increasingly be developed to help instructors and instructional designers understand what is possible in the Web of Learning. And the Web of Learning will continue to offer new technology choices, learning paths, and learning contents. As this occurs, the frameworks for online interaction, collaboration, resource selection, and learning styles will evolve as well.

Certainly, dozens of the 100+ strategies outlined in Chapters Three, Five, Seven, and Nine of this book can be applied in traditional FTF settings. There are no secrets here: many of these strategies have been used for decades; the Internet simply makes them more noticeable, and, for some of them, more implementable. In effect, these 100+ ideas highlight the importance of effective pedagogy while simultaneously describing emerging technology that can enhance or supplement such teaching. And perhaps the use of such online strategies will positively influence your FTF teaching and training situations.

As this occurs, there will be growing opportunities to share how you are using R2D2 in individual phases of the model as well as across the model. Such examples might foster a community of instructors and trainers who are concerned with their online teaching approaches and learning philosophies. Perhaps R2D2 is not important at all—what may be more crucial is that there is a framework you can use to think about how an online course or modules within such a course are designed and evaluated. We all need models and frameworks when entering a new area. For many instructors, online education is unquestionably a new endeavor that you never fathomed when first deciding to teach. We hope that R2D2 empowers you as well as your learners to learn, share, and grow online in ways that no one has before.

As shown by the R2D2 model, the Web of Learning is rich with instructional possibilities. Many of these undoubtedly replicate what currently occurs in FTF classroom settings. However, if it results in learning for those who previously did not have a chance to experience it—at least, learning within a particular course—then there should be wide acclaim and excitement. And, without a doubt, many of the activities and ideas elaborated on here extend well beyond traditional classroom settings and provide novel instructional events, activities, and resources. Still other pedagogical activities found in the Web of Learning offer new opportunities that are not reminiscent of those found in face-to-face courses.

Of course, the penultimate question regarding R2D2 use in the Web of Learning is whether it makes a difference in education and training: Does the use of it increase student learning satisfaction and retention, zest for learning, learning achievements, knowledge application and transfer, and lifelong learning interests and pursuits, as well as personal participation in such learning? In response, we welcome your feedback on its use. As indicated in the Preface, educational professionals we have met in our travels across this planet, in higher education as well as in K–12 education, nonprofit settings, military institutes, and corporate training, have welcomed it as a viable and understandable instructional framework or model for their online teaching and learning events and expeditions. Perhaps you will too! If so, mission accomplished.

In any event, we sincerely hope you enjoy your journeys with R2D2 into an awe-inspiring and highly empowering galaxy of e-learning opportunities. May the force be strong with you at all times in your online teaching and learning quests and adventures.

# WEB LINKS, EXAMPLES, AND RESOURCES

## Chapters Two and Three: Auditory and Verbal Learning (Phase 1)

### Adaptive and Assistive Technologies and Resources

Freedom Scientific (assistive and adaptive technology, including the JAWS screen reader): http://www.freedomscientific.com/

Section 508 of Rehabilitation Act of 1998: http://www.section508.gov/

### Language Learning Resources

Chinesepod: http://www.chinesepod.com/

Chinswing: http://www.chinswing.com/

Englishtown: http://www.englishtown.com/

Global English: http://www.globalenglish.com/

Japanesepod101.com: http://www.japanesepod101.com/

LangMedia: http://langmedia.fivecolleges.edu/index.html

LiveMocha: http://www.livemocha.com/

On Demand English: http://www.ondemand-english.com/

Online Mandarin Chinese Program (Michigan State University): http://ott.educ.msu.edu/confucius/test4/programs.asp

## Language Translation Resources

Babelfish: http://babelfish.altavista.com/

## Learning Object Repositories

Connexions (from Rice University): http://cnx.org/

Jorum (United Kingdom; teaching and learning materials): http://www.jorum.ac.uk/

Multimedia Educational Resource for Learning and Online Teaching (MERLOT): http://www.merlot.org/

## Literature Resources

Complete Works of William Shakespeare: http://wild-turkey.mit.edu/Shakespeare/

Edgar Allen Poe Webliography (by Heyward Ehrlich): http://andromeda.rutgers.edu/~ehrlich/poesites.html

Google Book (the writings of Charles Darwin): http://books.google.com/books?q=darwin

Google Book (the writings of John Dewey): http://books.google.com/books?q=dewey

Google Book (the complete plays of William Shakespeare): http://books.google.com/googlebooks/shakespeare/

Poetry teaching ideas: http://www.poets.org/page.php/prmID/85

Poets: http://www.poets.org/page.php/prmID/6

Romantic Poetry Project: http://ssad.bowdoin.edu:8668/space/snipsnap-index

## Mobile Learning Resources

Dot Mobile: http://www.dotmobile.co.uk/home/home.php

## Music-Related Resources

Musical Acoustics Training: http://www.phys.unsw.edu.au/music/

### Online Mentoring and Coaching

Ask a Mad Scientist: http://www.madsci.org/

Ask Dr. Global Change: http://www.gcrio.org/doctorgc/index.php

Ask Dr. Universe: http://www.wsu.edu/DrUniverse/

ePALS Classroom Exchange: http://www.epals.com/

IECC: http://www.iecc.org/

International Education and Resource Network (iEARN): http://www.iearn.org/

MentorNet (for engineering, science, and mathematics): http://www.mentornet.net/

My Language Exchange: http://www.mylanguageexchange.com/

NetMentors.org (for teen mentoring): http://netmentors.org/

Write to Dr. Math: http://mathforum.org/dr.math/ask/

### Online Tutorials

PubMed tutorial: http://www.nlm.nih.gov/bsd/pubmed_tutorial/m1001.html

### Online Video Repository Resources and Tools

TeacherTube: http://teachertube.com/

YouTube: http://www.youtube.com/

### Open Access Journals and Magazines

Campus Technology: http://campustechnology.com/

### Podcasting and Vodcasting Resources and Sites

Audacity: http://audacity.sourceforge.net/

Daily Source Code (Adam Curry): http://dailysourcecode.podshow.com/

Education Podcast Network (EPN): http://epnWeb.org/

Garageband: http://www.apple.com/ilife/garageband/

How to Create Your Own Podcast: A Step-by-Step Tutorial: http://radio.about.com/od/podcastin1/a/aa030805a.htm

Learning 2007 University (from Elliott Masie): http://www.learning2007.com/university

Making Your First Podcast (from Podcasting News): http://www.podcastingnews.com/articles/How-to-Podcast.html

NPR Podcast Directory (Beta): http://www.npr.org/rss/podcast/podcast_directory.php

Podcast Alley: http://www.podcastalley.com/

Podcast Directory: http://www.podcast.net/

Podcasting News: http://www.podcastingnews.com/forum/link_6.htm

Podcast.net: http://www.podcast.net/cat/47

SonoSite ultasound training: http://www.sonosite.com/trainingmodules/

Understanding RSS News Feeds (from Podcasting News): http://www.podcastingnews.com/articles/Understanding_RSS_Feeds.html

## Reading and Writing Resources

Classroom Practices: Research on the Web (from NCTE): http://www.ncte.org/collections/Weblit/strategies/117192.htm

National Council of Teachers of English (NCTE): http://www.ncte.org/

Oh, What a Tangled Web We've Woven: Helping Students Evaluate Web Resources (from NCTE): http://www.ncte.org/library/files/Free/Journals/ej/EJ0891What.pdf

Reading and Writing on the Web (from NCTE): http://www.ncte.org/collections/Weblit

## Synchronous Web Conferencing and Virtual Classroom Systems

Acrobat Connect Professional (formerly known as "Breeze"): http://www.macromedia.com/software/breeze/

Centra (from Saba): http://www.saba.com/centra-saba/

Elluminate™ Live! ™: http://www.elluminate.com/

Interwise (AT&T): http://www.interwise.com/

LiveMeeting (from Microsoft): http://www.microsoft.com/uc/livemeeting/default.mspx

WebEx: http://www.Webex.com/

Webinar (Nonprofit Technology Network): http://www.nten.org/Webinars

Wimba: http://www.horizonwimba.com/

### Technology Tools

Camtasia: http://www.techsmith.com/camtasia.asp?CMP=KgoogleCStm

Captivate: http://www.adobe.com/products/captivate/

Flash: http://www.adobe.com/products/flash/flashpro/

Socialtext: http://www.socialtext.com/company

### Video Resources and Portals

TeacherTube: http://www.teachertube.com/

You Tube: http://www.youtube.com/index

### WebQuests and Scavenger Hunts

Scavenger hunts (Spartanburg School District): http://www.spa3.k12.sc.us/Scavenger.html

WebQuest Lesson Template: http://WebQuest.sdsu.edu/LessonTemplate.html

WebQuest Portal: http://WebQuest.org/

WebQuest Template: http://www.spa3.k12.sc.us/WebQuestTemplate/Webquesttemp.htm

### Web Streaming Tools

ePresence TV: http://epresence.tv/

MediaSite Live (from Sonic Foundry): http://www.sonicfoundry.com/solutions/higher_education.aspx

Polycom: http://www.polycom.com/usa/en/home/index.html

Tegrity: http://www.tegrity.com/

Webcast Group: http://www.webcastgroup.com/

## Chapters Four and Five: Reflective and Observational Learning (Phase 2)

### Anatomy and Medical Web Sites and Resources

Anatomy and Physiology I Web sites: http://science.nhmccd.edu/BioL/ap1.html

Biology 129 Human Anatomy (self-tests; Dr. James Strauss): http://www.bio.psu.edu/people/faculty/strauss/anatomy/biology29.htm

MedCases: http://optionstraining.org/login

Muscular System (self-test): http://www.bio.psu.edu/people/faculty/
strauss/anatomy/musc/muscular.htm

## Bloggers in Education and Training

Jay Cross (Internet Time Blog): http://internettime.com/blog/

Stephen Downes (OLDaily): http://www.downes.ca/news/OLDaily.htm

Stephen's Web: http://www.downes.ca/

Weblogg-ed (blog by Will Richardson): http://www.Weblogg-ed.com/

## Blogging Software and Sites

Blogger: http://www.blogger.com/

Diaryland: http://www.diaryland.com/

Live Journal: http://www.sixapart.com/livejournal/

Movable Type: http://www.sixapart.com/movabletype/

Pitas: http://www.pitas.com/

TypePad: http://www.sixapart.com/typepad/pricing

Xanga: http://www.xanga.com/

## Collaborative Writing Tools

Groove (Microsoft Office): http://www.groove.net/home/index.cfm

Windows Sharepoint: http://www.microsoft.com/technet/windowsserver/
sharepoint/V2/default.mspx

## Content Management Systems and Portal Development Tools

Content Management Systems (list): http://en.wikipedia.org/wiki/
Comparison_of_content_management_systems

Daisy: http://cocoondev.org/daisy/index.html

Drupal: http://drupal.org/

Free and Open Source Software Portal: http://www.unesco.org/cgi-bin/
webworld/portal_freesoftware/cgi/page.cgi?d=1&g=Software/
Courseware_Tools/index.shtml

Joomla! http://www.joomla.org/

Mambo: http://mambo-foundation.org/

MediaWiki: http://www.mediawiki.org/wiki/MediaWiki

Netvibes: http://www.netvibes.com/

Pageflakes: http://www.pageflakes.com/

Squidoo: http://www.squidoo.com/

### Online Group Tools or Sites

Google Groups: http://groups.google.com/

MSN Groups: http://groups.msn.com/

Yahoo! Groups: http://groups.yahoo.com/

### Online Learner Readiness Checklists

Distance Learning Readiness Checklist (from the Nursing Program at the University of Alabama at Huntsville): http://onlinenurse.nb.uah.edu/distance/online/readiness_list.htm

Distance Learning Self-Assessment (from Manatee Community College): http://www.mccfl.edu/Self_Assessment/Self_Assessment.cfm

Online Readiness Checklist (San Juan College): http://www.sjc.cc.nm.us/documents/DistanceLearning/stu_or.htm

Questionmark Perception: http://www.questionmark.com/us/perception/

### Online Moderator Resources

eModerators.com: http://emoderators.com/

Moderator's Homepage: http://www.emoderators.com/moderators.shtml

Useful URLs for e-Moderators from e-Moderators: http://www.atimod.com/e-moderating/links.shtml

### Podcast Tours

Indianapolis Museum of Art: http://www.ima-digital.org/podcast/spurse/

Smithsonian American Art Museum: http://americanart.si.edu/collections/interact/gallery/coverage.cfm

Stephen's Web: http://www.downes.ca/

Walker Art Center (Minneapolis): http://newmedia.walkerart.org/aoc/index.wac

### Social Networking Sites and Resources

Classmates: http://www.classmates.com/

Facebook: http://www.facebook.com/

Friendster: http://www.friendster.com/

MySpace: http://www.myspace.com/

Orkut: http://www.orkut.com/GLogin.aspx?done=http%3A%2F%2Fwww
.orkut.com%2F

Tribe: http://www.tribe.net/

YouTube: http://www.youtube.com/

### Portfolio Tools and Resources

Avenet Web Solutions (efolio): http://www.avenet.net/

Chalk and Wire: http://www.chalkandwire.com/

Electronic Portfolio Consortium: http://www.eportconsortium.org/

Electronic Portfolios (Helen Barrett): http://electronicportfolios.com/

Electronic Portfolios (TaskStream): http://www.taskstream.com/pub/
electronicportfolio.asp

ePortaro: http://www.eportaro.com/

e-Portfolio (Pennsylvania State University): http://www.personal.psu.edu/
staff/g/f/gfj100/eportfolio/examples/

Folio Live (McGraw-Hill): http://www.foliolive.com/

iWebfolio: http://www.nuventive.com/products_iWebfolio.html

LiveText: http://college.livetext.com/college/index.html

NuVentive: http://www.nuventive.com/

PebblePad: http://www.pebblepad.co.uk/eportfolio/

Task Stream: http://www.taskstream.com/pub/

### Process Writing Tools

Process Writing (North Central Regional Education Laboratory
[NCREL]): http://www.ncrel.org/sdrs/areas/issues/methods/instrctn/
in5lk11.htm

Writing across the Curriculum in the Disciplines (Purdue University Online
Writing Lab): http://owl.english.purdue.edu/handouts/WAC/

### Technology Tools

Computer Assisted Learning Method (CALM): http://calm.indiana.edu/

Hot Potato from Half-Baked Software: http://hotpot.uvic.ca/

# Chapters Six and Seven: Visual Learners (Phase 3)

### Adventure Blogging and Interactive Expeditions

Adventure Weather: http://www.adventureweather.com/

Ben Saunders: http://www.bensaunders.com/

ExplorersWeb: http://www.explorersWeb.com/

Mark Fennell: http://www.markfennell.com/

Mark Fennell sample adventure: http://www.markfennell.com/panoramas/
frames.php?pan=http://www.markfennell.com/adventure/arctic/
index.html&lat=90.0000&long=90.0000

Mark Fennell sample video: http://www.markfennell.com/video/arktica/
index.html

Mount Everest: http://www.mounteverest.net/

The Oceans: http://www.theoceans.net/

One World Journeys/Expeditions: http://www.oneworldjourneys.com/
expeditions/

Polar Quest Ambassadors: http://polarquest.co.uk/
polar_ambassadors.php

The Poles (on ExplorersWeb): http://thepoles.com/

### Art, Design, and Photomedia

Icograda Education Network: http://www.education.icograda.net/web/
home.shtml

International Council of Graphic Design Associations (Icograda): http://
www.icograda.org/Web

Omnium Project: http://www.omnium.edu.au/project/

Omnium Project (Creative Waves): http://www.omnium.edu.au/promo/
creativewaves/

Omnium Project photomedia examples: http://www.omnium.edu.au/
project/galleries/creativewaves2005/photomedia/

### Blog Search Tools

Google Blog Search: http://blogsearch.google.com/

Technorati: http://www.technorati.com/

### Concept-Mapping Tools

BrainMine Standard (from Neural Matters): http://www.neuralmatters.com/

Cmap tools (University of Western Florida): http://cmap.ihmc.us/

FreeMind: http://freemind.sourceforge.net/wiki/index.php/Main_Page

Inspiration: http://www.inspiration.com/

Kidspiration: http://www.inspiration.com/productinfo/kidspiration/index.cfm

MindGenius: http://www.mindgenius.com/Website/presenter.aspx#topofpage

MindManager (from Mindjet): http://www.mindjet.com/us/

MindMapper: http://www.mindmapper.com/

Visual Mind: http://www.visual-mind.com/wv.htm?0015

Visual Understanding Environment (VUE, from Tufts University): http://vue.tccs.tufts.edu/

### Copyright and Intellectual Property Sites

Copyright Management Center, Indiana University, Purdue University at Indianapolis: http://www.copyright.iupui.edu/

Creative Commons: http://creativecommons.org/

University of Maryland University College, Center for Intellectual Property: http://www.umuc.edu/distance/odell/cip/cip.shtml

### Inquiry Learning and Global Collaboration (Science, Math, Engineering, and Inquiry)

The GLOBE (Global Learning and Observations to Benefit the Environment) Project: http://www.globe.gov/globe_flash.html

Inquiry Learning Forum: http://ilf.crlt.indiana.edu/

The Journey North: A Global Study of Wildlife Migration and Seasonal Change: http://www.learner.org/jnorth/

Kids as Global Scientists: http://www-personal.umich.edu/~mlhartma/kgs.html

PreK–12 Engineering (Massachusetts Science and Technology/Engineering Curriculum Frameworks): http://www.prek-12engineering.org/

## Interactive Multimedia Web Sites and Portals

Autopsy (HBO): http://www.hbo.com/autopsy/interactive/#

DNA from the Beginning: http://www.dnaftb.org/dnaftb

Valley of the Shadows: http://valley.vcdh.virginia.edu/

Virtual Autopsy (from the University of Leicester, United Kingdom): http://www.le.ac.uk/pa/teach/va/welcome.html

## Interactive News and News Documentaries

Altered Oceans (*Los Angeles Times*): http://www.latimes.com/news/local/oceans/la-oceans-series,0,7842752.special

BBC: http://www.bbc.co.uk/

BBC News: http://news.bbc.co.uk/

Becoming Human (explorative): http://www.becominghuman.org/

Behind the Scenes: NYTimes' multimedia reporter (Cyberjournalist.net): http://www.cyberjournalist.net/news/000887.php

Birth of a Tornado (MSNBC; instructive): http://www.msnbc.com/modules/tornado/default.asp

CNN: http://www.cnn.com/

CNN Video (*see also* Video Resources and Portals): http://www.cnn.com/video/

CurrentTV (*see also* Video Resources and Portals): http://www.current.tv/

DOT Earth (Andrew C. Revkin, *New York Times*): http://topics.nytimes.com/top/reference/timestopics/people/r/andrew_c_revkin/

Enron 101 (narrative): http://www.msnbc.com/modules/enron/

Google News: http://news.google.com/

MSNBC: http://www.msnbc.msn.com/

*New York Times*: http://www.nytimes.com/

Oil Safari (*Chicago Tribune*): http://www.chicagotribune.com/news/specials/broadband/chi-oilsafari-html,0,7894741.htmlstory

Postcards from the Arctic (Andrew C. Revkin, *New York Times*): http://www.nytimes.com/pages/science/sciencereport/index.html

A Scene from the Ice Age (Cyberjournalist.net): http://www.cyberjournalist.net/news/001450.php

Web Log of Interactive Narratives: http://www.interactivenarratives.org/

What Is a Print? (Museum of Modern Art): http://www.moma.org/whatisaprint/flash.html

Yahoo! News: http://news.yahoo.com/

## Lesson Plan Sites

Busy Teachers' WebSite K–12: http://www.ceismc.gatech.edu/busyt/

CEC (Columbia Education Center) Lesson Plans: http://www.col-ed.org/cur/

Education World: http://www.education-world.com/

Edutopia Instructional Modules (George Lucas Education Foundation): http://www.edutopia.org/foundation/courseware.php

Funderstanding (Constructivism): http://www.funderstanding.com/constructivism.cfm

Kathy Shrock's Guide for Educators (Discovery Education): http://school.discovery.com/schrockguide/

*New York Times* Learning Network (includes Daily Lesson Plan): http://www.nytimes.com/learning/index.html

PBS Teachers: http://www.pbs.org/teachersource/index.htm

Teachers Helping Teachers: http://www.pacificnet.net/~mandel/

Teachers.net: http://teachers.net/

Teaching Tips: http://www.teachingtips.com/

TechLearning: http://techlearning.com/

## Library and Museum Portals

LibraryShare: http://www.libraryshare.com/

The Metropolitan Museum of Art Timeline of Art History: http://www.metmuseum.org/toah/splash.htm?HomePageLink=toah_l

The Museum of Online Museums (MoOM): http://www.coudal.com/moom.php

Theban Mapping Project: http://www.thebanmappingproject.com/

## Reading Resources

E-Read Ohio: http://www.readingfirstohio.org/?pid=6

## Technology Tools

Adobe Authorware 7: http://www.adobe.com/products/authorware/

Adobe Captivate 3: http://www.adobe.com/products/captivate/

Adobe Creative Suite 3 Web Premium: http://www.adobe.com/products/creativesuite/web/

Adobe Dreamweaver CS3: http://www.adobe.com/products/dreamweaver/

Adobe Flash Player: http://www.adobe.com/shockwave/download/download.cgi?P1_Prod_Version=ShockwaveFlash

Camtasia Studio: http://www.techsmith.com/camtasia.asp?CMP=KgoogleCStmhome

LearnByDoing: http://www.learningbydoing.net/

Maplesoft: http://www.maplesoft.com/

Mathematics Visualization Toolkit MERLOT: http://www.cfkeep.org/html/snapshot.php?id=83229305765805

Microsoft FrontPage: http://office.microsoft.com/en-us/frontpage/default.aspx

## Timeline Tools

JRR Tolkien's Oxford: http://www.chem.ox.ac.uk/oxfordtour/tolkien-tour/index.html

Learning Tools (University of British Columbia): http://www.learningtools.arts.ubc.ca/timeline.htm

ReadWriteThink (a partnership among the International Reading Association (IRA), National Council of Teachers of English (NCTE), and the Verizon Foundation: http://www.readwritethink.org/materials/timeline/

TeAchnology: http://www.teach-nology.com/Web_tools/materials/timelines/(K–12)

## Video Resources and Portals

Alan Kay: Education in the Digital Age (Google Video): http://video.google.com/videoplay?docid=-1109203988787201616&q=alan+kay

BBC News: Video and Audio: http://news.bbc.co.uk/2/hi/video_and_audio/default.stm

BBC News: Video and News: http://news.bbc.co.uk/

CNN.com Video (*see also* Interactive News and News Documentaries): http://www.cnn.com/video/

CurrentTV (*see also* Interactive News and News Documentaries): http://www.current.tv/

Global Nomads Group: http://www.gng.org/

Google Video: http://video.google.com/

MIT World: http://mitworld.mit.edu/index.php

Moving Beyond the Classroom with Executive Education, and Distance Learning: What the Experts Think (Dorothy Leonard, Harvard Business School: http://hbswk.hbs.edu/pubitem.jhtml?id=3217&sid=0&pid=0&t=innovation

MSNBC Video (see link to videos): http://www.msnbc.msn.com/

Nomadsland: http://www.nomadsland.com/

SplashCast: http://web.splashcast.net/catalog/search.aspx

TeacherTube: http://www.teachertube.com/

Video Nation (BBC): http://www.bbc.co.uk/videonation/

The World Is Flat (Thomas Friedman's MITWorld lecture): http://mitworld.mit.edu/video/266/

Yahoo! Video: http://video.search.yahoo.com/

You Tube: http://www.youtube.com/index

## Virtual Archeology

Digital Archeology: http://www.digital-archaeology.com/

Discover Babylon: http://www.discoverbabylon.org/index.asp

UCLA Cultural VR Lab: http://www.cvrlab.org/

Virtual Archeology: http://www.mnsu.edu/emuseum/archaeology/virtual/

Virtual Archeology portal: http://www.ku.edu/~hoopes/virtual.htm

## Virtual Field Trips

Gettysburg National Military Park: http://www.nps.gov/gett/

How to Create a Virtual Tour: http://www.uen.org/utahlink/tours/tourFames.cgi?tour_id=6018

Internet4Classrooms Virtual Fieldtrips: http://www.internet4classrooms.com/vft.htm

Virtual Field Trip Hawaii: http://satftp.soest.hawaii.edu/space/hawaii/virtual.field.trips.html

Virtual Field Trip of the Landscapes of Nova Scotia: http://www.gov.ns.ca/natr/meb/field/start.htm

Virtual Field Trips: http://www.uen.org/utahlink/tours/fieldtrips2.htm

Virtual Field Trips at Tramline: http://www.field-guides.com/vft/index.htm

Virtual Gettysburg: http://www.virtualgettysburg.com/

Virtual Tours and Field Trips: http://www.theteachersguide.com/virtualtours.html

Where in Google Earth Is Matt: http://www.youtube.com/watch?v=BJbNuKvp0dY

Where in the Hell is Matt (blog): http://www.wherethehellismatt.com/

Where in the Hell Is Matt (video): http://www.youtube.com/watch?v=bNF_P281Uu4

## Virtual Tours

The British Museum: http://www.thebritishmuseum.ac.uk/explore/online_tours.aspx

Rome Reborn 1.0: http://www.romereborn.virginia.edu/

Second Life (*see also* Virtual Worlds): http://secondlife.com/

Smithsonian: National Museum of Natural History: http://www.mnh.si.edu/museum/VirtualTour/index.html

U.S. Capital Virtual Tour: http://www.senate.gov/vtour/index.html

Virtual Jerusalem Tour: http://www.md.huji.ac.il/vjt/

The Virtual Sun: http://www.michielb.nl/sun/

Virtual Tour of the Louvre: http://www.louvre.fr/llv/commun/home_flash.jsp?bmLocale=en

Virtual Tour of Oxford: http://www.chem.ox.ac.uk/oxfordtour/

Welcome to Antarctica!: http://astro.uchicago.edu/cara/vtour/

## Virtual Worlds

Active Worlds: http://www.activeworlds.com/

Active Worlds and Education: http://www.activeworlds.com/edu/index.asp

Second Life (*see also* Virtual Tours): http://secondlife.com/

# Chapters Eight and Nine: Hands-On Learners (Phase 4)

### Case-Based and Scenario Learning

Biz/ed: http://www.bized.co.uk/

Harvard Business School Case Studies: http://harvardbusinessonline.hbsp. harvard.edu/b02/en/cases/cases_home.jhtml

MedCases: http://www.medcases.com/Physician/cme_portal.asp

The Real-Time Case Method: http://www.sloan-c.org/effective/details2. asp?ACC_ID=32

WisdomTools: http://wisdomtools.com/

### Collaborative and Creative Writing Software

Collaboration tools: http://collaboration.qarchive.org/

Collanos: http://www.collanos.com/

Creative Writing Top Ten Software Reviews for 2007: http://creative-writing-software-review.toptenreviews.com/

Google Docs: http://www.google.com/google-d-s/intl/en/tour1.html

Groove: http://office.microsoft.com/en-us/groove/ FX100487641033.aspx

LetsPowwow Collaboration Software: http://letspowwow-collaboration-software.yugma-inc.qarchive.org/

Sharepoint: http://office.microsoft.com/en-us/groove/ FX100487641033.aspx

ThinkTank (GroupSystems): http://www.groupsystems.com/

Writer's Window: http://english.unitecnology.ac.nz/writers/

Writing.com: http://www.writing.com/page/writing_software/ writing_software.html

### Digital Storytelling

Center for Digital Storytelling: http://www.storycenter.org/

Digital Storytelling (Helen Barrett): http://electronicportfolios.com/digistory/

Educational Uses of Digital Storytelling: http://www.coe.uh.edu/ digital-storytelling/

Elements of Digital Storytelling: http://www.inms.umn.edu/elements/

### E-Learning Reports in K–12 and Higher Education

Educause: http://www.educause.edu/

Edutopia (George Lucas Education Foundation):
http://www.edutopia.org/

Hewlett Foundation Open Educational Resources (OER): http://www.hewlett.org/Programs/Education/OER/openEdResources.htm

Pew Internet and American Life Project: http://www.pewinternet.org/

The Sloan Consortium (Sloan-C): http://www.sloan-c.org/

### E-learning Development, Evaluation, and Consultation for Corporate Training

Allen Interactions: http://www.alleni.com/

Arjuna Multimedia: http://www.arjunamultimedia.com/

Brandon Hall Research: http://www.brandon-hall.com/

Chapman Alliance: http://www.chapmanalliance.com/

Dublin Consulting: http://www.lancedublin.com/

eLearning Guild: http://www.eLearningGuild.com

Granato Group: http://www.granatogroup.com/

Handshaw: http://www.handshaw.com/default.asp

Hezel Associates: http://www.hezel.com/index.html

InSync Training: http://www.insynctraining.com/

Learning Times: http://www.learningtimes.net/certified.shtml

Marc Rosenberg and Associates: http://marcrosenberg.com/

The Masie Center: http://www.masie.com

Option Six: http://www.optionsix.com/

The Thiagi Group: http://www.thiagi.com/

TrainingShare: http://www.trainingshare.com/

William Horton Consulting: http://www.horton.com/html/home.aspx

### Interactive Multimedia Web Sites and Portals

Human Intelligence: http://www.indiana.edu/~intell/index.shtml

## Online Games, Simulations, and Labs

BioKids (Kids' Inquiry of Diverse Species): http://www.biokids.umich.edu/

BrainPop: http://www.brainpop.com/

Cells alive!: http://www.cellsalive.com/

Chemistry Online (University of Oxford): http://www.chem.ox.ac.uk/it/

Free Online Games: http://puzzle-games.freeonlinegames.com/

General Chemistry Online!: http://antoine.frostburg.edu/chem/senese/101/index.shtml

The GLOBE Program: http://www.globe.gov/fsl/welcome.html

Halo: http://www.microsoft.com/games/halo/

Halo 2: http://www.xbox.com/en-US/games/h/halo2/

Human Embryology Animations: http://www.indiana.edu/~anat550/embryo_main/index.html

Intel IT Manager Game 2.0: http://itmg2.intel.com/eng/

The irYdium Project (online chemistry; Carnegie Mellon University): http://iry.chem.cmu.edu/irproject/

Lab Physics: http://lab-physics.com/

Learn Anywhere Anytime Physics (LAAP): http://www.laaphysics.org/

Lyryx Learning: http://lyryx.com/lyryx_interactive.php

The National Budget Simulation: http://www.nathannewman.org/nbs/)

National University of Singapore Internet Remote Experimentation (lab experiments): http://vlab.ee.nus.edu.sg/vlab/

Net Frog (dissection): http://curry.edschool.virginia.edu/go/frog/)

One Sky, Many Voices: http://www.ed.gov/pubs/edtechprograms/manyvoices.html

Online Psychology Laboratory (American Psychological Association and the National Science Foundation): http://opl.apa.org/

PsychExperiments: Psychology Experiments on the Internet: http://psychexps.olemiss.edu/

Puzzlemaker (Discovery Education): http://puzzlemaker.com/

Virtual Chemistry: http://www.chem.ox.ac.uk/vrchemistry/

Virtual Stock Exchange: http://virtualstockexchange.com/Game/Homepage.aspx

The Virtual U Project: http://www.virtual-u.org/

Voltage Circuit Simulator: http://jersey.uoregon.edu/vlab/Voltage/

## Role Play Tools and Resources

Fablusi: http://www.fablusi.com/

Role Play Explanation: http://www.trainingshare.com/download/roles.doc

## Technology Tools

VideoPaper Builder 3: http://vpb.concord.org/?version=print

World Clock: Time Zones: http://www.timeanddate.com/worldclock/

## Virtual Simulations, Labs, and Practica

The Interactive Patient (Marshal University School of Medicine): http://medicus.marshall.edu/mainmenu.htm

Laerdal SimMan: http://www.laerdal.com/simman/simman.htm

Medi-Smart Virtual Autopsy: http://medi-smart.com/tut-40.htm

Sim-Man at Case Western Reserve University: http://www.cwru.edu/pubaff/univcomm/vnr/spring02/nurse/Virtual_Reality_Nursing.mov

Simulation Development and Cognitive Science Lab (Penn State College of Medicine): http://www.hmc.psu.edu/simulation/available/ids.htm

Trauma Scenarios: http://www.trauma.org/resus/moulage/moulage.html

Virtual Nursing Learning Center (Valparaiso University): http://www.valpo.edu/nursing/facilities/lab.php

## Web-Based Survey Tools

Free Online Surveys: http://freeonlinesurveys.com/

Infopoll: http://infopoll.com/live/surveys.dll/Web

KeySurvey: http://www.keysurvey.com/

Survey Console: http://www.surveyconsole.com/

Survey Professionals: http://www.surveypro.com/

SurveyKey: http://www.surveykey.com/

SurveyMonkey: http://surveymonkey.com/

SurveyShare: http://www.surveyshare.com/

VoVici (online survey software): http://Websurveyor.com/gateway.asp

Zoomerang: http://info.zoomerang.com/

## Wiki Resources and Projects

Media Wiki: http://www.mediawiki.org/wiki/MediaWiki

Pbwiki: http://pbwiki.com/

Romantic Audience Project: http://ssad.bowdoin.edu:8668/space/snipsnap-index

Seedwiki: http://www.seedwiki.com/

Socialtext: http://www.socialtext.com/

TikiWiki: http://tikiwiki.org/tiki-view_articles.php

Wiki Resources (Participatory Media Literacy project): http://www.socialtext.net/medialiteracy/index.cgi?wiki_resources

Wikibooks: http://en.wikibooks.org/wiki/Main_Page

Wikimedia Commons: http://commons.wikimedia.org/wiki/Main_Page

Wikinews: http://en.wikinews.org/wiki/Main_Page

Wikipedia: http://en.wikipedia.org/wiki/Main_Page

Wikiquote: http://en.wikinews.org/wiki/Main_Page

Wikisource: http://en.wikisource.org/wiki/Main_Page:English

Wikispaces: http://www.wikispaces.com/

Wikispecies: http://species.wikimedia.org/wiki/Main_Page

Wikiversity: http://en.wikiversity.org/wiki/Wikiversity:Main_Page

Wiktionary: http://en.wiktionary.org/wiki/Wiktionary:Main_Page

# REFERENCES

Allen, I. E., & Seaman, J. (2004). *Entering the mainstream: The quality and extent of online education in the United States, 2003 and 2004*. Needham, MA: Sloan-C. Retrieved December 4, 2005, from http://www.sloan-c.org/resources/entering_mainstream.pdf

Allen, I. E., & Seaman, J. (2005). *Growing by degrees: Online education in the United States, 2005*. Needham, MA: Sloan-C. Retrieved December 4, 2005, from http://www.sloan-c.org/resources/growing_by_degrees.pdf

Alimohammadi, D. (2004, August). Designing Webliographies in an effective and simple manner: A step by step process. *Webology*, *1*(1). Retrieved September 19, 2007, from http://www.webology.ir/2004/v1n1/a2.html

Ausubel, D. P. (1978). In defense of advance organizers: A reply to the critics. *Review of Educational Research*, *48*(2), 251–257. Retrieved October 1, 2006, from http://www.jstor.org/view/00346543/ap040234/04a00040/0

Averill, D. S. (2005, April). Using mindtools in education. *THE Journal*, *32*(9). Retrieved September 17, 2006, from http://thejournal.com/articles/17216

Bandura, A. (1986). *Social foundations of thought and action: A social-cognitive theory*. Englewood Cliffs, NJ: Prentice Hall.

Bandura, A. (1997). *Self-efficacy: The exercise of control*. New York: W. H. Freeman.

Bean, J. C. (1996). *Engaging ideas: The professor's guide to integrating writing, critical thinking, and active learning in the classroom*. San Francisco, CA: Jossey-Bass.

Bereiter, C., & Scardamalia, M. (1987). *The psychology of written communication*. Hillsdale, NJ: Erlbaum.

Bienias, M. (2004, January 14). The offbeat traveler: Mark Fennell. *VR Mag*, *14*. Retrieved September 16, 2006, from http://vrm.vrway.com/issue14/THE_OFFBEAT_TRAVELLER_MARK_FENNELL.html

Blaisdell, M. (2006, March). Academic MP3s: Is It iTime Yet?*Campus Technology, 19*(7), 38–40, 42, 44, 46, 48, 50. Retrieved August 22, 2006, from http://www.campus-technology.com/print.asp?ID=18001

Bloom, B. S. (1956). *Taxonomy of educational objectives, Handbook I: The cognitive domain.* New York: David McKay.

Bonk, C. J. (2002, January). *Executive summary of online teaching in an online world.* United States Distance Learning Association (USDLA). Retrieved August 13, 2006, from http://www.usdla.org/html/journal/JAN02_Issue/article02.html

Bonk, C. J., Angeli, C., Malikowski, S., & Supplee, L. (2001, August). *Holy COW: Scaffolding case-based conferencing on the Web with preservice teachers.* Education at a Distance, United States Distance Learning Association, Retrieved September 29, 2006, from http://www.usdla.org/html/journal/AUG01_Issue/article01.html

Bonk, C. J., & Cunningham, D. J. (1998). Searching for learner-centered, constructivist, and sociocultural components of collaborative educational learning tools. In C. J. Bonk & K. S. King (Eds.), *Electronic collaborators: Learner-centered technologies for literacy, apprenticeship, and discourse* (pp. 25–50). Mahwah, NJ: Erlbaum.

Bonk, C. J., Daytner, K., Daytner, G., Dennen, V., & Malikowski, S. (2001). Using Web-based cases to enhance, extend, and transform preservice teacher training: Two years in review. *Computers in the Schools, 18*(1), 189–211.

Bonk, C. J., & Dennen, V. (2003). Frameworks for research, design, benchmarks, training, and pedagogy in Web-based distance education. In M. G. Moore & B. Anderson (Eds.), *Handbook of distance education* (pp. 331–348). Mahwah, NJ: Erlbaum.

Bonk, C. J., & Dennen, V. P. (2005). *Massive multiplayer online gaming: A research framework for military education and training.* (Technical Report # 2005–1). Washington, DC: U.S. Department of Defense (DUSD/R): Advanced Distributed Learning (ADL) Initiative. Retrieved September 26, 2006, from http://www.adlnet.gov/downloads/189.cfm

Bonk, C. J., Hara, H., Dennen, V., Malikowski, S., & Supplee, L. (2000). We're in TITLE to dream: Envisioning a community of practice, The Intraplanetary Teacher Learning Exchange. *CyberPsychology and behavior, 3*(1), 25–39.

Bonk, C. J., Kim, K. J., & Zeng, T. (2006). Future directions of blended learning in higher education and workplace learning settings. In C. J. Bonk & C. R. Graham (Eds.), *Handbook of blended learning: Global perspectives, local designs* (pp. 550–567). San Francisco, CA: Pfeiffer.

Bonk, C. J., Malikowski, S., Angeli, C., & East, J. (1998). Web-based case conferencing for preservice teacher education: Electronic discourse from the field. *Journal of Educational Computing Research, 19*(3), 267–304.

Bonk, C. J., Olson, T., Wisher, R. A., & Orvis, K. L. (2002). Learning from focus groups: An examination of blended learning. *Journal of Distance Education, 17*(3), 97–118.

Bonk, C. J., & Reynolds, T. H. (1992). Early adolescent composing within a generative-evaluative computerized prompting framework. *Computers in Human behavior, 8*(1), 39–62.

Bonk, C. J., Reynolds, T. H., & Medury, P. V. (1996). Technology enhanced workplace writing: A social and cognitive transformation. In A. H. Duin & C. J. Hansen (Eds.), *Nonacademic writing: Social theory and technology* (pp. 281–303). Mahwah, NJ: Erlbaum.

Bonk, C. J., & Zhang, K. (2006). Introducing the R2D2 model: Online learning for the diverse learners of this world. *Distance Education, 27*(2), 249–264.

Bowlin, W. (2001, Spring). Experiential learning: Benefits for academia and the local community. *Management Accounting Quarterly*, 21–27.

Branzburg, J. (2006, May 25). Use Google Maps mashups in K-12 education. *Technology and Learning Magazine.* Retrieved September 16, 2006, from http://www.techlearning.com/story/showArticle.jhtml?articleID=187002846

Brennan, M., & Kao, G. (2004, May). The promise and reality of technology-based simulations. *Chief Learning Officer, 3*(5), 52–55.

Briggs, T. W. (2007, September 7). Books not closed on text messaging. *Sci-Tech Today.* Retrieved September 19, 2007, from http://www.sci-tech-today.com/news/Book-s-Not-Closed-on-Text-Messaging/story.xhtml?story_id=0220002KEPJS

Bronstein, J., & Newman, A. (2006, February). IM 4 learning. *T+D Magazine, 60*(2), 47–50.

Brown, J. S., Collins, A., & Duguid, P. (1989). Situated cognition and the culture of learning. *Educational Researcher, 18*(1), 32–41.

Brumfield, R. (2006, January 19). Virtual schools offer clubs, field trips. *eSchool News,* Retrieved September 16, 2006, from http://www.eschoolnews.com/news/showStory.cfm?ArticleID=6065

Campus Technology. (2007, August 22). Webinar: Wikis and Web 2.0. Retrieved September 19, 2007, from http://campustechnology.com/articles/49909/

Carlson, S. (2004, November). Music students audition electronically in 'virtual practice rooms'. *Chronicle of Higher Education.* Retrieved October 10, 2005, from http://chronicle.com/weekly/v51/i12/12a03102.htm

Carmean, C., & Haefner, J. (2002, November/December). Mind over matter: Transforming course management systems into effective learning environments. *Educause Review, 37*(6), 27–34. Retrieved February 19, 2006, from http://www.educause.edu/ir/library/pdf/erm0261.pdf

Carmean, C., & Haefner, J. (2003). Next-generation course management systems. *Educause Quarterly, 26*(1), pp. 10–13. Retrieved August 12, 2006, from http://www.educause.edu/ir/library/pdf/erm0261.pdf

CBC News. (2007, February 9). Text-message course helps newcomers learn English. Retrieved September 19, 2007, from http://www.cbc.ca/canada/edmonton/story/2007/02/09/text-classes.html

Clark, R. A., Gjerde, K.A.P., & Skinner, D. (2003). The effects of interdisciplinary instruction on simulation performance. *Simulation & Gaming, 34*(1), 150–163.

The Cognition and Technology Group at Vanderbilt. (1990). Anchored instruction and its relationship to situated cognition. *Educational Researcher, 19*(6), 2–10.

The Cognition and Technology Group at Vanderbilt. (1991). Technology and the design of generative learning environments. *Educational Technology, 31*(5), 34–40.

Collins, A., Brown, J. S., & Newman, S. E. (1990). Cognitive apprenticeship: Teaching the crafts of reading, writing, and mathematics. In L. B. Resnick (Ed.), *Knowing, learning, and instruction: Essays in honor of Robert Glaser* (pp. 453–494). Hillsdale, NJ: Erlbaum.

Collis, B. (2006). Putting blended learning to work. In C. J. Bonk & C. R. Graham (Eds.), *The handbook of blended learning: Global perspectives, local designs* (pp. 461–473). San Francisco, CA: Pfeiffer.

Collison, G., Elbaum, B., Haavind, S., & Tinker, R. (2000). *Facilitating online learning: Effective strategies for moderators.* Madison, WI: Atwood.

Cross, J. (2002, April). Blogs. *Learning Circuits.* Retrieved August 26, 2006, from http://www.learningcircuits.org/2002/apr2002/ttools.html

Cross, J. (2007). *Informal learning.* San Francisco, CA: Pfeiffer.

Cummings, J. A., Bonk, C. J., & Jacobs, F. R. (2002). Twenty-first century college syllabi: Options for online communication and interactivity. *Internet and Higher Education, 5*(1), 1–19.

Daiute, C. A. (1986). Physical and cognitive factors in revising: Insights from studies in computers. *Research in the Teaching of English, 20*(2), 141–159.

Dede, C. (2005). Planning for neomillennial learning styles: Implications for investments in technology and faculty. In D. G. Oblinger & J. L. Oblinger (Eds.), *Educating the net generation.* Retrieved November 20, 2006, from: http://www.educause.edu/content. asp?page_id=6069& bhcp=1

Dennen, V. P. (2005) From message posting to learning dialogues: Factors affecting learner participation in asynchronous discussion. *Distance Education, 26*(1), 125–146.

Dennis, A., Bichelmeyer, B., Henry, D., Cakir, H., Korkmaz, A., Watson, C., & Brunnage, J. (2006). The Cisco Networking Academy: A model for the study of student success in a blended learning environment. In C. J. Bonk & C. R. Graham (Eds.), *Handbook of blended learning: Global perspectives, local designs* (pp. 550–567). San Francisco, CA: Pfeiffer.

Dev, P., et al. (2004–2005). Production of a multisource, real-time, interactive lesson in anatomy and surgery: CORN demonstration. *Journal of Educational Technology Systems, 33*(1), 3–10.

DeViney, N., & Lewis, N. J. (2006). On-demand learning: How work-embedded learning is expanding enterprise performance. In C. J. Bonk & C. R. Graham (Eds.), *Handbook of blended learning: Global perspectives, local designs* (pp. 491–500). San Francisco, CA: Pfeiffer.

Dewey, J. (1910). *The influence of Darwin on philosophy and other essays in contemporary thought.* New York: Holt. Retrieved May 26, 2007, from http://books.google.com/books?id= XJYYAAAAMAAJ& printsec=titlepage& dq=dewey

DiMascio, J. (2004, April 12). Ft. Benning soldiers among the first to sample commercial X-box game. *Inside the Army*, p. 1.

Downes, S. (2004, September/October). Educational blogging. *Educause Review, 39*(5), 14–26. Retrieved August 27, 2006, from http://www.educause.edu/pub/er/erm04/erm0450. asp?bhcp=1

Dye, S. (2006, May 15). Text messages to help students study by phone. *New Zealand Herald.* Retrieved August 22, 2006, from http://subs.nzherald.co.nz/topic/story.cfm?c_id=186& objectid=10381845

Edens, K. (2000). Preparing problem solvers for the 21st century through problem-based learning. *College Teaching, 48*(2), 55–60.

Educational Pathways. (2005, May 20). ePortfolios. *Educational Pathways, 4*(5).

EDUCAUSE Learning Initiative. (2005). 7 things you should know about blogs. *Educause.* Retrieved September 20, 2007, from http://www.educause.edu/ir/library/pdf/ELI7006.pdf

Ehman, L. H., Bonk, C. J., & Yamagata-Lynch, E. (2005). A model of teacher professional development to support technology integration. *Association for the Advancement of Computing in Education Journal, 13*(3), 251–270.

Ellis, R. (2006). Synchronous e-learning survey results. *Learning Circuits.* Retrieved August 22, 2006, from http://www.learningcircuits.org/2006/March/2006synch_poll.htm

Emigh, W., & Herring, S. (2005). Collaborative authoring on the Web: A genre analysis of online encyclopedias. *Proceedings of the Thirty-Eighth Hawaii International Conference on System Sciences (HICSS-38).* Los Alamitos: IEEE Press.

Encyclopedia Britannica. (2006, March). Fatally flawed: Refuting the recent study on encyclopedic accuracy by the journal *Nature.* Retrieved September 27, 2006, from

http://corporate.britannica.com/britannica_nature_response.pdf#search=%22Refuting
%20the%20recent%20study%20on%20encyclopedic%22

Evarts, L. (2003, January 30). College professors across the nation join the latest internet phenomenon: Weblogs. *Brown Daily Herald*. Brown University, Electronic document no longer retrievable.

Farmer, R. (2005, November/December). Instant messaging: IM online!: RU? *Educause Review, 40*(6), 48–63. Retrieved October 25, 2006, from http://www.educause.edu/apps/er/erm05/erm0562.asp

Fecarotta, T. (2007, May 11). E-animations bring to life anatomical complexities. *IU Home Pages*, p. 11.

Feder, B. J. (2002, February 10). I learn what people want, trade idea stocks. *New York Times*, Business, p. 4. Retrieved November 24, 2006, from http://cbcl.mit.edu/news/files/nytimes-idea-stocks.pdf

Finkelstein, J. E. (2006). *Learning in real time: Synchronous teaching and learning online*. San Francisco, CA: Jossey-Bass.

Fleming, N. D., & Mills, C. (1992). *VARK: A guide to learning styles*. Retrieved October 11, 2005, from http://www.vark-learn.com/English/index.asp

Flower, L., & Hayes, J. R. (1981). A cognitive process theory of writing. *College Composition and Communication, 32*, 365–387.

Foreman, J. (2006, January 31). Learning with visualizations. *Converge*. Retrieved September 17, 2006, from http://www.convergemag.com/story.php?catid=231& storyid=98168& aid=8219072

Frankola, K. (2001, August). Training e-trainers. *Learning Circuits*. Retrieved November 18, 2006, from http://www.learningcircuits.org/2001/aug2001/frankola.html

Giles, J. (2005, December 15). Internet encyclopedias go head to head. *Nature, 438*(7070), 900–901. Retrieved September 28, 2006, from http://www.nature.com/nature/journal/v438/n7070/full/438900a.html

Graham, J. (2006, June 14). Website designers want searches to work for free. *USA Today*. Retrieved August 27, 2006, from http://www.usatoday.com/tech/news/2006-06-13-Web-marketing_x.htm

Gredler, M. E. (1996). Educational games and simulations: A technology in search of a (research) paradigm. In D. H. Jonassen (Ed.), *Handbook of research for educational communications and technology* (pp. 521–540). New York: Simon & Schuster Macmillan.

Groth, D. P., & Robertson, E. L. (1999, November). *Its all about process: Project-oriented teaching of software engineering*. Technical Report No. 532. Bloomington, IN: Indiana University, Computer Science Department.

Guernsey, L. (2005, July 22). Soaring through ancient Rome, virtually: A compact version of existing technology lets archeologists and art historians revisit the past. *Chronicle of Higher Education*. Retrieved September 16, 2006, from http://chronicle.com/temp/reprint.php?id=2occrtqptrzi0jucx1639sc6sh2lmzp

Hall, B. (2006, July). Five innovation technologies. *Chief Learning Officer*. Retrieved September 27, 2006, from http://www.clomedia.com/content/templates/clo_article.asp?articleid=1443& zoneid=190

Harmon, A. (2003, April). More than just a game, but how close to reality? *New York Times*. Retrieved January 6, 2008, from http://query.nytimes.com/gst/fullpage.html?res=9B0CE3D81F39F930A35757C0A9659C8B63

Hayes, J. R., & Flower, L. S. (1986). Writing research and the writer. *American Psychologist, 41*(10), 1106–1113.

Henri, F. (1992). Computer conferencing and content analysis. In A. R. Kaye (Ed.), *Collaborative learning through computer conferencing: The Najaden papers* (pp. 115–136). New York: Springer.

Hillman, D.C.A., Willis, D. J., & Gunawerdena, C. N. (1994). Learner-interface interaction in distance education: An extension of contemporary models and strategies for practitioners. *American Journal of Distance Education, 8*(2), 30–43.

Hofmann, J. (2000, March). Designing for a synchronous learning session. *Learning Circuits.* Retrieved August 22, 2006, from http://www.learningcircuits.org/2000/mar2000/mar2000_synch.html

Hofmann, J. (2001, March). 24 hours in the day of a life of a synchronous trainer. *Learning Circuits.* Retrieved November 18, 2006, from http://www.learningcircuits.org/2001/mar2001/hofmann.html

Hofmann, J. (2003). *The synchronous trainer's survival guide: Facilitating successful live and online courses, meetings, and events.* San Francisco, CA: Pfeiffer.

Hofmann, J. (2004). *Live and online!: Tips, techniques, and ready-to-use activities for the virtual classroom.* San Francisco, CA: Pfeiffer.

Jayakanthan, R. (2002). Application of computer games in the field of education. *Electronic Library, 20*(2), 98–102.

Jonassen, D. H. (1996). *Computers in the classroom: Mindtools for critical thinking.* Columbus, OH: Merrill/Prentice-Hall.

Jonassen, D. H., Beissner, K., & Yacci, M. A. (1993). Structural knowledge: Techniques for conveying, assessing, and acquiring structural knowledge. Hillsdale, NJ: Erlbaum.

Jost, M., Mumma, P., & Willis, J. (1999). *R2D2:* A constructivist/interpretivist instructional design model. In J. Price et al. (Eds.), *Proceedings of Society for Information Technology and Teacher Education International Conference 1999* (pp. 1489–1494). Chesapeake, VA: Association for the Advancement of Computing in Education.

Ju, E., & Wagner, C. (1997). Personal computer adventure games: Their structure, principles, and applicability for training. *The DATA BASE for Advances in Information Systems, 28*(2), 78–92.

Kiegaldie, D., & White, G. (2006). The Virtual Patient—Development, implementation and evaluation of an innovative computer simulation for postgraduate nursing students. *Journal of Educational Multimedia and Hypermedia, 15*(1), 31–47.

Kiernan, V. (2006, May 12). Sign of the times: Deaf-education departments find new uses for online videoconferencing. *Chronicle of Higher Education.* Retrieved September 24, 2006, from http://chronicle.com/weekly/v52/i36/36a03701.htm

Kim, H. (2004). The relationship between online teacher immediacy behaviors and online instructional effectiveness. In G. Richards (Ed.), *Proceedings of World Conference on E-Learning in Corporate, Government, Healthcare, and Higher Education 2004* (pp. 1954–1959). Chesapeake, VA: Association for the Advancement of Computing in Education.

Kim, K.-J., & Bonk, C. J. (2006). The future of online teaching and learning in higher education: The survey says . . . *Educause Quarterly, 29*(4), 22–30. Retrieved November 18, 2006, from http://www.educause.edu/ir/library/pdf/eqm0644.pdf

Kirkley, J. R., & Kirkley, S. E. (2006). Expanding the boundaries of blended learning: Transforming learning with mixed and virtual reality technologies. In C. J. Bonk & C. R. Graham (Eds.), *Handbook of blended learning: Global Perspectives, local designs* (pp. 533–549). San Francisco, CA: Pfeiffer.

Kolb, D. A. (1984). *Experiential learning: Experience as the source of learning and development.* Englewood Cliffs, NJ: Prentice-Hall.

Langer, J. A., & Applebee, A. A. (1987). *How writing shapes thinking.* Urbana, IL: National Council of Teachers of English.

Lave, J., & Wenger, E. (1991). *Situated learning: Legitimate peripheral participation*. New York: Cambridge University Press.

Lawrence, G. (1993). *People types and tiger stripes: A practical guide to learning styles* (3rd ed.). Gainesville, FL: Center for Applications of Psychological Types.

Leemkuil, H., de Jong, T., & Ootes, S. (2000). *Review of educational use of games and simulations*. EC project KITS (Knowledge management Interactive Training System). EC project KITS (IST-1999–13078), KITS Deliverable D1, Enschede: KITS consortium. University of Twente, The Netherlands. Retrieved May 14, 2004, from http://kits.edte.utwente.nl/documents/D1.pdf

Lewis, N. J., & Orton, P. Z. (2006). Blending learning for business impact: IBM's case for learning success. In C. J. Bonk & C. R. Graham (Eds.), *Handbook of blended learning: Global perspectives, local designs* (pp. 61–75). San Francisco, CA: Pfeiffer.

Liang, M. Y., & Bonk, C. J. (in review). Enriching EFL learning experiences with Web-based interactions: A blended approach.

Lombardi, C. (2006). Belatedly, Britannica lambastes Wikipedia findings. *CNET News*. Retrieved September 27, 2006, from http://news.com.com/Belatedly,+Britannica+lambastes+Wikipedia+findings/2100-1025_3-6053754.html

MacDonald, C. (2006). State teens learn Chinese online. *Detroit News*. Retrieved August 22, 2006, from http://www.detnews.com/apps/pbcs.dll/article?AID=/20060510/SCHOOLS/605100395/1026

Malone, T. (1981). Toward a theory of intrinsically motivating instruction. *Cognitive Science, 4*, 333–369.

Martindale, T., & Wiley, D. (2005). Using Weblogs in scholarship and teaching. *TechTrends, 49*(2), 55–61.

Masie, E. (2006, September 18). *#402—Fingertip knowledge and lowered memorization Learning TRENDS*. Retrieved May 24, 2007, from http://trends.masie.com/archives/2006/09/402_fingertip_k.html

Mayer, R. E. (2003). The promise of multimedia learning: Using the same instructional design methods across different media. *Learning and Instruction, 13*, 125–139. Retrieved August 22, 2006, from http://www.unisanet.unisa.edu.au/edpsych/external/EDUC_5080/Mayer.pdf

McCarthy, B. (1987). *The 4MAT system: Teaching to learning styles with right/left mode techniques* (Rev. ed.). Barrington, IL: EXCEL.

Mitchell, M. (2002, February 1). Students getting hands-on experience designing unique teams. News Bureau, University of Illinois at Urbana-Champaign. Retrieved September 26, 2006, from http://www.news.uiuc.edu/gentips/02/02tourism.html

Moore, M. G. (1989). Editorial: Three types of interaction. *American Journal of Distance Education, 3*(2), 1–6.

MSNBC. (2005, November, 18). 2B? Nt2b? Shakespeare gets texting treatment: Company claims shrinking the classics will help students. Retrieved January 7, 2008, from http://www.msnbc.msn.com/id/10084329/

Nielsen/NetRatings. (2006, May). Social networking sites grow 47 percent, year over year, reaching 45 percent of Web users, according to Nielson/NetRatings. Retrieved August 27, 2006, from http://www.nielsen-netratings.com/pr/pr_060511.pdf#search=%22Top%2010%20social%20networking%20sites%20see%2047%25%20growth%22

Nielson, J. (2005, December 19). One billion Internet users. *Jacob Nielson's Alert Box*. Retrieved August 22, 2006, from http://www.useit.com/alertbox/internet_growth.html

North Central Regional Educational Laboratory (NCREL). (1997). *Learning with technology: Participant's manual*. Oak Brook, IL: NCREL.

Novak, J. D., & Gowin, D. B. (1984). *Learning how to learn*. Cambridge, UK, and New York: Cambridge University Press.

Novak, J. D., & Musconda, D. (1991). A twelve-year study of science concept learning. *American Educational Research Journal, 28*, 117–153.

Oblinger, D. (2003, July/August). Boomers, Gen-Xers, and Millennials: Understanding the "new students." *Educause Review, 38*(4), 37–47. Retrieved November 22, 2006, from http://www.educause.edu/ir/library/pdf/erm0342.pdf

Olsen, F. (2003, May 16). Internet2 at a Crossroads: The network has transformed research, teaching, and daily campus life, but can colleges afford its ambitions? *Chronicle of Higher Education*. Retrieved October 26, 2006, from http://chronicle.com/weekly/v49/i36/36a03201.htm

Organisation for Economic Co-operation and Development (OECD). (2004). *OECD broadband statistics*. Retrieved August 27, 2006, from http://www.oecd.org/document/60/0,2340,en_2825_495656_2496764_1_1_1_1,00.html

Organisation for Economic Co-operation and Development (OECD). (2005). *OECD broadband statistics*. Retrieved August 27, 2006, from http://www.oecd.org/document/39/0,2340,en_2649_34225_36459431_1_1_1_1,00.html

Ou, C., & Zhang, K. (2006). Teaching with databases: Begin with the Internet. *TechTrends, 50*(5), 46–51. Retrieved November 24, 2006, from http://www.springerlink.com/content/r553267768v73537/fulltext.pdf

Paivio, A. (1991). Dual coding theory: Retrospect and current status. *Canadian Journal of Psychology, 45*, 255–287.

Palloff, R. M., & Pratt, K. (2001). *Lessons from the cyberspace classroom: The realities of online teaching*. San Francisco, CA: Jossey-Bass.

Park, Y. J., & Bonk, C. J. (2007). Synchronous learning experiences: Distance and residential learners' perspectives in a blended graduate course. *Journal of Interactive Online Learning, 6*(3), 245–264.

Pea, R. D. (2002). Learning science through collaborative visualization over the Internet. In N. Ringertz (Ed.), *Nobel Symposium: Virtual museums and public understanding of science and culture*. Stockholm, Sweden: Nobel Academy Press.

Peffers, K., & Bloom, S. (1999). Internet-based innovations for teaching IS courses: The state of adoption, 1998–2000. *Journal of Information Technology Theory and Applications, 1*(1). Retrieved July 21, 1999, from http://clam.rutgers.edu/~ejournal/spring99/survey.htm

Penn State Live. (2005, January 6). *Professor's anatomy Web quiz garners quarter-million plus hits*. Retrieved August 27, 2006, from http://live.psu.edu/story/9593

Perseus Development Corporation. (2003, October). *The blogging iceberg: Of 4.12 million hosted Weblogs, most little seen, quickly abandoned*. Retrieved October 10, 2005, from http://www.perseus.com/blogsurvey/thebloggingiceberg.html

Perseus Development Corporation (2005, April). *The blogging geyser: Blogs blast from 31.6 million today to reach 53.4 million by year end*. Retrieved October 10, 2005, from http://www.perseus.com/survey/news/releases/release_blogginggeyser.html

Prensky, M. (2001). *Digital game-based learning*. New York: McGraw-Hill.

Putnam, J. (2007, March 20). Online Chinese coming to all Michigan high schools. *Mlive.com*. Retrieved May 10, 2007, from http://www.mlive.com/news/statewide/index.ssf?/base/news-8/1174342204100120.xml&coll=1

Raths, D. (2006, August). Virtual reality in the OR. *Training and Development, 60*(8), 36–40.

Read, B. (2005, July 15). Romantic poetry meets 21st century technology: With wikis, the new Web tool, everybody's an editor and a critic. *Chronicle of Higher Education,* A35–36. Retrieved September 26, 2006, from http://chronicle.com/free/v51/i45/45a03501.htm

Read, B. (2006, August 7). "Wikimania" participants give the online encyclopedia mixed reviews. *Chronicle of Higher Education.* Retrieved September 27, 2006, from http://chronicle.com/weekly/v53/i02/02a06201.htm

Reynolds, T. H., & Bonk, C. J. (1996). Creating computerized writing partner and keystroke recording tools with macro-driven prompts. *Educational Technology Research and Development, 44*(3), 83–97.

Rickard, W., & Oblinger, D. (2004). *Higher education leaders symposium: Unlocking the potential of gaming technology.* Redmond, WA: Microsoft. Retrieved April 11, 2004, from http://www7.nationalacademies.org/itru/Gaming%20Technology.pdf

Roebuck, D. B., Brock, S. J., & Moodie, D. R. (2004). Using a simulation to explore challenges of communicating in a virtual team. *Business Communication Quarterly, 67*(3), 359–367.

Salmon, G. (2000). *E-moderating: The key to teaching and learning online.* London: Kogan Page.

Salmon, G. (2002). *E-tivities: The key to active online learning.* Sterling, VA: Stylus.

Salomon, G. (1988). AI in reverse: Computer tools that turn cognitive. *Journal of Educational Computing Research, 4*(2), 123–139.

Sampson, H. (2006, March 8). Board ok's flip-flops, but iPods are out. *Miami Herald.* Retrieved March 26, 2006, from http://www.miamiherald/14042999.htm

Santo, S. (2006). Relationships between learning styles and online learning: Myth or reality? *Performance Improvement Quarterly, 19*(3), 73–88.

Savarese, J. (2006, March). Helping students help each other. *Campus Technology, 19*(7), 24, 26. Retrieved August 27, 2006, from http://www.campus-technology.com/article.asp?id=18005

Scardamalia, M., & Bereiter, C. (1986). Research on written composition. In M. C. Wittrock (Ed.), *Handbook of research on teaching* (3rd ed., pp. 778–803). New York: Macmillan Education.

Scardamalia, M., Bereiter, C., McLean, R. S., Swallow, J., & Woodruff, E. (1989). Computer supported intentional learning environments. *Journal of Educational Computing Research, 5*(1), 51–68.

Schrage, M. (1990). *Shared minds: The technologies of collaboration.* New York: Random House.

Seigenthaler, J. (2005, November 29). A false Wikipedia "biography." *USA Today.* Retrieved September 27, 2006, from http://www.usatoday.com/news/opinion/editorials/2005-11-29-wikipedia-edit_x.htm

Singh, H. (2006). Blending learning and work: Real-time work flow learning. In C. J. Bonk & C. R. Graham (Eds.), *Handbook of blended learning: Global Perspectives, local designs* (pp. 474–490). San Francisco, CA: Pfeiffer.

Sloan, G. (2006, October 2). Personal music players: An artwork in progress. *USA Today.* Retrieved May 24, 2007, from http://www.usatoday.com/travel/destinations/2006–08–24-ipod-museum-tours_x.htm

Snider, M. (2004, May 10). Hollywood at the controls: Video games feed off each other. *USA Today,* pp. 1D–2D.

Soo, K. S., & Bonk, C. J. (1998, June). *Interaction: What does it mean in online distance education?* Paper presented at Ed-Media & Ed-Telecom 98, Freiberg, Germany. (ERIC Document Reproduction Service No ED 428724)

Stevenson, R. (2003, May). U.S. Army creates video game to train soldiers. Technology—Reuters. *SignOnSanDiego.com.* Retrieved October 1, 2007, from http://www.signonsandiego.com/news/computing/20030515–1745-tech-army.html

Sugar, W. A., & Bonk, C. J. (1998). Student role play in the World Forum: Analyses of an Arctic learning apprenticeship. In C. J. Bonk, & K. S. King (Eds.), *Electronic collaborators: Learner-centered technologies for literacy, apprenticeship, and discourse* (pp. 131–155). Mahwah, NJ: Erlbaum.

Theroux, J., Carpenter, C., & Kilbane, C. (2004). Experimental online case study for a breakthrough in student engagement: Focus group results. *Journal of Asynchronous Learning Networks, 8*(3). Retrieved October 10, 2005, from http://www.sloan-c.org/publications/jaln/v8n3/v8n3_theroux.asp

van Dam, A., Becker, S., & Simpson, R. M. (2005, March/April). Next-generation educational software: Why we need it and a research agenda for getting it. *Educause Review, 40*(2), 26–32. Retrieved September 16, 2006, from http://www.educause.edu/apps/er/erm05/erm0521.asp

Wagner, E. D. (1994). In support of a functional definition of interaction. *American Journal of Distance Education, 8*(2).

Watkins, R. (2005, May/June). Developing interactive e-learning activities. *Performance Improvement, 44*(5), 5–7.

Weigel, V. (2005). From course management to curriculum capabilities: A capabilities approach for the next-generation CMS. *Educause Review, 40*(3), 54–67. Retrieved August 22, 2006, from http://www.educause.edu/apps/er/erm05/erm0533.asp

Wenger, M. S., & Ferguson, C. (2006). A learning ecology model for blended learning from Sun Microsystems. In C. J. Bonk & C. R. Graham (Eds.). *Handbook of blended learning: Global perspectives, local designs* (pp. 76–91). San Francisco, CA: Pfeiffer Publishing.

Wikipedia. (2006). *Wiki.* Retrieved September 27, 2006, from http://en.wikipedia.org/wiki/Wiki

Wikipedia. (2007). *Wikipedia: Statistics.* Retrieved May 23, 2007, from http://en.wikipedia.org/wiki/Special:Statistics

Wired News. (2003, October 3). *Military training is just a game.* Retrieved May 2, 2004, from http://www.wired.com/news/games/0,2101,60688,00.html?tw=wn_story_related.

Wisher, R. A. (2006). Blended learning in military training. In C. J. Bonk & C. R. Graham (Eds.), *Handbook of blended learning: Global perspectives, local designs* (pp. 519–532). San Francisco, CA: Pfeiffer.

Young, J. R. (2002a, March). E-portfolios could give students a new sense of their accomplishments. *Chronicle of Higher Education, 48*(26), A31–A32. Retrieved February 12, 2006, from http://chronicle.com/weekly/v48/i26/26a03101.htm

Young, J. R. (2002b, May 31). The 24-hour professor. *Chronicle of Higher Education.* Retrieved November 18, 2006, from http://chronicle.com/free/v48/i38/38a03101.htm

Young, M. (2003, May 30). Fashion and computer students collaborate to create a virtual runway. *Chronicle of Higher Education.* Retrieved May 24, 2007, from http://chronicle.com/weekly/v49/i38/38a03101.htm

Zhang, K., & Peck, K. L. (2003). The effects of peer-controlled or moderated online collaboration on group problem solving and related attitudes. *Canadian Journal of Learning and Technology, 29*(3), 93–112.

# INDEX